PERMANENT THINGS

Permanent Things

Toward the Recovery of a More Human Scale
at the End of the Twentieth Century

Edited by

Andrew A. Tadie
and
Michael H. Macdonald

WILLIAM B. EERDMANS PUBLISHING COMPANY
GRAND RAPIDS, MICHIGAN / CAMBRIDGE, U.K.

This book is dedicated
to the memory of

Russell Amos Kirk

October 19, 1918 - April 29, 1994

✠ R.I.P.

© 1995 Wm. B. Eerdmans Publishing Co.
255 Jefferson Ave. S.E., Grand Rapids, Michigan 49503 /
P.O. Box 163, Cambridge CB3 9PU U.K.

Printed in the United States of America

00 99 98 97 96 95   7 6 5 4 3 2 1

Library of Congress Cataloging-in-Publication Data

Permanent things / edited by Andrew A. Tadie and Michael H. Macdonald.
    p.   cm.
   ISBN 0-8028-3804-9
   1. English literature — 20th century — History and criticism.   2. Christianity and
literature — England — History — 20th century.   3. Christian literature, English —
History and criticism.   4. Chesterton, G. K. (Gilbert Keith), 1874-1936 — Ethics.
5. Eliot, T. S. (Thomas Stearns), 1888-1965 — Ethics.   6. Lewis, C. S. (Clive
Staples), 1898-1963 — Ethics.   7. Christian ethics in literature.
I. Tadie, Andrew A.   II. Macdonald, Michael H.
PR478.C45P47   1995
820.9'382 — dc20
                                           95-35842
                                           CIP

Contents

Preface   viii

Acknowledgments   x

Introduction   xii
Ian Crowther

The Great Mysterious Incorporation
of the Human Race   1
Russell Kirk

**From War to Affirmation:
The Literature of the Permanent Things**

Father Brown's War on the Impermanent Things   17
John Peterson

Chesterton's Dickens and the Literary Critics:
The Thing and the Theory   31
David Whalen

Contents

Waugh's Road to Affirmation   48
   David Dooley

"Little Systems of Order": Evelyn Waugh's Comic Irony   66
   Gregory Wolfe

C. S. Lewis Celebrates "Patches of Godlight"   82
   George Musacchio

The Permanent Things in the Public Square

Chesterton, Democracy and the Permanent Things   93
   Kent R. Hill

G. K. Chesterton and the Science of Economics   118
   William F. Campbell

Finding the Permanent in the Political:
C. S. Lewis as a Political Thinker   137
   John G. West, Jr.

Of Golden Threads: Poets "Set on the Marble of Exchange"

What Dorothy L. Sayers Found Permanent in Dante   151
   Barbara Reynolds

Perplexity in the Edgeware Road:
Four Quartets Revisited Yet Again   164
   Thomas T. Howard

G. K. Chesterton among the Permanent Poets   176
    Aidan Mackey

**Dying and Rising: Toward the Renewal
of the Permanent Things**

Darkness at Noon: The Eclipse of the Permanent Things   195
    Peter Kreeft

In Defense of Permanent Truth and Value   222
    John A. Sims

"There Are No 'Trees' . . . Only This Elm":
C. S. Lewis on the Scientific Method   240
    Evan K. Gibson

Some Ideas on a Christian Core Curriculum
from the Writings of G. K. Chesterton,
T. S. Eliot, and Dorothy L. Sayers   253
    Alzina Stone Dale

C. S. Lewis and the Conversion of the West   270
    William J. Abraham

The Recovery of the Permanent Things:
Eliot circa 1930   283
    Marion Montgomery

Contributors   306

Appendix of Conference Participants   310

Preface

The title of this volume, *Permanent Things: Toward the Recovery of a More Human Scale at the End of the Twentieth Century*, describes the motive of the editors both in preparing this collection of essays and in directing the conference which preceded it. We intended the conference to be a five-day forum of thoughtful dialogue exploring an aspect common to the thinking of certain twentieth-century Anglo-American writers. Regardless of their personal proclivities and idiosyncrasies, our writers believed Permanent Things really exist. Moreover, they agreed in general about what they are — those perennial or recurring attributes inherent in and characteristic of every real being, natural and supernatural. Their belief was founded upon the conviction that by experience human beings can discover and decipher enough about reality to know it to be fundamentally coherent and good. As Christian theists they knew the source and cause of the coherence and goodness.

The writers considered in the essays here, G. K. Chesterton, C. S. Lewis, Evelyn Waugh, T. S. Eliot, and Dorothy L. Sayers, lived at a time of great social ferment, and while they engaged in the disputes of the time, they resisted, unlike so many of their contemporaries, the appeals of fashionable ideological groups: world statists and chauvinistic nationalists, anarchists and social planners, socialists and fascists, materialists and gnostics, historical determinists and rugged individualists, social Darwinists and Spenglerians, militarists and pacifists, scientific progressives and Luddites, futurists and traditionalists, unionists and capitalists, industrialists and agrarians, extremists of all sorts and moderates in search of a shifting center. Our writers believed that this short list of the century's darling notions when applied to the human condition would prove to be ultimately insufficient and unsatisfying, and in the end they would sometimes cause more grief than they alleviated.

Permanent Things, on the other hand, are more salutary to the human condition. These recurring attributes of nature, including human nature, may recede temporarily as conditions change. Permanent Things for a time may even be suppressed, but they cannot be thwarted forever. Our writers came to believe (in spite of great differences in their personalities, interests, experiences, and predilections) in a rather uniform idea both of what constituted the Permanent Things and what distinguished seemingly permanent things from truly Permanent Things. This acquaintance with Permanent Things allowed our writers to resist being absorbed by narrow ideals and exaggerating or minimizing human potential. They kept their thinking on a more human scale.

To be useful, human ideals must be scaled to human nature, just as maps must be scaled to roads that actually exist. Like road maps, ideals must be accurately scaled if they are to be good for human beings. Our writers knew that a scale was necessary to keep one's perspective in balance. What they employed to evaluate the worth of an ideal was a type of balance scale. They placed its pedestal on solid reality, and into the pedestal they fixed a post straight and true, from the top of which pivot they connected arms with pans suspended at each end. In one pan they placed a known weight, human nature and the human condition; in the other, an ideal. In a balance scale the relative weight of the ideal can be discovered if a known weight is employed as a standard. The only reliable weight against which an ideal can be measured is a permanent standard. A standard that expects too much or too little of human beings or one that varies unpredictably will reveal on balance little about the true worth of an ideal.

Our writers, believing Christians, knew the ultimate worth of the standard of Christ. This standard, while compatible with the belief that human reason can know reality as good and coherent, is not ultimately derived from human reason. The standard is given by God, who reveals partially both himself and the expectations he has for his creatures. The Christian standard not only reveals the full potential for postlapsarian human beings but also foreshadows the fulfillment of a promise, the possibility of a fully perfected human life united to God and those in communion with him.

Andrew Tadie

Acknowledgments

The essays in this volume were among those presented at a conference hosted in June of 1990 by Seattle University and Seattle Pacific University. This was the second of three such conferences hosted jointly by these two universities, one Catholic and Jesuit, the other Protestant and Free Methodist.

The principal sponsor for the three conferences (1987, 1990, 1993) was the Intercollegiate Studies Institute, which for over forty years has supported scholars and students in the advancement and defense of the humanities and social sciences. Without the unfailing encouragement of two people at I.S.I., John Lulves, Executive Vice President, and Ann Wendig, Executive Assistant, these conferences, this volume, and its predecessor, *C. S. Lewis and G. K. Chesterton: The Riddle of Joy*, would have been ideas far less completely realized.

The provost of Seattle University, John Eshelman, and the dean of continuing studies of Seattle Pacific University, Ralph Kester, generously provided the essential administrative support. Kim Gilnett at Seattle Pacific University attended to countless details with a flourish that made him the *arbiter elegantiae* of the conference, which drew participants from various academic disciplines in the humanities and social sciences. These diverse scholars made the conference intellectually scintillating, yet made the task of selecting essays for this book daunting.

Many papers not included here merit publication. The ones selected for this volume were chosen to satisfy conflicting aims: (1) the essays should manifest the broad range of approaches taken in addressing the conference's theme, the Permanent Things in twentieth-century Anglo-American literature; and (2) they should form as much as possible a unified and coherent book.

At the final stage of the project, the editors benefited particularly from the counsel of Mark Shea, one of the conference participants. He recommended several refinements and suggested the titles for the book's four sections. Of course, this volume would not exist were it not for those who participated in the conference. (See the appendix to this volume.) Unlike the king in the parable who prepared the wedding feast, when we invited people to attend an intellectual feast to discuss the Permanent Things, they did come to form a most excellent company.

Andrew Tadie
Michael Macdonald
July 4, 1995

Introduction

Not the least of the benefits arising from the collapse of the Soviet Empire, and of communism as an ideology demanding to be taken seriously as much by its enemies as by its friends, is the removal of a massive intellectual distraction which has exercised some of the twentieth century's best minds, as well as some of its worst. Now that communism has been consigned to "the dustbin of history" which Marx reserved for capitalism, a new debate has begun — or rather an old debate has been resumed — between, on the one hand, those who hail the triumph of Western liberal democracy as marking the "end of history" and, on the other, those who question many of the liberal progressive assumptions upon which the modern project to build a "City of Man" apart from the "City of God" has been based.

The contributors to this volume belong firmly in the latter camp, as do the Christian writers whose work has served as inspiration for the essays presented here. This book reminds us that some of the century's most imaginative minds — G. K. Chesterton, T. S. Eliot, C. S. Lewis, Charles Williams, Dorothy L. Sayers, Evelyn Waugh — were profoundly out of sympathy with the secularist spirit of the age, seeing progressive enlightenment as ushering in, not a millennium of perfect freedom, but a Waste Land whose inhabitants — Waugh's "vile bodies," Eliot's "hollow men," Lewis's "men without chests" — can find refuge from their boredom and anomie only in the ceaseless acquisition of things or in the consoling illusions of pseudo religions: "distracted from distraction by distraction," as Eliot memorably put it.

How does one explain the desolation of a world which, though richly endowed with material comforts, is mentally and spiritually impoverished? The essayists here are united, as were their subjects, by a need to try to answer this question. Modern man's poverty of spirit, visible alike in so much of his art and architecture, his literature and philosophy and political science, reflects his loss of any *good* reasons for living; his loss of the Permanent Things or of what C. S. Lewis called the *Tao* to denote that eternal wisdom by which, in all the great civilizations, human lives have been ordered and ennobled. Of course, we moderns persuade ourselves that we do have good reasons for living: power, pleasure, wealth, success, limitless self-expression. But the sense of an objective good, a *telos*, has been lost along with the sense of any sacral order. Why? Because when all that is valuable is forced, by the advance of science, to migrate from the outer world to the inner, and in the process demoted to the lowly status of secondary, purely subjective qualities, it is left without any real means of support (or grounding in reality). We were not formed, modern science tells us, for any purposes higher than those encompassed by our urges for reproduction and survival. No wonder, then, that in the disenchanted world bequeathed to us by behaviorism and positivism, the only goals authorized by reality are health and wealth, or life, liberty and the pursuit of happiness! What was once objectively valuable now leads a wraith-like existence in the shape of personal "values" whose only authority resides in the fact of our having chosen them. We are all heretics now, that is to say, persons who have elevated arbitrary choice into the supreme value. The market-place, whose function in former times was to humbly minister to our material needs, has grown into a metaphor for the modern world as shopping mall of the mind. Consumer sovereignty extends to moral as well as material goods. Nothing is sacred, nor could it be when what belongs to the sacred, by definition, are unchosen goods: the Permanent Things.

Modern man is Protagorean man: the measure of all things. So deeply ingrained in our culture is the idea that all that pertains to value, to the good, begins subjectively in the mind and not in reality that we can barely conceive of anything which is given to us objectively other than the raw material of our animal nature. We are emboldened by the false promises of human happiness held out to us by the modern "engineers of the human soul," C. S. Lewis's "Conditioners," to experiment endlessly, as we do upon the "world's body," for the purpose of gratifying our material appetites. This has consequences for the whole of nature, including our own, which we are only now beginning to glimpse in all their enormity. The experiment, for that is what it is, of modern life has not transformed humanity for the better in the way the great prophets of modernity imagined it would; instead it has very nearly resulted in what C. S. Lewis called "the abolition of man," that is, the abolition of that creature who was once understood to be only a little lower than the angels, rather than just a little higher than the apes.

If we are tempted by the collapse of Soviet totalitarianism to crow about the now historically proven superiority of Western liberal democracies, we should remember that communist society has only embodied in a collectivist form the same secular humanism and immanentism which our own has embodied in an individualist form. This is not to postulate a "moral equivalence" between the two systems. Freedom is a precious thing; but only insofar as it serves precious purposes. Communism denied a person's right to plough his own as opposed to the collective's field. But this was a denial not simply of a human being's possessive instinct; it was a denial equally of a human being's purposive instinct. Freedom answers to the self-transcending ends as well as the self-regarding needs of a human nature cultivated not simply for its own sake but for the fruits it will yield. Unfortunately we no longer know with any certainty what these fruits should be; we no longer know what freedom is for. How can we continue in the West to value, or expect others to value, a freedom whose chief use is the opportunity it affords for transgressive behavior? Western man's claim to freedom originally rested upon the idea that human life is a drama or pilgrimage, in the course of which we are summoned to act out a God-given destiny. But if we reject the obligations placed on us by a natural, and ultimately a supernatural, order, yet still insist on keeping our individual freedom, then we are left with mere individualism, a euphemism for selfishness by whomsoever practiced.

The liberal theory of politics is predicated on the assumption that, essentially, the role of government should be restricted to the management and prevention of conflict, and that a government so restricted guarantees the "minimal state." What the liberal theory fails to contemplate is the possibility that the freedom encouraged by it may generate conflict on such a scale that any state forced to "manage" it will be far from minimal. The early liberal philosophers simply took for granted the existence of a virtuous people, or of freedom as anchored in a closed moral order. They did not envisage, as more pessimistically inclined thinkers did, a government having to cope with the kind of unbridled liberty now exercised in the moral playground which is modern Western society.

That the chief threat to our liberties comes today not from communism but from our own severely attenuated sense of moral order, and of the Permanent Things constituted by that order, is a principal theme linking together the essays collected here. All are informed and their prose animated by a moral urgency which betokens a more than academic concern with the issues and the writers addressed. Academically, indeed, this enterprise must appear hopelessly quixotic to those intellectual barbarians among us who see inscribed on every "text" the marks left there, not by the "author," but by the repressive or mythical or ideological structures to which said "author" has merely borne unconscious witness. According to this nihilistic view, one must not read the "texts" of great authors (whose greatness is in any case illusory) as though they were coherent testimonies to truth, or profound and imaginative renderings of the human condition.

Happily, the essayists here are moved not by a spirit of deconstruction, but of reconstruction. They are concerned to recover for us the works and thoughts of certain great writers of this century who saw Western civilization as having slipped its metaphysical moorings in Christendom, with the result that its people were whoring *After Strange Gods*, the title of Eliot's *Primer of Modern Heresy* whose preface begins, "*Le monde moderne avilit*. It also provincialises, and it can also corrupt." Esteeming individuality and contemporaneity above tradition, we moderns are provincials, tyrannized by our time and our pathetic desire to keep up with it.

The Christian writers whose work is eloquently interpreted in this book repay our attention for many reasons, but two especially are worth mentioning here. First is their ability to sharpen our awareness of what, by any previous civilized standards, by the *philosophia perennis*, must be called, quite literally, the abnormal condition of modern man. For example, particularly in Waugh's novels and Eliot's poetry, we repeatedly encounter vivid cameos of broken relationships and marriages, which mirror the larger breakdown of social bonds and mores, and of an organic, Christian society in which, as Eliot depicted it, "the natural end of man — virtue and well-being in community — is acknowledged for all, and the supernatural end — beatitude — for those who have the eyes to see it."

For Eliot, as for all the other writers to whom our attention is drawn by this book, it was never enough simply to capture the spiritual aridity of modern life. It was also necessary to speak of a moral order which, though only perhaps surviving in scattered remnants in contemporary society, may yet be restored by the expressive power and beauty of the written word. And this positive vision, set beside the negative, is our second basic reason for acquainting ourselves anew with the writers studied here. As we make our way through these pages, we meet Evelyn Waugh's "little independent system of order"; C. S. Lewis's *Mere Christianity*; Dorothy L. Sayers's Dante-inspired sacramentalism; G. K. Chesterton's *The Thing* (that reality which is given to us and in accordance with which, in any normal society, we would conduct our lives); and, the book's *leitmotiv*, T. S. Eliot's Permanent Things, albeit latterly reduced to "fragments I have shored against my ruins." All these things are, of course, versions of the same thing: the Truth that shall make us free. The essays that follow may be read as tributes to this truth, and to those who cared for it in a century that didn't.

Ian Crowther

The Great Mysterious Incorporation of the Human Race

Russell Kirk

The title of these remarks I owe to that great rhetorician Edmund Burke. By "the great mysterious incorporation of the human race" he meant the intricate continuity which joins the dead, the living, and those who will be born; he meant, too, the community of souls, transcending time; and he meant that nothing in the civil social order is either wholly old or wholly new, for Providence has arranged that change as the means of our preservations.

The men and women of letters whose talents and virtues we celebrate in this symposium[1] were champions of the Permanent Things; and they knew themselves to be shareholders in the great mysterious incorporation of the human race, and so they live far longer than this mortal envelope endures. Not one of them is still here below; but they are those dead who give us energy; and if any human creatures were made for the resurrection of the flesh and the life everlasting, surely these men and women were. Of Chesterton, Eliot, Lewis, Sayers, Tolkien, and Waugh, I knew only Eliot personally; and most people today have never looked upon the face of any of these talented writers. Here I give you some lines of moving verse by a Southern gentleman and scholar of the generation that is passing — by Professor George Burke Johnston, of Blacksburg, Virginia. His poem is entitled "On the Death of J. R. R. Tolkien."

---

1. *Editors' note:* All of the contributors to this book participated in a Conference in Celebration of Permanent Things held in June 1990 on the campuses of Seattle Pacific University and Seattle University.

Many a citizen of Good Queen Bess
Must have desired to see and touch the hand
Of Edmund Spenser, free of Faerie Land,
And must have felt a pang of deep distress
On hearing such a meeting could not bless
His fellow wanderer on this dark strand;
Then must have turned with signs from vision planned
Back to the pulsing lines' infiniteness.
We who walked Middle-Earth in Tolkien's time
And yearned in vain to meet him eye to eye.
Now that his sailing from Grey Havens ends
The hope of meeting here, may praise in rime
His word-lore, in this Age unlike to die,
And in the Fellowship be sealed his friends.[2]

Though we cannot see the faces of the men and women whose poetry and prose we so cherish, by an act of the moral imagination we may evoke them to renew our minds and consciences. They may delineate for us the Permanent Things, a phrase borrowed from T. S. Eliot. By "the Permanent Things" he meant those elements in the human condition that give us our nature, without which we are as the beasts that perish. They work upon us all in the sense that both they and we are bound up in that continuity of belief and institution called the great mysterious incorporation of the human race.

Can the great writers of the first half of the twentieth century — the fabulists of that age, if you will — help to redeem our time? Eliseo Vivas tells us that it is one of the marks of human decency to be ashamed of having been born into the twentieth century. The writers whom we honor here set their faces against the errors and vices of the century: as they and we were swept down by a flood toward the Dead Sea, those writers refused to sing Hallelujah to the river god. By the ghostly power of these great dead, may the literature of our bent culture be renewed?

As I put it in my book *Eliot and His Age*, "though here and there some stalwart Gerontion still writes, or some hopeful new talent starts up, for the most part we encounter literary ephemera, or else the prickly

---

2. George Burke Johnston, "On the Death of J. R. R. Tolkien," *Banked Fire, Poems: 1929-1976* (Blacksburg, Va.: The White Rhinoceros Press, 1988), 6.

2

pears and Dead Sea fruit of literary decadence."[3] Yet it does not follow as the night does day that there may not occur a renewal of high literary talents, illuminated by the moral imagination.

Permit me to suggest certain causes of our literary decadence; and then to speculate on whether, and how, it may be possible to conceive of a regeneration of humane letters.

I commence with a passage from the earliest of T. S. Eliot's better-known essays, "Tradition and the Individual Talent," published in 1917. Here he touches upon emotions expressed in poetry, a subject pertinent to the present dismal endeavor of various writers to probe pruriently into Eliot's private life:

> It is not in his personal emotions, the emotions provoked by particular events in his life, that the poet is in any way remarkable or interesting. . . . The emotion in his poetry will be a very complex thing, but not with the complexity of the emotions of people who have very complex or unusual emotions in life. One error, in fact, of eccentricity in poetry is to seek for new human emotions to express; and in this search for novelty in the wrong place it discovers the perverse.[4]

That last sagacious sentence may be applied to more than "poetry" in the sense of verse. Consider the very numerous schools of divinity or theology in this land, many of them richly endowed with capital assets, although not so lavishly supplied with spiritual insights. Handsome scholarships continue to attract young persons to these institutions, and those persons continue to pour out dissertations in the discipline of theology. Some element of originality is demanded in doctoral dissertations; but few young men and women, especially in our time, are capable of first-rate original contributions to the divine science, having been reared in an intellectual climate of vulgarized Darwinism and vulgarized Freudianism. What to do?

Why, the thing to do is to search for novelty in the wrong place, and discover the perverse in new aspects of an alleged "theology": liberation theology, black theology, chicano theology, feminist theology, theology of animals, gay theology, deconstructive theology, rock theology, Lord knows what else. Often the first trumpet-blast proclaiming

---

3. Russell Kirk, *Eliot and His Age: T. S. Eliot's Moral Imagination in the Twentieth Century,* second edition (Peru, Ill.: Sherwood Sugden and Co., 1988), 3.

4. T. S. Eliot, "Tradition and the Individual Talent," *The Sacred Wood: Essays on Poetry and Criticism* (London: Methuen and Co., Ltd., 1950), 57-58.

these new discoveries in the god-science is a denial of the dogmata upon which the old theology was founded. The perverse offers its rewards, for a time — although presently yet other and more startling shapes of the perverse must be unveiled, Dinos of the insatiable appetites being king when Zeus has been overthrown.

So it is with the writing of books in our bent world. A great many young people aspire to the condition of authors, both for emoluments and for celebrity. Whole departments — nay, schools — of "creative writing" proliferate; writers' workshops and colonies provide supplementary pay to college instructors serving on their staffs; community colleges offer courses in "How to Write the Novel" and "Writing Articles for Profit" for the edification of housewives and ambitious tool-and-die makers. Meanwhile it grows increasingly difficult to find any publisher who will bring out an author's first novel; probably the novel itself is a dying form of the literary art.

Then what is the would-be writer to do? Why, devise some literary novelty; to impress a publisher, take up a fresh form of perversity — although such innovations may be difficult to imagine, the changes already having been rung on the bells of morals and politics by well-paid literary men still in the land of the living. Let me turn again to T. S. Eliot, writing in 1933 about the attractions of Marxism for a New York writer:

> The literary profession is not only, in all countries, overcrowded and underpaid (the few overpaid being chiefly persons who have outlived their influence, if they ever had any); it is embarrassed by such a number of ill-trained people doing such a number of unnecessary jobs; and writing so many unnecessary books and unnecessary reviews of unnecessary books, that it has much ado to maintain its dignity as a profession at all. One is almost tempted to form the opinion that the world is at a stage at which men of letters are a superfluity. To be able therefore to envisage literature under a new aspect, to take part in the creation of a new art and new standards of literary criticism, to be provided with a whole stock of ideas and words, that is for a writer in such circumstances to be given a new lease of life. It is not always easy, of course, in the ebullitions of a new movement, to distinguish the man who has received the living word from the man whose access of energy is the result of being relieved of the necessity of thinking for himself. Men who have stopped thinking make a powerful force.[5]

5. T. S. Eliot, "A Commentary," *The Criterion* 12, no. 47 (January 1933): 244.

Those sentences were written more than half a century ago; the public that used to be called "the common reader" has diminished since then, and employment for persons with literary aptitudes is confined more and more to editorial labors for trade journals, "dumbing down" already dull manuals for school-textbook publishers, and copywriting for advertising agencies. Under such circumstances, the inducements to prostitution of literary skills loom large.

*   *   *

In a prosperous Michigan town about six years ago, I gave the dedicatory address at the opening of a new public-library building. That structure was very well equipped with the newest gadgets of library science. Just inside the entrance, close to the circulation desk, stood racks of paperbacks, hot off the press, hundreds of them in their glossy multicolored illustrated stridency. It was clear that many of them were pornographic; others pretended to be. They were placed in this conspicuous situation so that "young adults" — that is, teenagers — might be attracted to them. "The great thing is to get the kids reading; it doesn't matter so much what they read." So apologists tell us. If the kids didn't read, where would graduates of library schools find employment?

The purposes of reading for Eliot were different, as he explained in *After Strange Gods,* his lectures at the University of Virginia in 1933:

> The number of people in possession of any criteria for discriminating between good and evil is very small; the number of the half-alive hungry for any form of spiritual experience, or what offers itself as spiritual experience, high or low, good or bad, is considerable. My own generation has not served them very well. Never has the printing press been so busy, and never have such varieties of buncombe and false doctrine come from it. "Woe unto the foolish prophets, that follow their own spirit, and have seen nothing! O Israel, thy prophets have been like foxes in the waste places. . . . And the word of the Lord came unto me, saying, Son of man, these men have taken their idols into their hearts, and put the stumbling-block of their iniquity before their face: should I be inquired of at all by them?"[6]

6. T. S. Eliot, *After Strange Gods* (London: Faber and Faber, 1933), 61-62.

5

It is not necessary that, in the name of the public libraries' boasted "freedom to read," the rising generation be brought up on a diet of literary foulness which loathsomely misrepresents human nature and incites to gross acts of aggression or degradation. This mockery of freedom of choice has arisen only in recent decades. I remember with much affection the beautiful little library-room at Starkweather School, in Plymouth, Michigan, where I was a pupil. Of its hundreds of books on those handsome shelves of oak, every one in some degree was a Bright Book. Funds being limited in our railroad town, those books had been selected with much care by the school's principal, a woman of considerable presence and knowledge, and by the chairman of the school board, a bank manager who happened to be my grandfather. That library was kept open all summer, too, so that we children could read on our front porches, which we did, down there by the railroad yards. Instructed by certain heroic tales, notably the versions of Arthurian legends by Sidney Lanier and Howard Pyle, we boys battered one another with wooden swords after having garbed ourselves in cardboard armor: it was no bad preparation for the dawning age. Nobody pored over pornography, that kind of "freedom to read" not having been thoughtfully provided for our delectation.

Now what are we to make of the potboiling writers who turn out the pornography that becomes the daily literary diet of too many boys and girls, often with unhappy moral and psychological consequences for them, and with disagreeable consequences in society generally? Perhaps it may be said in lefthanded defense of such scribblers that they do not pretend to be serious writers; they are in the game merely for the money. What then of the people who write Dark Books on principle, it seems, and often are praised in major book-review media for the latest display of their original insights into delightful human depravity?

Edmund Fuller described such folk in 1958, in his book *Man in Modern Fiction:*

> What some writers have lost is not an external framework of values, not just this or that set of value concepts. They have lost the basic vision of the nature of their own kind. They not only do not know *who* they are, which is problem enough; they also do not know *what* they are — and that is the ultimate tragedy; for man not to know the nature of man. Indeed, if he knows not what he is, is he any longer man, until he has re-learned himself?[7]

7. Edmund Fuller, *Man in Modern Fiction: Some Minority Opinions on Contemporary Writing* (New York: Random House, 1958), 52.

Such writers are original in the sense that until the end of the eighteenth century no writer presumed to employ the language that the authors of the Dark Books habitually use, and no writer before Sade took so lunatic a view of the human person. Today, a good many such writers make real money by shocking the public by ingenious impudicities; but the love of money is not the sole root of their evil: some of them earnestly desire to degrade, to pull down, to destroy — the satanic impulse. Once people begin to call themselves intellectuals and cease to believe in the existence of Satan, the power of the Dark draws in about them.

What many writers of our present hour thrust upon us is a perverse vision of the Abyss — in which spectacle they rejoice, or pretend to rejoice. In the lines of the York Mystery plays, "There shalt thou naught but sorrow see, and sit by Sathanas the fiend."[8] As some of you know, I write mystical tales — taking ordinarily the form of ghost stories. My stories, too, offer glimpses of the Abyss; but they do not rejoice in damnation. In very recent years I have observed in anthologies of "horror stories" — anthologies, I mean, in which some tale of my own was included — a pervasive pseudo-eroticism of a most disagreeable nature. I say "pseudo-eroticism" because one encounters in those stories sexuality without love, sexual violation instead of fulfillment, sniggering descriptions of cruelties and perversions. The erotic impulse is bound up with love of life; but what we find in these horror stories is appetite for gory death. Like the learned researches of Alfred Kinsey, these stories might convert Casanova into a Puritan: they make sexuality seem utterly repellent.

So runs the current in one genre. A depraved literature reflects a growing depravity in a society generally; but also it nurtures that larger depravity and defiantly attempts to justify it. Sir Thomas Gresham instructs us that bad money drives out good. So it is, more and more, with the reading of our rising generation.

* * *

During what I have called the Age of Eliot — the period from the middle twenties to the middle sixties — Britain, France, and the United States

8. Canon J. R. Purvis, The York Mystery Cycle, 1952 version, quoted by Russell Kirk in "York and Social Boredom," *The Sewanee Review* 61, no. 4 (Autumn 1953): 657.

were endowed with a remarkable number of able writers, and some great ones. I knew certain of them — Eliot, Wyndham Lewis, Roy Campbell, Robert Speaight, George Scott Moncrieff, Max Picard, Robert Graves, Donald Davidson, Bernard Iddings Bell, Albert Jay Nock, Richard Weaver, Flannery O'Connor, Walker Percy. They no longer live; and their places have not been filled.

Of course, we still have among us some distinguished men of letters: I think of Andrew Lytle, Cleanth Brooks, Czeslaw Milosz, Malcolm Muggeridge. But they are older than I. There are some sound writers now rising to influence. Yet I know of no able critic who would venture to maintain that the literary arts in the English language stand in a healthy condition during these closing years of the twentieth century.

Or is this period of ours an interregnum, a pause, an interval between one era of high literary achievement and another era of a different character but of comparable worth? Cultures do suffer from fatigue and cease to wake the imagination; or they sometimes are broken by great changes, not necessarily military. There came a time, in the fifth century of the Christian era, when polite literature in the Latin language ceased to be written — totally ceased; there had come a time, three centuries earlier, when imaginative and original literature in classical Greek had dried up. Is it conceivable that after eight centuries of achievement the English language may cease to be the instrument of great poetry and prose? It comes to mind that Italian, which rose to influence throughout Europe during the Renaissance, has lost the dominion it enjoyed in the times of Dante, Aristo, and Tasso. Yet what language might supplant English — now the commercial and diplomatic tongue internationally, having supplanted French — as the chief body of literature during the twenty-first century?

Or is it conceivable that the literatures of all nations may be flung into the dustbin, humane culture being overwhelmed by materialism, the total state, and the full intellectual affliction which Robert Graves, in *Seven Days in New Crete*, denominated Logicalism? May getting and spending usurp the whole of life, and may "literature" be reduced to mere diversion during an idle hour — on a beach, say, when television is unavailable — and that diversion of rather a nasty character, *a la* Huxley's *Brave New World?*

Before we turn to some reflections upon alternatives to this dismal prospect, let us look briefly at causes of our literary decadence. Some causes are obvious to everybody. The coming of elaborate diversions — television in particular — led the majority of people away from most forms of reading. When the weekly or monthly magazine ceased to appear in middle-income houses, middlebrow culture became wholly subject to Demon TV.

The participants in a tolerable literary culture, moreover, have been much diminished in number by the loss of standards in public instruction, from kindergarten up through graduate school. In my book *Decadence and Renewal in the Higher Learning* and elsewhere, I have described the consequences of the wretched anthologies used in nearly all American schools during recent decades. Young people who have been introduced to almost no good books during their school years are bewildered when they emerge from the dungeons of free and compulsory public instruction: they lack literary norms.

Another cause of literary decadence has been the centralization of writing and publishing, which has tended to reduce diversity and discussion in the realm of letters, has put powerful influence into the hands of very small circles of writers, reviewers, and publishers, has ignored the literary interests of a great part of the population, and has forced those outlanders to conform their tastes to the notions prevalent in the literary capital. In these United States, the hegemony of New York literary circles and publishing firms is nearly absolute. Eliot said once that the worst form of expatriation for an American writer is residence in New York City. Yet it is New York's book reviews in major newspapers and magazines that determine the fate of nearly every new book published in this country. A major reason why the writings of nihilists and people possessed by the diabolic imagination sell well is that the New York book-review media consistently puff up such books and authors, apparently on principle, in part, a principle politically perverse.

The underlying cause of decadence, in any society, has been the decay of religious belief and the religious imagination. Culture arises out of the cult; and when the cult's belief has altogether evaporated, after some lapse of time the society disintegrates. One may turn to the pages of Toynbee, of Voegelin, of Dawson for historical confirmation of this.

"Decadence" is the loss of an object, an end, in existence. Literary decadence commonly is bound up with a general intellectual and moral disorder in a society — resulting, before very long, in violent social disorder. The decay of literature appears often to result from a widespread decay of the religious imagination, from a rejection of the ancient human endeavor to apprehend a transcendent order in the universe and to live in harmony with that order. That rejection is conspicuous in the nihilistic writers of our day.

Religious assumptions about the human condition having been abandoned by the writer, the moral imagination starves. And presently that moral imagination is supplanted by the diabolic imagination, infecting both the best-educated and the worst-schooled classes in our society. Upon this corrupted imagination the clever charlatan and the writer who relishes the diabolic can prey. Unscrupulous originality thus terminates in a universal boring nihilism — or, yet more catastrophic than the pose of nihilism, the common collapse of all standards, of all authority visible or invisible: the ruin of culture, the ruin of life.

And now, after having loosed upon you all those noxious things out of Pandora's box, am I about to lift the lid a final time and release Hesiod's ironic consolation — *delusory* hope? A doubtful hope, perhaps; but not a deluding one that never can be gratified.

Civilizations commonly pass through alternating periods of decay and renewal in the course of their history. One may trace this process in most literatures that have a continuity extending over some centuries. It is not unreasonable to hope for a renewal of our civilization — from causes, perhaps, as yet not possible to specify — and a concomitant reinvigoration of the influence of great literature, even the appearance of new great literature.

Even if it is true that a literature decays when the religious apprehension of life is lost and when the moral imagination has withered, there may be observed nowadays certain phenomena of green shoots springing up in the Waste Land.

It seems worth remarking that for the past three decades the most popular series of books for children, available everywhere, has been C. S. Lewis's *Chronicles of Narnia*.

It seems worth remarking that for nearly the same length of time, the authors most popular with teenage boys who read have been J. R. R. Tolkien and Ray Bradbury, writers possessed of moral imagination.

It seems worth remarking that for the past decade, the writer most popular with teenage girls (or with those given to reading morally imaginative books, at least) has been Madeleine L'Engle, a fabulist of the high dream.

All life is an allegory, and we can understand it only in parable,

G. K. Chesterton tells us. The rising generation increasingly turns to fable for its reading — and to fantasy more than to science-fiction: one has only to look at the paperback racks of any popular bookshop. Most of that fable is far inferior in substance and style to the books of Lewis, Tolkien, Bradbury, and L'Engle, true; nevertheless, this great mass of paperback fantasies is evidence that young people want something more genuinely imaginative than the pseudo-serious boring books or the pornographic rubbish that have been pressed upon them.

As the political inclinations of the present rising generation are notably or notoriously different from the frantic politics of college students twenty years ago, so literary preferences of the youthful — those of them who read seriously at all — seem to be shifting. And the young do not stay young: they become dominant within a few years. As Disraeli put it, prevailing opinions generally are the opinions of the generation that is passing. When it becomes clear that the public's taste has altered greatly, even New York publishers make changes in their lists; why, even New York review media, after some uneasy interval, condescend to review books they would prefer to ignore.

Thus it seems worth noting that the two American writers of recent years most seriously discussed by serious literary critics nowadays are Flannery O'Connor and Walker Percy — both Christians endowed with moral imagination, both political conservatives, both Southerners and defenders of the traditions of the South. Also it seems worth noting that the European man of letters, Solzhenitsyn aside, who is most honored among us is Czeslaw Milosz, whose prose and poetry are suffused with the tragic sense of life.[9]

In the dawning era of the twenty-first century, it may come to pass that an old orthodoxy will seem happily attractive to the surviving friends of humane letters. It may be that the recovery of norms will be more exciting than surrender to the perverse. It may be that the Permanent Things, those norms and standards and institutions and beliefs and customs and conventions that enable us to live as moral beings, will be respected more in the observance than they ever could in the breach.

It may be that once more the literature of the English language will be strongly marked by that ethical end which rose up so strong in

9. See Miguel de Unamuno, *The Tragic Sense of Life in Men and Nations* (Princeton, N.J.: Princeton University Press, 1972), 21-22, 38-39, 69, 138-139.

Ben Jonson and Samuel Johnson and many another great writer. It may be that the fabulists, the creators of allegory and parable and fable and poetic fiction, will supplant those authors of our day who see man as the Naked Ape.

It may be that even those in journalism — and even the clerisy of the twenty-first century — will come to apprehend the great mysterious incorporation of the human race. Those in newspaper and classroom and pulpit will acknowledge the truth that we moderns are dwarfs standing upon the shoulders of giants; they will learn to look backward toward their ancestors so that they may look forward to their posterity. They may swallow the hard old truth that men and women are more than the flies of a summer; that generation does link with generation; and that a principal means for that connection among the dead, the living, and the unborn is our inheritance of humane letters. It may be that the third century of the American Republic will become a regenerate Augustan age.

Or it may be that future generations, having cast out the literature of affirmation, will come to read nothing but technical manuals, comic books, and obscene fantasy. What direction our society may take, by the beginning of the twenty-first century, must depend upon the energies and the imagination, for good or ill, of the people who only in recent months have entered upon the duties and opportunities of the bent world of the nineties.

Eugene Ionesco, creator of the theater of the absurd, received in 1985 the Eliot Award of the Ingersoll Prizes. In accepting the prize, the old dramatist expressed clearly for the first time his purpose in prancing absurdities across the stage. "If I have shown men to be ridiculous or ludicrous," he said, "it was in no way out of any desire for comic effect, but rather to proclaim the truth . . . to show what man may become when he is cut off from all transcendence."[10]

These words, like the literary preferences of the more thoughtful among the rising generation, offer us hope for a regenerate literature that regards human beings as standing somewhat closer to the angels than to the naked apes. The votaries of the ephemeral things are blown about by every wind of doctrine; the enthusiasts for mere appetite are confuted, in the long run, by the great mysterious incorporation of the

10. Eugene Ionesco, "Realism and the Spirit," *Chronicles of Culture* 10, no. 2 (February 1986): 24-25.

human race, which exacts severe penalties from its defeated adversaries. Imagination it is that shapes society — moral imagination, or idyllic imagination, or diabolic imagination. The writers whose works we celebrate here were endowed with the moral imagination. Let us read them through, all over again, and then draw the sword of imagination, and endeavor to redeem the time.

> Pens are most dangerous tools, more sharp by odds
> Than swords, and cut more keen than whips or rods.[10]

So we are instructed by old John Taylor, the Water Poet, in *News from Hell, Hull, and Halifax*. So we friends of the moral imagination in humane letters are formidably armed as were our preceptors from the first half of this dying century. In letters as in life, abide by the counsel of Edgar:

> "Take heed o' the foul fiend: obey thy parents; keep thy word justly; swear not; commit not with man's sworn spouse; set not thy sweet heart on proud array. . . . Keep thy foot out of brothels, thy hand out of plackets, thy pen from lenders' books, and defy the foul fiend."[11]

The foul fiend denominated Screwtape has besmirched a great many of the books of the twentieth century. Set him at defiance, cast him into the outer darkness, far beyond the confines of the republic of letters, and posterity may celebrate the victory of high-spirited writers over the vegetative and sensual errors of their time.

---

10. John Taylor (1580-1653), "News from Hell, Hull, and Halifax," *All the Workes of John Taylor, the Water Poet* (1630) (London: The Spenser Society, 1868-1878).

11. William Shakespeare, "King Lear," *The Riverside Shakespeare* (Boston: Houghton Mifflin, 1974), III, 4, lines 71-74, 96-98.

From War to Affirmation:
The Literature of the
Permanent Things

Father Brown's War on the Impermanent Things

John Peterson

Father Brown, the sleuth in Chesterton's detective stories, is often
described as rather a passive character, a sort of a quiet dumpling
of a person. That is the way Chesterton first introduces him to us in
the opening story of the series, "The Blue Cross." Ronald Knox described the matter accurately enough when he said of our general
reaction to Father Brown that "a man like that will never be able to
get at the truth."[1]

But after that first glimpse of him, the reader must quickly adjust
to a more active and even noisily indignant Father Brown, a man who
had the habit of bursting suddenly into loud and vehement harangues.
He did this at odd times and to the general surprise of his listeners. At
these times his purpose was to condemn the ungodly and the immoral,
and it was his method to denounce them in a ringing voice described
variously by Chesterton as a drum roll or a pistol shot. Here is one of
his typically emotional tirades:

> "Do you think I don't know that the love of a man and a woman was
> the first command of God and is glorious forever? Are you one of
> those idiots who think we don't admire love and marriage? Do I need
> to be told of the Garden of Eden or the wine of Cana? It is just because
> the strength in the thing was the strength of God, that it rages with
> that awful energy even when it breaks loose from God. When the

---

1. Ronald Knox, introduction to *Father Brown: Selected Stories* by G. K. Chesterton (London: Oxford University Press, 1955), vii.

Garden becomes a jungle, but still a glorious jungle; when the second fermentation turns the wine of Cana into the vinegar of Calvary."[2]

You will find many more of these "preachments," as Larry Clipper called them,[3] embedded in Chesterton's fifty-three Father Brown short stories. These impromptu mini-sermons, messages of censure and rebuke delivered in a stentorian voice, were characteristic acts of the stumpy Catholic priest.

Detective stories are not usually considered part of serious, lasting literature or as part of Permanent Things of man and God which great literature celebrates. Yet even if we take Chesterton's stories very seriously, they are nonetheless not a celebration of Permanent Things. Father Brown is not a celebrator; he is a warrior. He is at war with the *im*permanent things. That is what his stories are about.

The most recent Father Brown bibliography lists more than 150 books, articles and book chapters discussing or critiquing the Father Brown stories.[4] As one might expect, most interpreters in this growing body of criticism have been one or other of two kinds: those primarily interested in detective stories and those primarily interested in Chesterton. The majority opinion of both groups, I am sorry to say, has not treated the little priest's moralistic outbursts as integral to the stories; that is, as an integral part of Father Brown's character or as playing an integral role in the narrative structure. The Chestertonians tend to see Father Brown's sermonizing as a simple reflection of Chesterton's own thoughts: thoughts which he expressed in his other writings and which are independent of the Father Brown character. In Gertrude White's phrase, the stories are "a mirror and a microcosm of Chesterton's philosophical world."[5] On the other hand, the aficionado of the detective story is primarily interested in clues, alibis, testimony, disguises, deductions — in short, the apparatus of the detective story. He is likely to find the moralizing an intrusion. "Too frequently," wrote Howard Hay-

2. Gilbert Keith Chesterton, *The Father Brown Omnibus* (New York: Dodd Mead, 1951), 970.

3. Lawrence J. Clipper, *G. K. Chesterton* (New York: Twayne, 1974), 124.

4. John Peterson, "A Father Brown Bibliography," in *The Mask of Midas* by G. K. Chesterton (Trondheim: Classica, 1991), "Part Three: Father Brown Criticism and Discussion," 49-62.

5. Gertrude M. White, "Mirror and Microcosm: Chesterton's Father Brown Stories." *The Chesterton Review* 10, no. 2 (May 1984): 184.

craft, Chesterton "seizes the occasion to intrude personal dogma and mystification."[6]

There is something to be said for these views, but there is something very unsatisfying about them also, especially to anyone who thinks Father Brown's "preachments," if that is a good word, are among the best things in the stories. To these readers the idea that the preachments represent an artistic lapse, or a mere intrusion of Chesterton's personal beliefs, is unacceptable.

It should be made clear that I am not speaking specifically about the theme of the stories or about the Chestertonian ideas that may be implied there in the abstract, but about a distinctive kind of Father Brown speech. Another example may serve to identify the kind of speech I mean, and about which a few obvious and uncritical remarks may be made. This comes at the end of "The Purple Wig," from *The Wisdom of Father Brown*, the second of Chesterton's five Father Brown collections. Our priest is in high dudgeon:

> "I know the Unknown God. . . . I know his name; it is Satan. The true God was made flesh and dwelt among us. And I say to you, wherever you find men ruled merely by mystery, it is the mystery of iniquity. If the devil tells you something is too fearful to look at, look at it. If he says something is too terrible to hear, hear it. If you think some truth unbearable, bear it. . . . The cross of Christ be between me and harm."[7]

The first obvious remark to be made is that this is not the voice of Gilbert Chesterton. Father Brown's peculiar tone of angry indignation is almost entirely absent from Chesterton's other writings and from his private life as well. Just two brief examples will illustrate this. His most persistent opponents, Bernard Shaw and H. G. Wells, were also his personal friends, in spite of decades of unremitting public disagreement. Chesterton would meet a bombastic threat from Shaw with what Vincent Brome called "a glorious gurgle of delight" and laughter. "It's your intellectual magnanimity which destroys me," Chesterton would say between chuckles, disarming Shaw as could no one else.[8] And to a

6. Howard Haycraft, *Murder for Pleasure: The Life and Times of the Detective Story*, 2nd ed. (New York: Biblo and Tannen, 1951), 76.

7. G. K. Chesterton, "The Purple Wig," in *The Father Brown Omnibus*, 344.

8. *Six Studies in Quarrelling* (London: Cresset, 1958), 154.

19

peevish letter from Wells, Chesterton once answered, altogether typically, "Any quarrel between us will not come from me," while charitably putting Wells' ill temper down "to an emotion of loyalty to another friend." Wells replied, sheepishly enough, "Also, I can't quarrel with you."[9]

All published recollections of Chesterton are the same in regard to his remarkable equanimity. But Father Brown is not Chesterton. The priest has a voice of his own; his displeasure, on provocation, is personal, cutting, and utterly devoid of Chestertonian good humor. Here is another example.

> "So the dog denounced him, did he? [he asks a visitor]. The oracle of the dog condemned him. Did you see what birds were flying? Did you consult the augers about the sacrifices? Surely you didn't omit to cut open the dog and examine his entrails. That is the sort of scientific test you heathen humanitarians seem to trust, when you are thinking of taking away the life and honour of a man."[10]

Father Brown had just then forgotten himself. His sarcasm was perhaps something more than this young man deserved, and Chesterton has the priest quickly apologize. It should be obvious from the apology that the outburst was something more than a Chestertonian meditation or a narrative break designed for a didactic message.

In fact, there is an important technical problem in writing detective stories that these preachments of Father Brown's were designed to answer. That is to say, the preachments have an integral function in the structure of the stories. They are as integral to understanding Father Brown as those opening interviews-in-his-quarters are to Sherlock Holmes, or those speeches-of-summation-in-the-library are to Lord Peter Wimsey.

The Father Brown stories are part of the subclass of crime fiction respectfully known as "The Classic British Detective Story" and disrespectfully as the "Whodunit." Few literary genres, if we dare call formula detective stories a genre, have been bounded by such rigid customs and prohibitions. Dennis Porter gives the recipe for the required plot components, six of them, in his 1981 study, *The Pursuit of Crime:*

9. Maisie Ward, *Gilbert Keith Chesterton* (New York: Sheed & Ward, 1943), 411-13.
10. "The Oracle of the Dog," in *The Father Brown Omnibus,* 487.

"[1] The initial situation that is about to be or has just been disrupted, [2] the discovery of the crime that disrupts, [3] the appeal to and the arrival of the detective, [4] the pursuit of the unknown criminal via a series of investigations, searches, and interrogations, . . . [5] the progressive elimination of suspects, and [6] the final unmasking and arrest of the criminal."[11]

This formula is almost identical to the one Chesterton himself outlined in 1911:

A policeman, stupid but sweet-tempered, and always erring on the side of mercy, walks along the street; and in the course of his ordinary business finds a man in a Bulgarian uniform killed with an Australian boomerang in a Brompton milk-shop. Having set free all the most suspicious persons in the story, he then appeals to the bull-dog professional detective, who appeals to the hawk-like amateur detective. The latter finds near the corpse a boot-lace, a button-hook, a French newspaper, and a return ticket from the Hebrides; and so, relentlessly, link by link, brings the crime home to the Archbishop of Canterbury.[12]

Such rigid formulization is certain to produce artistic problems of various kinds. Father Brown himself, as the Whodunit's first clerical detective, was an influential solution to one of these problems. Chesterton's solution was so successful that it has been cloned or reincarnated dozens of times, as Vicar Westerham, Father Dowling, Sister Ursela, Rabbi Small, and many more. The clerical detectives, Father Brown and the others as well, depart from the formula by seeing the crime from a religious point of view. The investigation is, in their hands, both the unraveling of a crime and a study of irreligion and sin.

In that sense the invention of the clerical detective was a master stroke, for it enabled Chesterton and his imitators to escape the first of the formula detective-story cul-de-sacs: the idea that fictional detectives succeed by applying their highly refined powers of logical deduction, the idea that the one acceptable way for an author to create a superior sleuth is to endow him with greater and ever greater powers of scientific

11. Dennis Porter, *The Pursuit of Crime: Art and Ideology in Detective Fiction* (New Haven: Yale, 1981), 87-88.
12. G. K. Chesterton, "Duties of the Police," *Illustrated London News, 1911-1913*, vol. 29 of *The Collected Works of G. K. Chesterton* (San Francisco: Ignatius Press, 1988), 82.

logic. To escape this cul-de-sac, Chesterton had long searched for and experimented with the idea of what he called "The Philosophical Detective" or a "transcendental Sherlock Holmes,"[13] an idea that surfaced but did not quite jell in such early works as *The Club of Queer Trades* and *The Man Who Was Thursday*. The inspiration had been provided in a famous and oft-told encounter between Chesterton and the Catholic priest John O'Conner. Father O'Conner jolted Chesterton by combining in himself an accustomed religious outlook with an unsettling practical knowledge of evil. That paradoxical combination was the essential idea behind the character of Father Brown.[14]

Of the many excellent attributes of the Father Brown stories, the one most universally praised, and certainly the one most crucial to their success, is the ingenuity with which Chesterton contrived his puzzles. Plot ingenuity is the foremost requirement of the classic detective story formula, and Chesterton excelled in impossible murders, locked rooms, contradictory witnesses, air-tight alibis, hoaxes, disguises, disappearances, practical jokes, impersonations, mistaken identities, and even a dog which, in parody of the celebrated Sherlock Holmes clue, enlightened Father Brown because, in fact, he did bark.

But an excess of the ingenious does create a problem: it is the danger of anticlimax. It has often been said that a detective story resembles a conjuring trick, and the resemblance is this: both author and magician depend on misdirection, on clever ways of making the audience look the wrong way at the right time. Of the two, however, the author finds himself at a distinct disadvantage at the end of the performance, for the magician is never expected to betray his secrets; and, as Chesterton put it, "The true object of an intelligent detective story is not to baffle the reader, but to enlighten the reader. . . ."[15] The problem stemming from the demand for ingenuity is the risk that the cleverness of the solution will not live up to the cleverness of the puzzle. Thus the Whodunit must not merely mystify us, but it must somehow avoid the deflation that comes when all the secrets are told, and the

13. Anonymous [Cecil Chesterton], *Gilbert K. Chesterton: A Criticism* (New York: John Lane, 1909), 209.

14. Maisie Ward, 251-53.

15. G. K. Chesterton, "Errors about Detective Stories," *Illustrated London News, 1920-1922*, vol. 32 of *The Collected Works of G. K. Chesterton*, ed. George Marlin (San Francisco: Ignatius Press, 1989), 80.

contrivances and machinery of mystification have been exposed. Moreover, part of the machinery is the detective's method of detection, and that also must be exposed.

Father Brown used many of the standard Holmesian techniques, but his essential method was something entirely his own. It has been variously described as intuition, empathy or some form of pattern recognition. Undoubtedly it is all of these things, but perhaps the best phrase for it would be not pattern recognition but pattern rejection. Father Brown senses, as the others do not, that events have taken on "the wrong shape"; the obvious explanation has struck a false note.

". . . There's something wrong [he says to Flambeau]. I feel it in my bones."[16]

"It's all too neat and correct."[17]

It is important to ask why the other characters accept the false pattern — why they are misled. In general, they are misled because they have no proper philosophy or religious faith to guide them. Thus, in the face of an enigma, they helplessly fall into superstition or relax into a comfortable class prejudice. They superstitiously accept oracles and curses and doom. They intolerantly accuse the vagabond or the failure, and not the magistrate or the millionaire. Compared to them, Father Brown is a rock of disbelief, a disbelief solidly based on proper philosophy and religious faith. "I do believe some things, of course," he tells a dissembler, "and therefore, of course, I don't believe other things."[18] He is not blinded by superstition; he is not blinded by prejudice. Thus, false religion and errant philosophy have an integral part to play in the development of each of the mysteries.

This means that Father Brown's methods of detection are fundamentally entangled with formal questions of belief and disbelief. Father Brown alone was theologian enough to discard the "oracle of the dog."[19] Father Brown alone was moralist enough to see "the invisible man."[20] His rejection of scientism saved him from "the mistake of the machine,"[21] and his rejection of superstition saved him from "the blast of

16. "The Sins of Prince Saradine," *The Father Brown Omnibus*, 150.
17. "The Duel of Dr. Hirsch," *The Father Brown Omnibus*, 279.
18. "The Dagger with Wings," *The Father Brown Omnibus*, 574.
19. "The Oracle of the Dog," *The Father Brown Omnibus*, 481-504.
20. "The Invisible Man," *The Father Brown Omnibus*, 82-100.
21. "The Mistake of the Machine," *The Father Brown Omnibus*, 298-314.

the book."[22] It would require a very fine scalpel indeed to remove all traces of moral doctrine from the Father Brown stories.

As a matter of technique, the difference in outlook between Father Brown and the other characters is a crucial element in the narrative structure. To be sure, the fictional detective is expected to expose the crime, but we should not be too quick in a Father Brown story to say exactly what the crime is. Father Brown himself reminds us in "The Donnington Affair," that "in a murder case the guiltiest person is not always the murderer."[23] The surprising truth of the Father Brown series is how rarely the guilt of the guiltiest person refers to murder, theft, blackmail or any other official crime.

It is no secret that half of Father Brown's criminals simply escape. Sometimes it is with the priest's help. On two occasions, after persuading a thief to return the loot, the priest conceals the crime from the authorities. This is not the formula detective story ending, and it demands an explanation. The explanation usually given is that Father Brown as a priest is interested in the criminal's soul and not in his police record. As W. D. Spencer put it in his recent study of the clerical detectives,

> He [Father Brown] brings the culprit before God's bar, himself serving first the role of prosecutor, then defense attorney, passing judgment and giving penance. He is arresting officer, prosecution, defense, judge, and jailer, incarcerating his convicts in the prison of God's mercy, sentenced to a life of repentance.[24]

This is a very attractive idea and one that figures prominently in several of the earlier and more frequently anthologized stories — as, for example, in the story of "The Invisible Man" which ends with Father Brown walking

> . . . snow-covered hills under the stars for many hours with a murderer, and what they said to each other will never be known.[25]

22. "The Blast of the Book," *The Father Brown Omnibus*, 857-72.

23. G. K. Chesterton: *Thirteen Detectives*, selected and arranged by Marie Smith (New York: Dodd Mead, 1987), 246.

24. William David Spencer, *Mysterium and Mystery: The Clerical Crime Novel* (Ann Arbor: UMI Research Press, 1989), 98.

25. *The Father Brown Omnibus*, 100.

Unfortunately for the theory, this is a scene rarely repeated after the first collection of stories. The priest is otherwise engaged. Of the fifty Father Brown stories, only ten show the priest counseling the criminal, and only four of these come after the first volume.[26] As the series developed, Chesterton evidently decided that criminals are hardly the worst people around, and his priest became indifferent to both criminals and police investigators. As Father Brown told the police inspector in "The Quick One,"

> "I've never had anything to do with setting police machinery at work, or running down criminals, or anything like that."[27]

If Father Brown's murderers and thieves are not the center of guilt in the stories, then who is? Chesterton's third Father Brown story, "The Queer Feet," is instructive in this regard. Having solved the crime and disposed of the criminal long before the story is half over, Father Brown finds himself among the robbery victims, the aristocratic members of an exclusive club. Although he has some respect and even a kind of admiration for the robber, he finds it somewhat difficult to hide his contempt for the wealthy men who have been robbed.

> "Odd, isn't it," he said, "that a thief and a vagabond should repent, when so many who are rich and secure remain hard and frivolous, and without fruit for God or Man?"[28]

In short, Father Brown has just insulted them roundly.

---

26. In *The Innocence of Father Brown* (1911), Father Brown counsels the criminal in six stories: he counsels Flambeau in "The Blue Cross," *The Father Brown Omnibus*, 18-23, "The Queer Feet," *The Father Brown Omnibus*, 54, and "The Flying Stars," *The Father Brown Omnibus*, 79-81; and he counsels James Welkin in "The Invisible Man," *The Father Brown Omnibus*, 100; Dr. Harris in "The Wrong Shape," *The Father Brown Omnibus*, 130-31; and Rev. Wilfred Bohun in "The Hammer of God," *The Father Brown Omnibus*, 174-75. In the later stories, Father Brown counsels the criminal in four stories: in *The Wisdom of Father Brown* (1914), the priest counsels Parkinson in "The Man in the Passage," *The Father Brown Omnibus*, 296; in *The Incredulity of Father Brown* (1926) he counsels Mr. Wilton in "The Arrow of Heaven," *The Father Brown Omnibus*, 477; in *The Secret of Father Brown* (1927), he counsels Tommy Hunter in "The Red Moon of Merus," *The Father Brown Omnibus*, 778, and Maurice in "The Chief Mourner of Marne," *The Father Brown Omnibus*, 798-800.

27. *The Father Brown Omnibus*, 845.

28. Ibid., 61.

There are other stories in which the not-so-innocent bystanders receive a hearty rebuke from Father Brown. One thinks of his harsh words for the American businessmen at the end of "The Arrow of Heaven,"

"Take your wild justice or our dull legality; but in the name of Almighty God, let there be an equal lawlessness or an equal law."[29]

or of his even harsher words for the gentry at Marne Mansion in "The Chief Mourner of Marne,"

"Go on your own primrose path pardoning all your favorite vices and being generous to your fashionable crimes; and leave us in the darkness. . . ."[30]

These speeches demonstrate Father Brown's characteristic refusal to condemn legal criminals for their legal crimes, coupled with his impatience with the spiritual criminals and their spiritual crimes. He sums it up beautifully for us in "The Actor and the Alibi," when he tells Ashton Jarvis that Mrs. Mandeville was "something very much worse than a murderess," and when Jarvis asks him what is worse than a murderess, Father Brown's answer is "An egoist."[31] Egoism and murder. Father Brown sees each of his mysteries as a double crime — a legal mystery wrapped in a spiritual mystery; crime wrapped in sin. But this, it must be emphasized, is not merely the well-worn notion that a legal crime has a spiritual aspect. The idea is, rather, that each of the two mysteries is a distinct puzzle in itself. In Father Brown tales, the reader not only learns that the Marquis murdered his brother, but the reader also learns that the Marquis' friends are a pack of cold-blooded hypocrites. It is a question of the legal criminal with whom we might sympathize and the spiritual criminals with whom, it is Father Brown's business to explain, we must not sympathize.

Chesterton will often have Father Brown choose someone on the fringe of the mystery as his sounding board, someone whom we readers might accept as a surrogate for ourselves. If the confidant is not the priest's friend Flambeau, as in the earlier stories, then it might be a detective or a reporter, a doctor or other neutral observer, as when

29. Ibid., 480.
30. Ibid., 803.
31. Ibid., 720.

Father Brown expostulates to his companion Evan Smith in "The Vanishing of Vaudrey":

> "What a horrible tale of hatred! What a vengeance for one mortal worm to take on another! Shall we ever get to the bottom of this bottomless human heart where such abominable imaginations can abide?"[32]

Smith, of course, and also the readers think he is speaking of the killer. But we are all mistaken. In this story Father Brown's sympathies were entirely with the murderer. His moral outrage and invective were reserved for the dearly departed victim — the man whose throat had been so recently cut.

The same comedy of misunderstanding is repeated in a number of other stories in which, much to the surprise of his companions, and perhaps to the surprise of the reader, Father Brown turns his back on the official criminal and on official crime to direct his anger toward those other actors in the mystery whose wrongheadedness somehow contributed to the crime or somehow prevented its solution. Father Brown's guilty ones are the secret fools of each case, wrong-headed fools who swallow superstitions and false science, worship money, chase intellectual fads and religious frauds, embrace barbarism, or whose vain ideals of democracy are an insult to the dignity of man. Father Brown sees through the cloud of foolishness and illogic; he sees the crime that surrounds the crime. As he said when so solemnly asked his opinion of the terrible "Doom of the Darnaways,"

> "Yes, we are dealing with something terrible; with the most terrible thing I know; and the name of it is nonsense."[33]

Or his opinion of the "actor's alibi,"

> ". . . damned nonsense and more than damned nonsense — nonsense that can damn."[34]

We might end this discussion where the Father Brown series begins — with the adventure of "The Blue Cross." Let us say we have followed

32. Ibid., 741.
33. Ibid., 596.
34. "The Actor and the Alibi," *The Father Brown Omnibus*, 724.

the story through its long sequence of seemingly meaningless and inexplicable events. And then, just as we reach the point of resolution and explanation, we are confronted with one more inexplicable event. There is an abrupt pause in the action of the story so that Father Brown might preach a brief sermon.

> "Look at those stars. Don't they look as if they were single diamonds and sapphires? Well, you can imagine any mad botany or geology you please. But don't fancy all that frantic astronomy would make the smallest difference to the reason and justice of conduct. On plains of opal, under cliffs cut out of pearl, you would still find a notice-board, 'Thou shalt not steal.'"[35]

Reading the story for the first time, we accept the speech, I suppose, as an attempt by Chesterton to give Father Brown a distinctively religious voice. But we are anxious to get on with the matter at hand. We are still perplexed about the bizarre turns and twists of the story that as readers we know are about to be resolved. Why was the soup spilled, and why was the window broken? Mystery stories excite us, as Chesterton once pointed out, by the explanations we have not yet heard.[36] As readers, we want to hear them. And so Father Brown explains.

> "At every place we went to, I took care to do something that would get us talked about for the rest of the day. I didn't do much harm — a splashed wall, spilt apples, a broken window. . . ."[37]

Having learned with what clever maneuvers the priest has trapped the thief, the reader might well marvel at the intricacies of plot and at the abrupt and complete reversal with which the story ends. But it is to be remembered that artificial contrivances of plot are not to be revealed without risk of anticlimax, and "The Blue Cross," it is also to be remembered, is packed with the wildest and most outlandish coincidences.

Curiously enough, however, the reader is not disappointed. There is one final exchange between Flambeau and Father Brown. Father

---

35. *The Father Brown Omnibus*, 19.

36. "Civilization and Progress," *Illustrated London News, 1911-1913*, vol. 29 of *The Collected Works of G. K. Chesterton* (San Francisco: Ignatius Press, 1988), 396.

37. *The Father Brown Omnibus*, 22-23.

Brown tells Flambeau that something in the priestly trade made him see through the other's disguise. Flambeau asks what that might have been, and Father Brown replies with this: "You attacked reason. . . . It's bad theology."[38]

It is my belief that the reader finds this warmly satisfying. I do not mean that it is satisfying as an idea or a lesson in theology, although it might be that as well. I mean that it is satisfying as a part of the detective-story machinery, a part of Dennis Porter's six-step recipe of Chesterton's parallel formula with its tell-tale clues of bootlace, button hook, French newspaper, and return ticket from the Hebrides. Long after we have forgotten the bootlace, or, in "The Blue Cross," long after we have forgotten that Father Brown put salt into the sugar bowl, we remember the surprising clue of the criminal's "bad theology." It goes beyond the revelation that the tall man in the clerical garb is an international jewel thief. The story puts into play another kind of falsity altogether. It adds to the fraud of a contrived and improbable theft, a greater and more familiar fraud of religious nonsense. Theologically speaking (we are happy to learn) the renowned international jewel thief is a commonplace prig and something of a fool.

This is the way to avoid deflation and anticlimax, and this is the way Chesterton ended his Father Brown stories. In story after story, the priest turns his back on the legal crime to rail against the immoral and irreligious atmosphere in which the legal crime has taken place and in which the truth has been hidden. He does not condemn the crime that makes the headlines. His preachments implicate everyone who shares in the larger issues of guilt — the fools and liars who misconstrue events while talking damned nonsense and hypocrisy. It is not enough to say of a Father Brown plot that there is a "moral to the story." There is a moralizer, and a very aggressive one at that — a moral warrior who makes the "moral to the story" a part of the action.

Father Brown's preachments are not a departure from the classic formula, but an original contribution to the formula. The voice of the preachments is not that of the jolly author insinuating a pet theory, but the voice of an angry priest denouncing the criminals for their foolishness and bad faith. In his own unmistakable style Father Brown has a war to wage, as he does in his final warning to his favorite professional jewel thief, Flambeau:

38. Ibid., 23.

"Men may keep a sort of level of good, but no man has ever been able to keep on one level of evil. That road goes down and down. The kind man drinks and turns cruel; the frank man kills and lies about it. Many a man I've known started like you to be an honest outlaw, a merry robber of the rich, and ended stamped into slime. . . . Your downward steps have begun. You used to boast of doing nothing mean, but you are doing something mean tonight. You are leaving suspicion on an honest boy with a good deal against him already; you are separating him from the woman he loves and who loves him. But you will do meaner things than that before you die."[39]

That was a very good warning to give to a jewel thief. It is also a very good warning to give anyone, even readers of common detective stories. A reader might pause just at that point to consider his own personal road that goes down and down — as Flambeau paused just long enough to fling the stolen gems at Father Brown's feet.

Chesterton remarked in 1908, "It is not that we have not got enough scoundrels to curse, but that we have not got enough good men to curse them."[40] Father Brown is Chesterton's idea of the good man who curses scoundrels. Chesterton said many things about scoundrels and stories, and one of the most important things he said for those who discuss Father Brown is a phrase he used about fairy tales. He said, ". . . there really is a dragon somewhere."[41] The official criminals, legal criminals — murderers, blackmailers and thieves — are not the dragon. The dragon is Father Brown's secret criminal, the fool and liar who worships the nonsense of the impermanent things. And there really is a dragon.

39. "The Flying Stars," *The Father Brown Omnibus*, 80-81.
40. "Public Confessions by Politicians," *Illustrated London News, 1908-1910*, vol. 28 of *The Collected Works of G. K. Chesterton*, ed. George Marlin and Lawrence Clipper (San Francisco: Ignatius Press, 1987), 64.
41. "On Adventure Stories for Boys," *Illustrated London News, 1920-1922*, vol. 32 of *The Collected Works of G. K. Chesterton*, ed. George Marlin (San Francisco: Ignatius Press, 1989), 454.

Chesterton's Dickens and the Literary Critics: The Thing and the Theory

David Whalen

It is a happy fact that we are witnessing a steady resurgence of interest in the works of G. K. Chesterton. Aidan Mackey has noted that no one would be more surprised than Chesterton himself, his humility being as great as his girth. But the resurgence of interest in Chesterton is often regarded as indicative of his particular relevance to our times. Today, we often find that our contemporary "hot topics" were ably addressed more than sixty years ago by a man whose intellect and liberality elevate the controversy to a high level of thought and art. Chesterton's relevance is widely affirmed and lauded, but here I wish to do the same for his *irrelevance*. In the largely academic world of literary criticism, Chesterton's copious literary criticism stands amidst a kind of saintly glow of irrelevance. By means of a few general points about Chesterton's criticism, especially his works on Charles Dickens, I wish to draw attention to the importance and influence of Permanent Things in that criticism. Specifically, I hope to address a way in which Chesterton is wholly irreverent, out of step, desynchronized with our times and, I suggest, rightly so.

What is meant by Permanent Things is, I hope, quite well known to the reader. It includes, for instance, what Josef Pieper and Etienne Gilson call the *"philosophia perennis"* — the perennial philosophy. It also refers to the good, the true, the beautiful, the honorable, the four cardinal virtues of justice, temperance, courage, and prudence, the three supernatural virtues of faith, hope, and charity, the seven gifts of the Holy Ghost, and every other numbered thing learned by medieval schoolboys with the ready aid of fingers and toes. Likewise, Permanent

Things include love, romance, courtesy, courtship — things learned, no doubt, by said schoolboys with the ready aid of yet another permanent thing: the opposite sex. Of all these things Chesterton is stout in defense because, for him, they are grounded in reality itself. They are simply true.

In a sense it is perhaps redundant to speak of Permanent Things at all. We could speak merely of "things" in the sense of the Latin word for "thing," *res*. It is a charged word in Latin. *Res* occurs in our words "real" and "reality." The *res-publica*, the "public thing," comes to us as "republic," the very word for government and statecraft — two things not at all trivial to the Roman mind. When the great Roman poet, Virgil, says *"Sunt lacrimae rerum"* — there are tears of *things* — he is not merely saying that sometimes things just don't go well. He is alluding to the essential sadness and tragedy of human life, the impossibility of perfection in this world, a note the Fathers of the Church deemed an appropriate precursor to the arrival of the only One capable of rendering this world a comedy.

As Chesterton well knew, the "thing," *res*, is reality itself. It is no coincidence that "the thing" was employed by him as the title of a book, for intrinsic in the *res* or "thing" is the idea of both the ending point, the term, and the beginning point, the principle. In the suggestive and evasive manner of poetic language, "The Thing" alludes to the fact that these beginnings and ends are identical — we move out only to return; we grasp the Alpha and are shocked to discover that we hold the Omega as well. "The thing" is reality, our created world and its Creator, luminous in the brilliance of existence, dazzling and even blinding, as Pieper notes, in its sheer intelligibility. We are ordered to reality, and thus a life lived in accordance with reality is one of sanity, sanctity, and at least moderate happiness. Reject reality and "hark what discord follows." It is the principle of all good thought and truth; it is the subsistence of all being, existence, and essence. We are in the realm, of course, of metaphysics, metaphysical realism to be exact, and Gilson's famous comments on Chesterton and St. Thomas Aquinas attest to G. K.'s lively apprehension of the importance of this realism. If Chesterton was rather shaky about certain aspects of reality, such as whether the book he had pocketed had been paid for, or whether his shoes matched, he was extraordinarily sensitive to the respect due to things merely because they exist. If he had once felt the power and fatal circularity of solipsistic metaphysical skepticism, it made him all the more sensitive to and all the more grateful for reality, such that he embraced God as the only Being capable of supporting his "immense and terrible gratitude." But to return to the mundane realm of literary criticism, Chesterton's realism is precisely the reason that his criticism is so "irrelevant," so out of step with the other common critical practices for the greater part of this century.

It is no secret that since the days of Descartes and particularly eighteenth-century critical epistemology, reality has seen difficult times. The history of skepticism and philosophical solipsism in the last four hundred years is too well known to belabor here, but it must be said that for at least the last 150 years, a deep metaphysical malaise has settled upon the Western world born of an often vague but general acceptance of doubt as the only reasonable starting point for thought. It is now *de rigueur* in academic or intellectual circles to regard objective truth as a highly improbable terminus. By and large, philosophy has become logical positivism, a great, mathematical rule-game of "let's pretend." We are surrounded by "would be's," "could be's" and "might be's." We are pommeled with "suggests," "implies," and the ubiquitous "perhaps." And who can forget that sly dog of intellectual discourse, "seems?" Alas, unlike Hamlet, we know "seems" only too well. In all of this we swim, adrift, longing for the sight of terra firma, the indicative statement. Even the honest interrogative has been subverted. Pilate's infamous question "What is truth?" is not a question at all but, paradoxically, a kind of sly, backwards statement. The contemporary practitioners of literary criticism have twisted the question, the interrogative mood, into a supporting rod for their indeterminacy and doubt. Legal thought is mostly positivist as well, the idea of natural law considered hopelessly antiquated and naive. The forsaking of an immediate and accessible reality is on every hand, and the halls of literary scholarship are no exception.[1]

---

1. See Eugene Goodheart, *The Skeptic Disposition in Contemporary Criticism* (Princeton, N.J.: Princeton University Press, 1984). See also Goodheart's *The Failure of Criticism* (Cambridge: Harvard University Press, 1978) in which he discusses the irrational obsession back to Descartes who, in freeing the mind from the body, actually subverted the powers of the mind, giving birth to a "critical machine of extraordinary destructive power" (13). G. Douglas Atkins, in *Reading Deconstruction Deconstructive Reading* (Lexington: University Press of Kentucky, 1983) discusses the "dehellenizing" of criticism. Atkins claims that criticism, like literature itself, cannot appeal to "reason, logic, and order . . ." since the idea of the "objective" is illusory (35, 36). Finally, see Steven E. Cole's "The Dead-End of Deconstruction: Paul de Man and the Fate of Poetic Language," *Criticism* 30, no. 1 (1988): 91-112.

The results of a nebulous metaphysical and epistemological skepticism in this field are many, and often even amusing. Who has not
noticed in academic prose the unyielding tyranny of the grammatical
subjunctive mood? There is an even more insidious effect of our professional metaphysical skepticism. It is more difficult to describe, but
more important as well, for it is the key to the distinction between
Chesterton's critical writing and the majority of that which literary
professionals must endure. When reality is problematic at best, when a
writer cannot really presume on our living, as A. D. Nuttall would say,
beneath "a common sky,"[2] a literary critic cannot reason nor write freely.
He is forced, rather unconsciously I believe, to engage in what I call
"logical fantasism," that is, the arbitrary and capricious creation of an
intellectual "world" in which to play out his ideas. Because he has
implicitly rejected this world, so he must invent one with its own rules,
patterns, values, criteria for valid inferences, and so forth. He must,
with great labor and difficulty, display for the reader what kinds of ends
he deems appropriate to pursue, what kinds of means his fantasy realm
of reasoning holds valid, what sorts of evidence may be used to "prove"
what sorts of points. Make no mistake, I do not speak of the well-worn
rhetorical practice of merely introducing the audience to the matter at
hand. What occurs in the subtext, as it were, of critical prose is something like this: "Behold, idle reader, I am aware that we operate in
separate and incommunicable worlds. I know that my observations and
reasonings are unfathomably individual and idiosyncratic, so before I
begin let me tell you the rules I have arbitrarily chosen to observe in
thinking about (fill in the blank) and then we can proceed." Of course,
approaches of this kind involve a contradiction: if reasonings are hopelessly individual and incommunicable, one cannot communicate one's
arbitrary criteria for reasoning. The metaphysical skepticism behind the
approach is wholly contradictory, as Maritain, Nuttall, and Gilson have
ceaselessly shown.[3] But this is indeed what obtains. Logical fantasism
is a fantasy world of reasonings, a world without a common field of
discourse where reasonable men intelligently discuss a text from essen-

2. A. D. Nuttall, *A Common Sky: Philosophy and the Literary Imagination* (Berkeley:
University of California Press, 1974).
3. Nuttall, *A Common Sky*; Etienne Gilson, *The Unity of Philosophical Experience*
(London: Sheed & Ward, 1938); Jacques Maritain, *An Introduction to Philosophy* (New
York: Sheed & Ward, 1937).

tially common principles. The critic is alone in the void of solipsism; what he considers reasonable has no objective claim — not even upon himself. So, he must create *ex nihilo* a world, an order, a "system of reasoning," apologize for it with an admission of its arbitrariness, and proceed. He is reduced to fantasy because he has lost reality.

As you might expect, these logical fantasists often come together into schools that operate on principles so idiosyncratic there can be little consistent intercourse between them: the New Critics, feminists, Marxists, structuralists, deconstructionalists, happily adrift (or as Walker Percy might say, happily *lost*) each in his own cosmos. These last, the structuralists and deconstructionists, have even codified their chaos, and pronounced all "communication" to be solitary, be-fluxed solipsistic exercises in fleeting language structures which, even when left in their linguistic hermitage, self-destruct in a kind of frenzy of love for the void. All acts of language deconstruct. They de-exist.[4]

Because Chesterton's literary criticism is of a different type, he is often given merely token notice, and sometimes he is even violently repudiated. The eminent Edmund Wilson said that Chesterton melts away "into that peculiar pseudo-poetic booziness which verbalizes with

---

4. Another intellectual consequence of skepticism — pointed out by Gilson and Nuttall — is the emergence of "method" as the *sine qua non* of thought. Method expands to fill the vacuum left by the knowing subject, and it supplants understanding or wisdom. Method becomes reason itself. I think it no coincidence that, as skepticism sinks deeper into the cultural consciousness, discourse upon literature comes to require a *method* of criticism in order to be legitimate. Thus, even New Critics like William K. Wimsatt, John Crowe Ransom, Allen Tate, and others, for all their excellences, made a "method" out of treatment of the text alone. Though by so doing they were trying to restore the legitimacy of genuine literary judgment (Rene Wellec, *A History of Modern Criticism: 1750-1950*, 6 vols. [New Haven: Yale University Press, 1986], 6: 144-48), they actually prepared the ground for other "methods" far less benign. Older critics like Max Eastman, Granville Hicks, and Raymond Williams and more recent critics like Erwin Pracht, Werner Mittenzwei, and Robert Weimann employ a Marxist methodology in their work. It is a method designed to spawn yet another methodology: one for making literature a vehicle of social revolution.

Structuralism may be regarded as language method gone mad and deconstructionism as a refusal to allow structuralism to forget its nihilistic consequences. Whatever the school, feminist, deconstructionist, New Critical, or Marxist, literary thought is nothing if not a "method." So much is this the case that a critic like Bert G. Hornback is constrained to defend himself for not employing a definite method and for suggesting that "wisdom" is the object of literary art and thought (*The Hero of My Life: Essays on Dickens* [Athens, Ohio: Ohio University Press, 1981], xi).

large conceptions and ignores the most obtrusive actualities."[5] Never mind that this statement is itself a boozy one which ignores rather obtrusive actualities, and never mind as well the persistent paradox that confirmed relativists feel free to speak of actualities. When Chesterton writes on Dickens, he does something so different that many critics can only quote him, refer to him, and ultimately dismiss him as unworkable, inexact, and incomplete. This dismissal is often respectful and even sympathetic. Alexander Woollcott, in his introduction to the Reader's Club edition of Chesterton's study, *Charles Dickens: The Last of the Great Men,* praises Chesterton highly, but finally recommends Wilson as a "corrective to Chesterton."[6] A frequent feature of commentary on Chesterton's criticism roundly denounces, as if from moral superiority, Chesterton's infamous inaccuracies. We must not chaff at this, for the master of paradox himself would delight in the fact that readers steeped in metaphysical doubt should so pride themselves upon punctilious accuracy. Let them master the footnotes; Chesterton will master the text. More particularly, the issue of Chesterton's inaccuracies is a telling one for it reveals a bit of what he believed was important in the role of "critic." Chesterton is not interested in data, but in that kind of fact that doesn't lend itself to systematization. Concerning data and exactitude, Chesterton says:

> [We] are all exact and scientific on the subjects we do not care about. We all immediately detect exaggeration in an exposition of Mormonism or a patriotic speech from Paraguay. We all require sobriety on the subject of the sea serpent. But the moment we begin to believe a thing ourselves, that moment we begin easily to overstate it; and the moment our souls become serious, our words become a little wild.[7]

In fact, Chesterton's literary criticism differs from the bulk of this century's literary criticism because he is not affected, except negatively, by the doubt of reality. Chesterton has no truck with metaphysical doubt

5. Edmund Wilson, "Dickens: The Two Scrooges," in *The Wound and the Bow* (New York: Oxford University Press, 1965), 4.

6. Alexander Woollcott, foreword to *Charles Dickens, The Last of the Great Men,* by G. K. Chesterton (New York: Reader's Club Press, 1942), xi.

7. G. K. Chesterton, "Charles Dickens: His Life," in *Charles Dickens, The Last of the Great Men* (*Encyclopedia Britannica,* 14th ed.; reprint, New York: Reader's Club Press, 1942), 15.

and the effect on his "critical" writings is profound. As an advocate of Permanent Things and a realist not merely in theory but in instinct and habit, Chesterton's literary writings cannot conceive of a text as an isolated language structure awaiting analysis. A text is a part of and a reflection of reality, and that reality is shared by, for instance, traditional Western theology, dogma, the Church. It is all part of *res*, "reality," "the thing." The ancient principle that *ars imitatio naturae est* is the very connection between art and the world, literature and reality, and it throws open the doors for Chesterton's criticism. Throughout his commentary, Chesterton displays a love for ideas, varieties, and truths both in and out of the author being studied. It is, not surprisingly, a paradox. For Chesterton, reality is the ideal judgment seat for art, because reality, like art, is poetic, dazzling, colorful, and dogmatic. For Chesterton, dogma that is true liberates; anarchic "freedom" is an ill-disguised prison. There is order in the universe, and a truth to be known. The order is deep and mysterious, and truth is often surprising. When Chesterton says, "Dream for one mad moment that grass is green," he gives the key to all his criticism.[8]

Many critics have seen Chesterton's poetic quality, his sublimity, his insight, but few have really understood the relation between Chesterton and reality. When, for instance, Chesterton digresses, he does so out of the conviction that the truth in a story is the same as the truth in a store, and when discussing one there is no inordinate leap in discussing the other. Where he digresses, he actually only shifts the viewpoint or angle of inspection; what he is studying is the same.[9] For

---

8. G. K. Chesterton, *Charles Dickens, The Last of the Great Men*, 1906; reprinted as *Charles Dickens: A Critical Study* (New York: Reader's Club Press, 1942), 18.

9. There are many times when Chesterton is at his best in a digression. In his *Charles Dickens*, for example, when he addresses the "Alleged Optimism of Dickens," he says that Dickens treated his characters rather as a host treats his guests — with great care for their material well-being. He then digresses briefly on the proper physical benevolence of a host, a benevolence justly aimed at the material requirement men have in common (1906 version, tenth edition, 197). But a real digression, a full-blown essay in the midst of his Dickens commentary, occurs shortly after the mention of "physical benevolence." In explaining how Dickens actually effected social reform, Chesterton launches into a four-and-a-half page discussion of contemporary reformers who underscore the misery and debased condition of the poor. This does not work, says Chesterton. The optimist or "contented reformer" is more effective since the optimist "keeps alive in the human soul an invincible sense of the thing being worth doing, of the war being worth winning, of the people being worth their deliverance" (203). As long as one stresses that "human life is valuable because it is human," one will accom-

Chesterton, the whole of the created order is God's great and glorious digression, and his criticism is a variation on this "ontological theme." Chesterton might say that to exclude those comments of his that do not bear directly on the text would be to exclude the text; the text itself doesn't bear on the text, it bears (poorly or well) on reality. This reality is the one great, liberating, even wild yet unifying source of art and art's criticism. The continuity between the world and the world of art (not a univocal continuity but an analogical one) is the very playground of the intellect. Hence, on the same page, Chesterton can discuss the form of the novel and the creation of the universe, the quality of a character and the nature of greatness, or even the redeemed Scrooge and the irredeemable eugenicist. Chesterton's ontological and theological principles are definite and "concrete," and thus so are his critical statements and viewpoints; it would be hypocritical of Chesterton to be otherwise. This is a quality which makes conventional literary scholarship nervous. Gone are the subjunctives and in come the indicatives, the imperatives, the genuine interrogatives. Chesterton's Dickens criticism illustrates his liberty upon the common ground of reality, for it constantly bounces from the text to the world without apology. Where critics methodically tally images and postulate themes, Chesterton merely surmises; where critics supply examples from the text, Chesterton supplies examples from the taxi he took yesterday. To many it appears that Chesterton's comments are undisciplined and lack the rigors of critical thought.[10]

---

plish more reform than the "compassionate pessimists" for whom human life often "ceases to be human" (204). In all of this, Dickens' name is scarcely mentioned. Had Chesterton's subject been Dickens purely and simply, it would have been sufficient to note that Dickens brought the plight of the downtrodden into public view, thus stimulating reform. But Chesterton dives into what might be called the psychology or rhetoric of social change, for the objective truths inherent in encouraging such change are as much his subject as is Dickens.

10. In *The Textual Life of Dickens's Characters* (London: Macmillan Press Ltd., 1989) James A. Davies compares Chesterton unfavorably with authors who write "more critically-aware analyses . . ." (78). Noel C. Peyrouton names Chesterton as belonging to the early critics whom Dickens "may be said to have survived not because of the critics but despite them" (*Dickens Criticism Past, Present, and Future Directions: A Symposium* [Cambridge, Mass.: The Charles Dickens Reference Center, 1962], vii). Though he admires Chesterton, it is clear that critical methodology is king for Peyrouton. He rejoices that modern critics are "not as limited, self-contained or absolute" as the early critics (viii). Indeed, the process of criticism seems most important as Peyrouton considers its perfection "the impossibility of its ever being complete" (2). In the same volume

Chesterton himself, I am sure, would plead guilty to these charges, but his prose "disorganization" and lack of critical methodology is defensible when it is understood that as a writer he has all of the created — and creating — reality in which to cavort. Again, G. K. might interject that if a man of his bulk is to cavort at all, all of reality is required. Chesterton refuses to approach a book any differently than he approaches a butcher, cab-driver, relative, or potted plant. In a real sense, he is simple; he is all of a piece. He really has no literary "mode," husband "mode," or recreation "mode." Woollcott relates that when he first saw Chesterton, he was furiously writing and splashing burgundy on a tavern's tablecloth while waiting with his wife to attend a wedding.[11] Chesterton writes about romance and violence, and he strides about with a swordcane; he writes drinking songs, and he sings them in taverns. But this freedom of range usually results in critics extracting from Chesterton's criticism choice observations and expressions while being careful to abjure his "mode." At the risk of repeating myself, the defect in such an approach is that Chesterton doesn't properly have a "mode," he has a mundus, a world, the real world of fish and fanatics, saints and sausages, texts and taxis. He is not restricted to the fantasy world of self-created structures of thought and theory designed to address the metaphysically doubtful text.

Needless to say, Chesterton is hopelessly out of step, marvelously desynchronized and gloriously irrelevant in a literary-intellectual cli-

---

Edgar Johnson agrees with George H. Ford that Chesterton's Dickens was a "beery Christmas-card Dickens" (16). Presumably, a properly critical or methodological critic would round out such a simplistic view. Similarly, in *The Dickens Aesthetic* (New York: AMS Press, 1989) Richard Lettis has little use for Chesterton and asserts that G.K.C. limited Dickens to being an "inspired cockney" (1-2). While disagreement with or criticism of Chesterton is often quite justified — he is by no means above criticism — what these critics exhibit is a disdain for the insufficiently systematic, rigorous method behind Chesterton's commentary. It must not be thought that Chesterton is universally reviled or that critics have no use for him at all. Quite the contrary. His status as a Dickens critic is rather like that of the "grand old man" in politics. His writings are so vast and aphoristic, that virtually every Dickens critic finds something in Chesterton to agree with and quote. In fact, G.K.C. has become a kind of *locus classicus* for critics. If one wants an idea or useful quote, go to Chesterton. But like the aged family pianist who — still capable of playing a few tunes — is rolled out at gatherings for an obligatory performance (and trolleyed back again into obscurity), Chesterton's criticism is to be admired but not imitated. He is too unmethodical for scholarly emulation.

11. Woollcott, foreword, x.

mate such as this. Fortunately for the adherents to Permanent Things, the permanence does not depend upon continuous acceptance within the groves of academe. As we move into a brief and general look at Chesterton's Dickens criticism, we can see that G. K.'s freedom of range derives from his constant focus upon what is here called Permanent Things. "Truth of whatever kind is the proper object of the intellect," Newman says, and Chesterton writes in full harmony with this proposition, with emphasis, perhaps, on the oft-overlooked "whatever kind."[12]

Stephen Marcus, in an introduction to a recent edition of Chesterton's *Charles Dickens: A Critical Study,* describes G. K.'s critical writing as being

> an older form of literary composition or criticism. He ruminates, he associates, he lets his pen carry him where it will. He is often inconsequent, and his arguments are not conducted along large, distinct logical lines. He almost never enters upon the critical analysis of a specific text, and his conclusions do not arise immanently out of his handling of the concrete material, out of his demonstrations. These objections, which are made in behalf of the admirable austerity of modern literary criticism, certainly have their point. They may in part be met, however, if we consider that the logical procedures of modern criticism — which in any event had not yet been really developed — were not germane to Chesterton's purpose. His book is largely polemical and hortatory; it is a piece of literary propaganda on the highest level. And the reader will soon see that the work is not about Dickens alone. At certain points Dickens is only a pretext, a point of departure for Chesterton's presentation of his own views about this, that, and everything, about modern life in general. These views, it may be added, rarely fail to be of intrinsic interest.[13]

While Marcus clearly perceives that Chesterton has a historical place in letters that belong to "an older form," he doesn't characterize what, for Chesterton, is the virtue of that older form. By calling Chesterton "polemical," "hortatory," and a literary propagandist, he skews notice

12. John Henry Cardinal Newman, *The Idea of a University* (London: Longmans, Green, and Co., 1896), 151.

13. Steven Marcus, introduction to *Charles Dickens: A Critical Study,* by G. K. Chesterton (New York: Schocken Books Inc., 1965), 11.

away from the universally accessible reality Chesterton feels free to romp within, and chooses instead to cast a murky light upon the dubious realm of motivation and ideology.

Likewise, it is easy to mistake the invitational aspect of Marcus's criticism for "propaganda," because where conventional critics seek to open a text with analysis, Chesterton seeks to open one's eyes with a text. "If the test of a great critic is a capacity to lure readers back to his subject," Ford notes, "then Chesterton indeed is a great critic.[14] The invitations to read, to consider, are rarely presented argumentatively; Chesterton's observations carry great force because they are presented as virtually self-evident. They are held aloft, like first principles for simple apprehension. Note the presumption behind such a manner: that there are valid first principles, that apprehension and recognition — which Aristotle places at the heart of artistic activity — are within human reach. But as Aristotle also notes, the self-evident is not without mystery, and mystery is one of those Permanent Things Chesterton gives full due, even in literature. Of Dickens in general and the role of a critic G. K. moans: "There is no way of dealing properly with the ultimate greatness of Dickens, except by offering sacrifice to him as a god; and this is opposed to the etiquette of our times."[15] Throughout his critical writings Chesterton is consistent in his idea of the critic's task, the mystery of his subject, and in particular, the nature of Dickens' greatest strength:

> But when we come to him [Dickens] and his work itself, what is there to be said? What is to be said about earthquake and dawn? . . . He has created creatures who cling to us and tyrannize over us, creatures whom we would not forget if we could, creatures whom we could not forget if we would.[16]

Dickens participated in that great divine activity of creation by pouring forth characters so vast and unimaginable, they defy comment. According to Chesterton, a mute silence seems to be the highest praise a critic can offer Dickens, and he openly professes and confesses:

14. George Ford, *Dickens and His Readers* (Princeton: Princeton University Press for the University of Cincinnati, 1955), 241.

15. Chesterton, *Great Men*, 174.

16. G. K. Chesterton, *Appreciations and Criticisms of the Works of Charles Dickens* (Port Washington, N.Y.: Kennikat Press, 1911; reprint, 1966), 138.

We can only walk round and round him wondering what we shall say. All the critics of Dickens, when all is said and done, have only walked round and round Micawber wondering what they should say. I am myself at this moment walking round and round Micawber wondering what I shall say. And I have not found out yet.[17]

It is this very staggering quality of Dickens' characters that impresses Chesterton the most; he devoted an entire chapter of his study to these characters and declares that they all call for "incoherent gratitude."[18] But criticism is not limited to a mute silence:

The function of criticism [Chesterton pronounces], if it has a legitimate function at all, can only be one function — that of dealing with the subconscious part of the author's mind which only the critic can express, and not with the conscious part of the author's mind, which the author himself can express. Either criticism is no good at all (a very defensible position) or else criticism means saying about an author the very things that would have made him jump out of his boots.[19]

Chesterton's use of "subconscious" is not deeply psychological or deterministic. As seen here and in the large body of Chesterton's writing, "subconscious" means unexamined opinions, or more properly, unexamined predispositions. Thus he does not give license to a deluge of psychological criticism but simply says that a critic can see the whole, on occasion, where an author may only see a part. In fact, the deep-rooted ontology behind Chesterton's literature and criticism is made plain in an often overlooked passage where he displays the relation of criticism to objective truth:

If truth is a plan or pattern of things that really are, or in other words, if truth truly exists outside ourselves, or in other words, if truth exists at all, it must be often possible for a writer to uncover a corner of it which he happens not to understand, but which the reader does happen to understand. The author sees only two lines; the reader sees where they meet and what is the angle. The author sees only an arc or fragment or a curve; the reader sees the size of the circle.[20]

17. Ibid., 139.?
18. Chesterton, *Great Men*, 174.
19. Chesterton, *Appreciations and Criticisms*, 51.
20. Ibid., 79-80.

Dickens' characters are, according to Chesterton, the highest work of his genius. It is not enough to say that character was Dickens' strong suit; Chesterton uses the words "creator" and "creation" in an obvious attempt to deepen the impact of the artistic accomplishment. Dickens does not characterize, he creates, "It is not a matter of making a man a little taller or a morning a little colder; the challenge to imagination is not whether he can exaggerate, but whether he can find anything worth exaggerating."[21] Dickens does not paint psychological, Jamesian portraits of people and their motives; he merely paints parts of them so large that they burst outside the covers of the books. They cannot be contained even within the broad limits of the story. Chesterton declares that the gods are about in England, and those gods are the product of Dickens' hand.

It is not surprising that Chesterton should notice the novelist's excellence in finding things "worth exaggerating," for the emphasis rests upon the reality of what is exaggerated. What Dickens exaggerates are qualities that truly inhere in people. These may be idiosyncratic qualities, "eccentric" qualities, or they may be qualities that, to a larger extent, are shared by all. The universally shared attributes Dickens takes up for artistic exaggeration are those things that Chesterton liked to call "democratic." Though the term today is clouded by connotations of party politics and rather inexact references to systems of government, for our critic its meaning is simple and consistent: democratic means "common" or universal. The things he calls democratic are usually what we would call permanent: love is universal — it is democratic; rage is common — it is democratic; even wine and the wine-dark sea are attuned to those qualities in men which are noblest and best. Heaven, for Chesterton, is democratic for it is available to all. Conversely, American politics is not quite so democratic for there is precious little of the common or universal in it, in spite of the vote. Dickens' universal tastes and passion for the ordinary give him, paradoxically, an uncommon brilliance:

> Commonness means the quality common to the saint and the sinner, to the philosopher and the fool; and it was this that Dickens grasped and developed. . . . And both his humour and his horror are of a kind strictly to be called human; that is, they belong to the basic part of

21. Chesterton, *Great Men*, 232.

us, below the lowest roots of our variety. His horror for instance is a healthy churchyard horror, a fear of the grotesque defamation called death; and this every man has, even if he also has the more delicate and depraved fears that come of an evil spiritual outlook. . . . In the same way the Dickens mirth is a part of man and universal. All men can laugh at broad humour, even the subtle humorists. Even the modern 'flaneur,' who can smile at a particular combination of green and yellow, would laugh at Mr. Lammle's request for Mr. Fledgeby's nose. In a word — the common things are common — even to the uncommon people.[22]

However, common or universal does not mean uniform. Dickens and his critic both are intensely sensitive to the universality of variety and its intimate companion, hilarity. Chesterton's chief "proof" of Dickens' greatness lies not in a novel, but in the variety of his people in the streets. The people may be foolish, but they can always be suffered gladly — with Dickens, very gladly.[23] Moreover, the novelist shared with his own creations the traditional virtue of a happy philosophy despite sad experience. Though he was intense about everything, he was intense in the right direction; he lifted the truly human pleasure of conversational drinking into a sacred tavern ritual. He had an adult's taste in humor and a child's fascination with horror; he had common sense matched with uncommon vigor which kept him, for the most part, from both sententious dogmatism and prosaic profundity. In short, he had a violent grip on human virtues (as well as some vices) which gave life and soul to his artistic virtues of exaggeration, pictorial framing, and character painting. Chesterton underscores all of these things, but as usual, the emphasis is on the soul. It is the real human virtue and the real artistic merit that produces the mythology, the larger-than-life eternal characters, the Dickens world. "In short, the Dickens novel was popular, not because it was an unreal world, but because it was a real world; a world in which the soul could live."[24]

Though Chesterton suggests we sacrifice to Dickens as a god, he means a pagan god; that is, a god who can be a nuisance and often rather shallow. Critics note Chesterton's exuberant praise of Dickens, but rarely do they notice his realism with regard to Dickens' weaknesses.

22. Ibid., 79-80.
23. Ibid., 182.
24. Ibid., 74.

Dickens had numerous personal difficulties for which the responsibility is probably his; Chesterton is not really interested in these. He is interested in those faults that may have affected his art, and of these, there are two primary weaknesses. Artistically, some of Dickens' worst work was the product of ambition. "[T]here is something a little vulgar about professing to be a Universal Provider; a man who writes not only something that he wants to write, but anything that anybody wants to read."[25] Too often Dickens tried to show his power and please every reader. He had the kind of ambition that wishes to be everything to everybody. His humor was genuine, but his pathos was often for effect. Dickens wanted to be able to milk and manipulate readers by tears and tragedies; too often he only distracts them. The other great weakness Dickens had was an intellectual one. Chesterton does not believe, as many of his contemporaries did, that Dickens was a shallow man gifted only in description. But in the order of ideas and theories, Dickens was flawed:

> One grave defect in his greatness is that he was altogether too indifferent to theories. On large matters he went right by the very largeness of his mind; but in small matters he suffered from the lack of any logical test and ready reckoner. . . . Dickens . . . was really deep about human beings; that is, he was original and creative about them. But about ideas he did tend to be a little superficial. He judged them by whether they hit him, and not by what they were trying to hit.[26]

About history particularly, Dickens was predisposed to believe that anything old was antidemocratic. "In theory at any rate, he had no adequate conception of the importance of human tradition; in his time it had been twisted and falsified into the form of an opposition to democracy. In truth, of course, tradition is the most democratic of all things, for tradition is merely a democracy of the dead as well as the living."[27]

There is, of course, a difficulty in speaking of Permanent Things with those skeptical that there are such things. It invariably appears that the advocate of Permanent Things has only assembled a series of attributes, qualities, and orders as random and unconnected as the next fellow's

25. Chesterton, "Charles Dickens: His Life," 221.
26. Chesterton, *Appreciations and Criticisms*, xxviii-xxix.
27. Ibid., 104.

particular values, but for which a transcendence is invoked by employing the specious euphemism, "Permanent Things." However, the things called permanent are neither random nor arbitrary. They are all of a piece, integrated by their situation in our created human natures and the created order as a whole. And there, as they say, is the rub. Immersed in metaphysical murk, much of contemporary criticism treats ideas such as "order" and "nature" with contempt at worst, wistful regret at best. Exceptions exist but the generality is a fair one. In such times Chesterton's criticism is, happily, irrelevant. It must be. He is at home in the world and need not postulate one in order to feel free or move his thoughts. His ontology is secure, and reality remains a given which, as he knew, is quite properly akin to being a gift. Chesterton's literary view is an integrated one, his system for critical judgment being the same as his system for life. Jacques Derrida (one hopes) does not treat his own name as a self-referential entity having no meaning outside itself; Wimsatt and Beardsley, it is certain, had definite intentions when they theorized that intention is a literary fallacy. Chesterton, contrariwise, simply believes that the nature of literature and the nature of the world are related and that there is no disparity in speaking about both, referring one to the other.

In all fairness, many critics who fail to see Chesterton's essential and realist thrust do recognize his importance in general. Woollcott and Marcus praise Chesterton quite highly, while Ford, Christopher Hollis, and even Wilson recognize his weight as a Dickens critic. However, concerning Chesterton's approach and the reason for his weight as a critic, most critics become vague or, perhaps appropriately, "appreciative" in their comments. However, as a Dickens critic he is inescapable, provocative, sensitive, perceptive, and to many critics even irritating.

Chesterton's world is a world of Permanent Things, a world teeming with truth and reality, mystery and depth. It is a world of paradox. He finds the world definite and dogmatic yet almost recklessly free and fresh; he writes in paradox because he believes he lives in it.[28] For

---

28. Cleanth Brooks finds it necessary to rescue paradox from the critical dustbin. He comments that few are willing to accept the idea that paradox is intellectually serious. Critics are "willing to allow" paradox as a weapon that someone like "Chesterton may *on occasion* exploit" ("The Language of Paradox" [from *The Well Wrought Urn*] in *The Art of the Critic*, 10 vols., ed. Harold Bloom [New York: Chelsea House Publishers, 1989], 9: 499, emphasis mine). He speaks with obvious and well-aimed irony, for he then attempts to rehabilitate paradox. It seems, then, that paradox was hardly the choice instrument in the critical toolbox.

Chesterton, the paradox becomes doxology — truth gives way to song, and in the case of Dickens it is a song of praise; he virtually bellows and cavorts among pages, much as Dickens did. There is much about Chesterton that is Dickens-like, and more than once he writes about the novelist and leaves us with the impression that both the novelist and his critic have been described. Chesterton may well have said of himself what he says of Dickens: ". . . the man who has found a truth dances about like a boy who has found a shilling; he breaks into extravagances, as the Christian churches broke into gargoyles."[29] Indeed, Chesterton is Dickens' gargoyle, he is "breaking out" everywhere, hanging over Dickens' gutters and stained glass windows equally, grinning broadly over each one. Though some do not like the look of the gargoyle, no one can deny nor diminish his huge and unassailable grin.

29. Chesterton, *Great Men*, 134.

Waugh's Road to Affirmation

David Dooley

Two well-known assessments by Edmund Wilson will serve to frame our consideration of Waugh's road to affirmation in his novels. In a famous tribute to Waugh's artistry which appeared in the *New Yorker* in March 1944,[1] Wilson described Waugh as the only first-rate comic genius to appear in English writing since Shaw. Wilson called attention to Waugh's brazen audacity, his skill in creating an atmosphere by implication, and his detachment: in *A Handful of Dust,* which Wilson thought Waugh's best novel, there was no word of explicit illumination from the author. Because Waugh approached the aristocracy from the outside, he said, his snobbery works; he is a Catholic and a conservative, but his political, religious, and moral opinions do not mar his fiction.[2]

In the same month, Wilson wrote to a friend commenting on Waugh's religion:

> A propos of what you say about Waugh's Catholicism: I have never really been able to see any Catholic point of view in his novels. He might equally well, it seems to me, be a Church of England conservative. If I had not been told that he was a Catholic convert, I should certainly never have known from reading his books.[3]

1. Edmund Wilson, "'Never Apologize, Never Explain': The Art of Evelyn Waugh," *New Yorker* 20 (4 March 1944): 75-76.
2. Ibid.
3. Edmund Wilson, letter of March 10, 1944 to Edouard Roditi, *Letters on Literature and Politics,* ed. Elena Wilson (New York: Farrar, Straus & Giroux, 1977), 429.

With the appearance of *Brideshead*, Wilson's opinion of its author suddenly changed. He wrote a scorching review of the book in the *New Yorker* for January 5, 1946, under the heading "Splendours and Miseries of Evelyn Waugh." When Waugh departed from the comic vein and became serious, Wilson said, he lapsed into banal romantic fantasy. Snobbery was his true religion; though his novel was a Catholic tract, it lacked genuine religious experience. Wilson concluded that Waugh's comic anarchy had been disciplined and destroyed by faith.[4]

In his early novels, Waugh was clearly fascinated by the social chaos he depicted; still, at least obliquely, he did show that it involved degeneration. Even if a specifically Catholic perspective was not apparent, the disorder implied a concept of order, the immorality implied a concept of morality, the faithlessness (as in Eliot's *Waste Land*) implied the need for faith. The gay antics of the Bright Young People in *Vile Bodies* had serious consequences: the novel ended on the biggest battlefield in the history of the world. Absence, especially in *A Handful of Dust*, implied the possibility of presence; the novel was a parable or a paradigm. *Brideshead Revisited* was really an answer to or completion of *A Handful of Dust*; it moved from negation and emptiness to affirmation and fulfillment. In writing it, Waugh showed much more artistry than Wilson and many of Waugh's other critics noticed, especially in the hints he gives of underground currents, of the inner turmoil of his central characters, a turmoil resulting from the tension between the pull of religion and the pull of the world.

Disorder is apparent on the first page of *Decline and Fall*, in which the Bollinger Club, "all that was most sonorous of name and title," has gathered at Scone College, Oxford, for a beano. What that means is quickly explained: "A shriller note could now be heard rising from Sir Alastair's rooms; any who have heard that sound will shrink at the recollection of it; it is the sound of the English county families baying for broken glass."[5] So it is the upper class, those who should be the pillars of the establishment, which is breaking up pianos, smashing china, and throwing a Matisse into a water jug.

What are the authorities doing to stop them? Nothing at all. Mr. Sniggs, the Junior Dean, and Mr. Postlethwaite, the Domestic Bursar,

---

4. Edmund Wilson. "Lesser Books by Brilliant Writers," *New Yorker* (13 July 1946): 73-74.

5. *Decline and Fall*, Uniform Edition (London: Chapman & Hall, 1948 [1928]), 14.

are rejoicing at the destruction; the fines they will be able to levy will give them a whole week of Founder's port on their table. They even resort to blasphemous prayer: "It'll be more if they attack the Chapel," said Mr. Sniggs. "Oh, please God, make them attack the Chapel."[6]

Underlying the destructiveness of the Bollinger Club and the irresponsibility of the college officials is the disease of the present, characterized by a loss of the values of the past. In a world from which all coherence is gone, Paul Pennyfeather can be deprived of his trousers by the Bollinger, sent down for indecent behavior, whirled around by fortune's wheel and eventually sent to prison for white slavery, only to undergo a "death" and a "resurrection" and return to Scone College once again. It is significant that at the beginning and end of the novel he is studying to become a clergyman, a clergyman preoccupied with ancient heresies — "So the ascetic Ebionites used to turn towards Jerusalem when they prayed. Paul made a note of it. Quite right to suppress them"[7] — and obviously incapable of helping to stop the decline and fall of the Permanent Things in English culture.

As is usual in Waugh, the decline is illustrated by the treatment of buildings. King's Thursday, the finest specimen of domestic Tudor in England, is bought by Margot Beste-Chetwynde and torn down; she wants it replaced by "something clean and square." The architect of the new house, Otto Silenus, considers that the problem of all art is the elimination of the human element from the consideration of form. Consequently, he takes a famous soliloquy of Hamlet and turns it upside down. Hamlet says, "What a piece of work is a man! how noble in reason! how infinite in faculty! in form and moving how express and admirable! in action how like an angel! in apprehension how like a god!"[8] A twentieth-century mechanical man can only parody such a vision of man's worth:

> "I suppose there ought to be a staircase," he said gloomily. "Why can't the creatures stay in one place? up and down, in and out, round and round! Why can't they sit still and work? Do dynamos require staircases? Do monkeys require houses? What an immature, self-destructive antiquated mischief is man! How obscure and gross his

6. Ibid.
7. Ibid., 239.
8. *Hamlet*, II, 2, ll. 315-20.

prancing and chattering on his little stage of evolution! How loath-
some and beyond words boring all the thoughts and self-approval of
this biological by-product! this half-formed, ill conditioned body! this
erratic, maladjusted mechanism of his soul. . . ."[9]

Can religion restore man to a conviction of his own importance
and dignity? The answer is that religion, too, is affected by the modern
world. In a humorous way, this is illustrated by the Welsh bandmaster,
who plays *Men of Harlech* at the Llanabba games for half an hour
straight, and refuses Dr. Fagan's request for a different tune because all
the others are holy and it would be blasphemy to play them while a lady
is smoking a cigarette.

> "This is most unfortunate," says Dr. Fagan. "I can hardly ask Mrs.
> Beste-Chetwynde to stop smoking. Frankly I regard this as imperti-
> nence."
> "But no man can you ask against his Maker to blaspheme whatever
> unless him to pay more you were. Three pounds for the music is good
> and one for the blasphemy look you."

So the Doctor gives him another pound and in a few minutes the silver
band begins playing "In Thy courts no more are needed Sun by day and
moon by night."[10]

A more telling examination of religion's corruption is the career
of Mr. Prendergast, an Anglican clergyman living comfortably in a
pleasant rectory in Worthing when he began to have doubts: *"I
couldn't understand why God had made the world at all."*[11] His doubts
took him right out of the Church, but after a spell as a completely
ineffectual schoolmaster he learned that there was a species of being
called a modern clergyman, who did not have to commit himself to
any definite beliefs whatsoever. So he became a prison chaplain, only
to be betrayed by the advanced theories of the prison governor, Sir
Wilfred Lucas-Dockery, and to suffer the sad fate described in a
parody of "O God, our help in ages past" in a chapter entitled "The
Death of a Modern Churchman."[12] The implication is clear: when

9. *Decline and Fall*, 136-37.
10. Ibid., 93-94.
11. Ibid., 41.
12. Ibid., 204. "Oh God, our help in ages past," sings Paul. "Where's Prendergast
to-day?" "What, ain't you 'eard? 'e's been done in," comes the reply — followed by a

religion compromises with the modern world, it loses its head; it suffers decapitation.

In *Vile Bodies,* where the fun is even wilder but despair never very far away, there are many references to religion. The American evangelist Mrs. Melrose Ape, whose favorite motto is, "Salvation doesn't do them the same good if they think it's free,"[13] arrives in England with her angels, named after the conventional virtues, plus others of her own devising: besides Chastity, Fortitude, Prudence, and so on, there are Divine Discontent and Creative Endeavour. There is a Jesuit priest, Father Rothschild, partly a parody of the cloak-and-dagger Jesuit of much popular fiction, partly a wise observer of historical trends and contemporary loss of faith. There is an extraordinarily unhistorical film dealing with the founder of Methodism, John Wesley. The film is being shot at Doubting Hall (a name taken from Bunyan's *Pilgrim's Progress*), which the taxi driver who takes Adam Fenwick-Symes there calls "Doubting 'All."[14] Martin S. Cohen has written, "Alone among Waugh's novels in this respect, A *Handful of Dust* relies almost entirely on dialogue to make its major points (one cannot truthfully say that the dialogue-filled *Vile Bodies* has any major points to make)."[15] But the number of religious references which I have pointed out (and there are many more) ought to make the reader just a little bit suspicious that beneath the surface of the novel there is a great deal of hidden meaning.

In fact, a racing-car episode which epitomizes the wild ride and inevitable crash of the younger generation has religious overtones. Before the race, an elderly man is walking among the cars carrying a banner inscribed, "Without Shedding of Blood Is No Remission of Sin." Since Agatha Runcible happens to be wearing a brassard saying "Spare Driver," she takes over when one of the drivers is put out of action, and the car she is driving is soon out of control. It shoots right off the track, runs right across a field, and eventually crashes — not into a war memorial, as one writer thinks probably happened, but into a market cross.[16] When Miss

---

line of the hymn — "And our eternal home." The second singer continues to tell, in gruesome detail, how a mad carpenter, allowed to have a saw by the prison governor, murdered the prison chaplain.

13. *Vile Bodies,* Uniform Edition (London: Chapman and Hall, 1948 [1930]), 21.

14. Ibid., 64.

15. Martin S. Cohen, "Allusive Conversation in A *Handful of Dust* and *Brideshead Revisited,*" *Evelyn Waugh Newsletter* 5 (Autumn 1971): 1-6.

16. *Vile Bodies,* 169, 174.

Runcible is in a nursing home in London, the Bright Young People who come to cheer her up have a party in her room, and soon have her in a state of delirium.

Elsewhere in London, Nina Blount is finding Adam very depressed:

> Later he said, "I'd give anything in the world for something different."
>
> "Different from me or different from everything."
>
> "Different from everything . . . only I've got nothing . . . what's the good of talking?
>
> "Oh, Adam, my dearest . . ."
>
> "Yes?"
>
> "Nothing."[17]

A few pages further, we switch back to Agatha Runcible, thinking she is still in the motor race:

> "Faster," cried Miss Runcible, "Faster."
>
> "Quietly, dear, quietly. You're disturbing every one. You must lie quiet or you'll never get well. Everything's quite all right. There's nothing to worry about. Nothing at all."
>
> They were trying to make her lie down. How could one drive properly lying down? . . .
>
> *"Faster. Faster."*
>
> The stab of a hypodermic needle.
>
> "There's nothing to worry about, dear . . . *nothing at all . . . nothing.*"[18]

So the novel describes, very vividly, a state of nothingness. One well-known passage sums up the lives of the Bright Young People: ". . . Masked parties, Savage parties, Victorian parties . . . dull dances in London and comic dances in Scotland and disgusting dances in Paris — all that succession and repetition of massed humanity. . . . Those vile bodies. . . ."[19] These are simply bodies coming and going, bodies in motion going round and round to no purpose; they are vile bodies because they know nothing of soul.

17. Ibid., 185.
18. Ibid., 193.
19. Ibid., 118.

The title of A *Handful of Dust* suggests that it has a similar theme to the nothingness and desperation of *Vile Bodies*; but again the thematic significance of the novel is often neglected. For example, in an article which appeared in the autumn 1988 issue of the *Evelyn Waugh Newsletter*, Edwin J. Blesch, Jr., gave an interesting account of the film version of the novel. He pointed out that Carlton Towers, the Yorkshire home of the seventeenth Duke of Norfolk, became Tony Last's beloved Hetton Abbey with very little change; that the old railway station at Windsor, still used by the Queen, became the setting for Brenda Last to see her dim lover John Beaver off for London; that the period furnishings in the movie represented very faithfully those of the 1920s, and so on. In his opinion, the combination of Derek Granger and Charles Sturridge which was responsible for the television version of *Brideshead* had done it again: the film was a brilliant and faithful adaptation of the novel. "Some Waugh fans may cavil with questions of emphasis and interpretation," he wrote, "but most, I think, will find it inspired filmmaking."[20]

It was indeed a successful film, but the major themes of the novel were almost entirely ignored. In particular, the religious dimension, which should have been there by implication or as a felt absence, was not there at all.

The whole of *Decline and Fall* and most of *Vile Bodies* were written while Waugh was considering becoming a Catholic. Later, in an article entitled "Converted to Rome: why it has happened to me," which appeared in the *Daily Express* on October 20, 1930, he ridiculed three popular errors with regard to conversion to Catholicism: "The Jesuits have got hold of him," "He is captivated by the ritual," "He wants to have his mind made up for him." The deeper reason, as he understood it, was related to the themes of the first two novels we have discussed.

"It seems to me," he wrote, "that in the present phase of European history the essential issue is no longer between Catholicism, on one side, and Protestantism, on the other, but between Christianity and Chaos." He regarded Europe's loss of faith as the active negation of all that Western culture had stood for:

> Civilization — and by this I do not mean talking cinemas and tinned food, nor even surgery and hygienic houses, but the whole moral and

20. Edwin J. Blesch, Jr., "(W)awe-Inspiring: Waugh's *Handful of Dust* on Screen," *Evelyn Waugh Newsletter*, Autumn 1988, 3-6.

artistic organization of Europe — has not in itself the power of survival. It came into being through Christianity, and without it has no significance or power to command allegiance. The loss of faith in Christianity and the consequential lack of confidence in moral and social standards have become embodied in the idea of a materialistic mechanized state, already existent in Russia and rapidly spreading south and west. It is no longer possible, as it was in the time of Gibbon, to accept the benefits of civilization and at the same time deny the supernatural basis upon which it rests.[21]

In Eliot's *Waste Land,* from which he took his title *A Handful of Dust,* Waugh found a similar treatment of the downfall of civilization. The poem shows modern man living a lonely, neurotic, and empty life because of the absence of a common core of values in society, the absence in fact of any faith which might produce regeneration. Man possesses only "a heap of broken images" — fragments from past cultures in which such values were a living reality. Waugh's use of Eliot went well beyond the choice of title; in fact, the more one looks for correspondences the more one finds them.

For example, Mme. Sosostris, famous clairvoyante, "with a wicked pack of cards," has her counterpart in Mrs. Rattery, who plays patience by herself and animal snap with Tony Last. The death by water in the poem has its parallel in Dr. Messenger's death by drowning, the fire and hallucinations in the poem in the fever and hallucinations of Tony. The dry bones of Ezekiel, of great importance in two sections of the poem — "The Burial of the Dean" and "What the Thunder Said" — are found in the novel too; Brenda's brother Reggie comes home from Tunisia "where he was occupied in desecrating some tombs." As a result of his archaeological depredations, his house in London is indeed full of broken images — "fragmentary amphoras, corroded bronze axeheads, little splinters of bone and charred stick, a Graeco-Roman head in marble. . . ."[22] But perhaps the clearest example in the novel of Eliot's "withered stumps of time"[23] is the jumble of objects, many of them

21. "Converted to Rome: Why It Has Happened to Me," *Daily Express* (London), 20 October 1930, 10. Reprinted in *Essays, Articles and Reviews of Evelyn Waugh,* ed. Donat Gallagher (London: Methuen, 1983), 103-5.

22. *A Handful of Dust* (London: Chapman and Hall, 1964 [1934]), 167.

23. T. S. Eliot, *The Waste Land,* 1. 104, in *The Waste Land and Other Poems* (London: Faber and Faber, 1952 [1940]), 30.

misapplied because their significance is not understood, in Princess Jenny Abdul Akbar's room: "swords meant to adorn the state robes of a Moorish caid were swung from the picture rail; mats made for prayer were strewn on the divan; the carpet on the floor had been made in Bokhara as a wall covering . . ." and so on for a long paragraph.[24]

In the poem London is an "unreal City"; in the novel it is a jungle, a counterpart of the jungle in Brazil — a correspondence not sufficiently established in the film. The initial scene in both novel and film brings out the predatory nature of Mrs. Beaver, rejoicing at news of a fire which may bring her an interior decorating commission if she can beat out the competition. Hetton is a sanctuary, a clearing in the jungle; a line near the end of Eliot's poem — "Shall I at least set my lands in order?"[25] — explains what Tony Last attempts to do — to preserve the traditions of Hetton, bogus though some of them are, and to preserve a way of life which finds room for generosity and responsibility.

As Frederick Stopp puts it, Tony is the Innocent who, by sheer selflessness and dedication to a principle, becomes the instrument of a moral judgment:

> The principle is Hetton and all that for which it stood: the integrity of marriage, responsibility towards the tenantry, the village, the Church, the house and its contents, poor relatives and next-of-kin, something which one can love unreservedly with that trust which comes of an undisturbed belief in its stability. The remoteness of this principle is expressed by the preposterous nature of its embodiment: Hetton Abbey, pure English nineteenth-century Gothic. . . . The very quality of childish illusion of immaturity, in the ideal, is a judgment on the grown-up, matured savagery of others.[26]

In the long run, Tony cannot keep out the London savages; Hetton is invaded, and Mrs. Beaver threatens to cover the walls with chromium plating. The primitive Indians in Brazil, when they decamp, take nothing that is not theirs; they have their principles, they know their limits. In contrast, the London savages take all they can get; Brenda, under their influence,

24. *A Handful of Dust*, 131.
25. *The Waste Land*, 41, l. 371.
26. Frederick J. Stopp, *Evelyn Waugh: Portrait of an Artist* (London: Chapman & Hall, 1958), 92.

demands a large amount of alimony from Tony (with which to buy Beaver), even though she realizes that it will force him to sell his beloved Hetton.

Most of these correspondences are lost when the novel is translated into film; in fact, by leaving out one important character in the novel, the film ignores the effects of spiritual ignorance in the modern world. The marvelous sermons of Mr. Tendril, first delivered in the far reaches of the Empire during the reign of Queen Victoria, illuminate this theme in the novel in a number of ways. As his name indicates, he himself makes only a slight impact upon an almost completely secularized society. Though the villagers enjoy his sermons, (he is considered the best preacher for miles around), "few of the things said in church seemed to have any particular reference to themselves."[27]

Tony's regular attendance at church is merely a formal ritual with no religious meaning; during the service his thoughts drift from subject to subject: "Occasionally some arresting phrase in the liturgy would recall him to his surroundings, but for the most part that morning he occupied himself with the question of bathrooms and lavatories. . . ."[28] He listens to the Vicar's Christmas sermon with pleasure, but it has implications which neither the preacher nor his congregation can possibly understand:

> "How difficult it is for us," he began, blandly surveying his congregation, who coughed into their mufflers and chafed their chilblains under their woolen gloves, "to realize that this is indeed Christmas. Instead of the glowing log fire and windows tight shuttered against the drifting snow, we have only the harsh glare of an alien sun; instead of the happy circle of loved faces, of home and family, we have the uncomprehending stares of the subjugated, though no doubt grateful, heathen. Instead of the placid ox and ass of Bethlehem," said the vicar, slightly losing the thread of his comparisons, "we have for companions the ravening tiger and the exotic camel, the furtive jackal and the ponderous elephant. . . ."[29]

Inappropriate as may be its references to the harsh glare of an alien sun in an English midwinter, the sermon is very revealing. It is indeed difficult for people to realize that this is Christmas, for they live in a heathen land, dominated by ravening and exotic creatures instead of

27. *A Handful of Dust*, 37.
28. Ibid.
29. Ibid., 69-70.

by Christian influences and symbols. These people are indeed far from home, far from their spiritual home.

So alien is religion to Tony's thinking that when the Vicar comes to call after John Andrew's death, Tony finds the meeting with him very embarrassing: "I only wanted to see him about arrangements. He tried to be comforting. It was very painful . . . after all the last thing one wants to talk about at a time like this is religion."[30] The point is given additional emphasis by the ritual he goes through with Mrs. Rattery — not prayers for the dead but a game of animal snap. When Albert the butler comes in to draw the curtains, Mrs. Rattery is saying, "Bow-wow" in imitation of a dog and Tony is saying "Coop-coop-coop" in imitation of a hen. "Sitting there clucking like a 'en," Albert reports to his fellow servants, "and the little fellow lying dead upstairs." In the absence of a spiritual dimension, men are merely animals and behave as such.

"What is the city over the mountains,"[31] asks the speaker in the fifth section of The Waste Land. Under the guidance of Dr. Messinger, Tony goes in search of a lost city in South America which the Pie-wies call the "Shining," and the Arekuna the "Many Watered," while the Warau use the same word for it as for a kind of aromatic jam they make. Tony can envisage it only in terms of what he has heard and what he is familiar with:

> For some days now Tony had been thoughtless about the events of the immediate past. His mind was occupied with the City, the Shining, the Many Watered, the Bright Feathered, the Aromatic Jam. He had a clear picture of it in his mind. It was Gothic in character, all vanes and pinnacles, gargoyles, battlements, groining and tracery, pavilions and terraces, a transfigured Hetton, pennons and banners floating on the sweet breeze, everything luminous and translucent; a coral citadel crowning a green hill-top sown with daisies, among groves and streams; a tapestry landscape filled with heraldic and fabulous animals and symmetrical disproportionate blossom.[32]

The implications are clear enough. Tony should be in search of the heavenly city, the City of God, but with no knowledge of it and with

---

30. Ibid., 133.
31. The Waste Land, 41, l. 371.
32. A Handful of Dust, 184.

the wrong kind of guide he cannot possibly find it. Instead he searches for a grotesque parody, an aromatic jam, a transfigured Hetton. In a moment of bitter realization, even in delirium, he concludes that "there is no City. Mrs. Beaver has covered it with chromium plating and converted it into flats. Three guineas a week with a separate bathroom. Very suitable for base love."[33]

Part of the irony related to the monument erected to him at Hetton before he is dead is that he is called "Explorer," but his journey has been circular rather than one of discovery; it has taken him from his Victorian house at Hetton to the reading of Victorian novels in the Brazilian jungle, from one kind of enchantment — suggested by the fact that his bedroom is named after Morgan le Fay, a witch or enchantress in the Arthurian legends — to another, under the spell of Mr. Todd (played so superbly by Alec Guiness in the movie).

What Granger and Sturridge failed to bring out in their film was the underlying message of the novel, which was really a fictional illustration of Waugh's contention in "Converted to Rome" that European civilization cannot exist without Christianity. Again, Frederick Stopp points this out very well:

> Of this book Mr. Waugh said, many years later, "A *Handful of Dust* . . . dealt entirely with behavior. It was humanist and contained all I had to say about humanism." All Mr. Waugh had to say about humanism in 1934 was that it was helpless in the face of modern savagery. Decency, humanity and devotion have failed, civilized life has degenerated into "the all-encompassing chaos that shrieked about his ears." . . . Man is doomed to remain in his wire cage, reinforced against escape, unless some other principle is found to restore to him his liberty and to banish fear. Instead of the ravening tiger and the furtive jackal, the ox and ass of Bethlehem.[34]

Excellent as the film was, it was not faithful to the novel, because its makers did not see that the book was really about the importance of faith.

As we have seen, Edmund Wilson wrote a scathing review of *Brideshead*, in which he declared that snobbery was Waugh's true religion and that the novel was a Catholic tract. Even though that novel

---

33. Ibid., 238.
34. Stopp, 99-100.

won Waugh a far wider readership than he had previously had, similar
criticisms were made when *Brideshead* first appeared, and have continued to be made. He has repeatedly been accused of snobbery, of
nostalgic conservatism (striving to maintain a social pattern known and
loved in youth), and of trying to reduce the formidable problems of the
human spirit and of the universe to parochial terms. Rose Macaulay
said that he was trying to pour the ocean into a holy water font.[35] By
the title of his article assessing the television version of *Brideshead*,
Kingsley Amis showed how he interpreted the account of Charles
Ryder's conversion — "How I Lived in a Very Big House and Found
God."[36] Martin S. Cohen writes that *A Handful of Dust* and *Brideshead*
are the only Waugh novels based on potentially tragic situations, "but
otherwise two totally dissimilar books"[37] and to attempt to establish any
thematic similarity would be far-fetched.

But as I have said, I consider the later book to be a completion of
and a reply to the earlier one. A consideration of the parallels between
them will lead to an understanding of that most criticized, indeed most
abused, of Waugh's novels. *Brideshead* opens on a wasteland atmosphere:
". . . whatever scenes of desolation lay ahead of us, I never feared one
more brutal than this. . . ."[38] All that survives of an orchard is half an
acre of mutilated old trees, and not far from the army camp is the
municipal lunatic asylum. The prophetic tone of Ezekiel which resounds
frequently in Eliot's poem has its counterpart in the passage from the
lamentations of Jeremiah — "Quomodo sedet sola civitas" — which
comes into Ryder's mind; and the idea expressed — "How desolate is
the city" — is very close to Tony's "There is no city. Mrs. Beaver has
covered it with chromium plating. . . ."[39] Like Tony, Ryder lives for a
time in a world of enchantment — "Et in Arcadia ego,"[40] like him he
lives in ignorance of religion, and like him he goes on a voyage of
discovery which proves fruitless. Tony is a semi-civilized man in a world
of barbarians, and so is Ryder; Tony dines with Reggie St. Cloud, who

35. Rose Macaulay, "Evelyn Waugh," *Horizon* 14 (December 1946): 360-76.
36. Kingsley Amis, "How I Lived in a Very Big House and Found God," *TLS*,
20 November 1981, 1352.
37. Cohen, "Allusive Conversation," 1.
38. Evelyn Waugh, *Brideshead Revisited* (Boston: Little, Brown and Company,
1945), 3.
39. Ibid., 351. The expression had previously been used by Cordelia, 220.
40. This is the title of book 1 of the novel.

tries to persuade him to sell Hetton in order to buy Beaver for Brenda and who greedily eats what other people usually leave on their plates, like chicken bones, peach stones, and the heads and tails of fish, and Ryder dines with Rex Mottram, reflecting that the Burgundy they drink is a reminder "that the world was an older and better place than Rex knew, that mankind in its long passion had learned another wisdom than his."[41] The difference between Tony and Charles, of course, is that the one is static and the other develops.

In *Brideshead*, we are asked to take the perspective of Charles Ryder; but we must sometimes see beyond him and make connections which he is not yet able to make. We are meant to see a process of gradual change going on in him, in a hidden way, from the time when he first meets the Marchmains and is captivated by them. He hardly believes his friend Sebastian, who is rebelling against his family and drinking too much, when Sebastian tells him that religion is never very far away from his thoughts. The more he sees of Lady Marchmain and her eldest son Bridey, the more he dislikes their church. "It seems to me that without your religion," he tells Bridey, "Sebastian would have the chance to be a happy and healthy man." When the younger daughter, Cordelia, says, "I sometimes think when people wanted to hate God they hated Mummy," he is interested but not really moved: ". . . I had no patience with this convent chatter."[42]

By this time, he has found something to dedicate himself to: art. His vocation is to paint the great houses surviving from the past before the present destroys them. When this inspiration fails, he seeks renewal in the jungle-covered ruins of Mexico and Central America. He also finds another reason for living when he falls in love with Sebastian's sister Julia — neither his own marriage nor Julia's having proved satisfactory. In other words, he has found several sources of meaning in life, as substitutes for the ultimate concern which involves belief in God. If he is supposed to be seeking divine grace, he does not realize it — not until the end of the story. Without his realizing it, grace has been pursuing *him* all along; he must go beyond both art and human love.

The real subject of the novel therefore is the search for faith, and the survival of faith, in the modern world. This is the Age of Hooper, the young man in the prologue with little imagination and no sense of history,

41. *Brideshead Revisited*, 175.
42. Ibid., 145, 221, 222.

who surveys the world from a "general, enveloping fog." It is the age of Julia's husband Rex Mottram, who wants a big church wedding with as many cardinals as can be brought to England and is not at all abashed when the matter of his previous marriage is disclosed: "All right then, I'll get an annulment. What does it cost? Who do I get it from? Has Father Mowbray got one? I only want to do what's right. Nobody told me."[43] It takes Julia a year of marriage to realize that Rex is not really all there; he is Waugh's comment on the nature of modern man without God — a person from whose life a whole dimension is missing.

The references to adolescent nostalgia in *Brideshead* have a certain point, but again this element in the novel has to be put in perspective. Early on, the aesthete Anthony Blanche warns Charles Ryder against succumbing to the Marchmain charm. Later, when Charles paints his Central American pictures, Anthony rushes to see them, only to find them, as usual, charming. "It was charm again, my dear, simple, creamy English charm, playing tigers."[44] The culture and traditions which the Marchmain family represent and which are symbolized by their great house, Brideshead, may help people in their quest for values, because they testify to the existence of an inner life. But they may be a stopping place rather than a way station. Charles is captivated by charm for far too long a time. He must come to realize that the house is less important than the chapel, the chapel itself less meaningful than the sanctuary lamp glowing in it.[45]

His progress towards faith is a reluctant one. When he and Julia begin to live in sin, and Bridey refers to the fact that they are doing so, Charles is outraged — but he is astonished to find that Julia takes Bridey's comments deeply to heart. Later, Lord Marchmain comes home from Venice to die. Years before, his mistress Cara had told Charles that Marchmain's life was dominated by hatred — hatred of his wife, "a good and simple woman who has been loved in the wrong way."[46] Such hatred, she says shrewdly, really springs from hatred of oneself: "When people hate with all that energy, it is something in themselves they are hating. Alex is hating all the illusions of boyhood — innocence, God, hope."[47]

43. Ibid., 196.
44. Ibid., 273.
45. Ibid., 351 — the last page of the novel, in which a "small red flame" is burning in a sanctuary lamp, "a beaten-copper lamp of deplorable design."
46. Ibid., 103.
47. Ibid.

But when he is on his deathbed, he still refuses to see the local priest, and Charles Ryder rejoices at his refusal: "'Mumbo-jumbo is off,' I said, 'the witch-doctor has gone.'"[48] After Lord Marchmain has been lingering near death for several months, it becomes obvious that the end is near; the "witch-doctor" is summoned again, over Charles' protestations. Eventually the cumulative pressure of years of thought about the place of religion in life affects him; in spite of himself he finds himself longing for a sign that Lord Marchmain accepts the absolution proffered him: "Then I knelt, too, and prayed: 'O God, if there is a God, forgive him his sins, if there is such a thing as sin.'"[49] Now the meaning of the "twitch upon the thread" passage, from one of Chesterton's Father Brown stories read aloud years earlier by Lady Marchmain, becomes clear: God could indeed let a man wander to the end of the earth, and then call him home with a twitch upon the thread — except that in this case two threads are intertwined, and the single twitch serves for Charles as well as Lord Marchmain.

When Waugh went to Hollywood to work on a film version of *Brideshead*, he wrote a memorandum for M-G-M explaining his concept of the story. Discussing this memorandum in an article in *America* several years ago, Father Pacificus Kennedy commented, "It reads as if he felt bound in conscience to tell them about their Unknown God." Waugh said in part,

> The Roman Catholic Church has the unique power of keeping remote control over human souls which have once been part of her. G. K. Chesterton has compared this to the fisherman's line, which allows the fish the illusion of free play in the water and yet has him by the hook; in his own time the fisherman by a "twitch upon the thread" draws the fish to land. This metaphor appears twice in the novel and should be retained. It is only bit by bit throughout the action that Charles realizes how closely the Flyte family are all held by the Catholic religion, and the book ends with Charles becoming a Catholic.[50]

He also wrote,

> The Grace of God turns everything in the end to good, though not to conventional prosperity. I regard it as essential that after having

48. Ibid., 327.
49. Ibid., 338.
50. Pacificus Kennedy, O.F.M., "Romance and Redemption in 'Brideshead Revisited,'" *America* 146 (May 1, 1982): 335.

led a life of sin Julia should not be immediately rewarded with conventional happiness. She has a great debt to pay, and we are left with her paying it.[51]

He also gave explicit instructions concerning the priest summoned to Lord Marchmain's deathbed:

It is important that the priest should be as unlike as possible to any priest hitherto represented in Hollywood. He must be a practical, simple man, doing his job in a humdrum way.[52]

So much for the notion that Waugh was attracted to the Catholic Church because of the alleged glamour associated with it. It is important to notice too that when Ryder is first taken to Brideshead, it is not to meet a member of the titled family which owns this magnificent house, but to meet a governess — Nanny Hawkins; and that at the end of the novel, he again sees Nanny Hawkins, the embodiment of a simple faith.

A great deal more could be said about *Brideshead* — the marvelous evocation of the Oxford atmosphere, perhaps modeled on and certainly reminiscent of those in Compton Mackenzie's *Sinister Street* and Max Beerbohm's *Zuleika Dobson;* the presentation of a whole range of alternatives to religious belief, other possible sources of meaning in life, from art to politics and scholarship, all of them examined and ultimately found unsatisfying; the range of responses to the conflict between religion and the world in the Flyte family, from the piety of Cordelia to the revolt of Sebastian, sinking farther and farther into the depths and yet finding grace there (almost, as Angus Wilson says, like a character out of Dostoevsky);[53] the subtle use of water imagery, discussed in an excellent *Evelyn Waugh Newsletter* article by Nicholas Kostis;[54] and so on. A comment by Graham Greene, however, is well worth quoting:

A writer of Evelyn's quality leaves us an estate to walk through: we discover unappreciated vistas, paths which are left for our dis-

51. Ibid.
52. Ibid., 337.
53. Angus Wilson, Canadian Broadcasting Corporation radio program, "Anthology," Nov. 7, 1981.
54. Nicholas Kostis, *"Brideshead Revisited:* The Saga of Water and Spirit," *Evelyn Waugh Newsletter* 19, no. 3 (Winter 1985): 1-7.

covery at the right moment, because the reader, like the author, changes. And I, for one, had been inclined to dismiss *Brideshead Revisited*. When he had written to me that the only excuse for it was Nissen huts and Spam and the blackout I had accepted that criticism — until the other day when I reread all his books and to my astonishment joined the ranks of those who find *Brideshead* his best, even though it is his most romantic.[55]

Whether or not one agrees that this is Waugh's best novel, it is clear that Edmund Wilson's depreciation of it was evidence of that excellent critic's blind spot, and that Waugh showed clearly in *Brideshead* that he could bring his own strong religious beliefs into his novels without destroying their artistry.

55. Graham Greene, *Ways of Escape* (New York: Simon & Schuster, 1980), 268-69.

"Little Systems of Order": Evelyn Waugh's Comic Irony

Gregory Wolfe

At first glance, it would appear that nothing could be easier than to prove that Evelyn Waugh, the brilliant and wickedly funny author of satirical novels, was a staunch defender of what T. S. Eliot called the Permanent Things. When Waugh converted to Catholicism in 1930 at the age of 26, he explained himself in terms that closely parallel those of Eliot's own famous statements in "Thoughts After Lambeth" and *The Idea of a Christian Society:* "It seems to me," Waugh wrote, "that in the present phase of European history the essential issue is no longer between Catholicism, on one side, and Protestantism, on the other, but between Christianity and Chaos."[1] For Waugh, as for Eliot, the Permanent Things were preeminently the moral and spiritual principles of the Judeo-Christian tradition of Western civilization. In his book *Robbery Under Law,* Waugh added an appendix titled "Conservative Manifesto," in which he linked his belief in Original Sin to the need for strong but limited government, the inevitability of hierarchy, and the dangers of social engineering.[2]

If Waugh's public statements of his beliefs are clear, it should come as no surprise that his readers got the message. Waugh's conservative pronouncements offended the intellectual class of his own day, and he would surely be delighted to know that they continue to evoke paroxysms of disgust. John Carey, one of Britain's leading literary critics,

---

1. "Converted to Rome," in *The Essays, Articles, and Reviews of Evelyn Waugh* (Boston: Little, Brown, 1984), 103.
2. "Appendix: Conservative Manifesto," *Essays,* 161-62.

titled his review of Waugh's posthumously collected essays and reviews "Evelyn Waugh: Who Needs Thought?" Carey's opening sentence sets the tone of the review: "Here is a social history of the modern era, viewed through a steadily accumulating fog of rage, bile and black humor." Waugh, writes Carey, was a "malignant right-wing satirist" who uses his religious beliefs as a screen behind which he was able to "outrage every decent feeling." "The disadvantage of Catholicism," Carey concludes, "is that it stopped him thinking."[3]

It is not surprising that Carey, a secular liberal, should find himself on the opposite side of the fence from Waugh on nearly every major issue. But in the course of his review, Carey raises a question that has troubled even those who share many of Waugh's convictions. Behind the religious principles and the reactionary stance, behind the stiletto-sharp wit and knockabout farce of his novels, was Waugh nothing more than a misanthrope? Those who know something of his life are aware that he could be contentious and at times nearly paranoid. He once admitted to Edith Sitwell: "I know I am awful. But how much more awful I should be without the Faith."[4] Christopher Hollis, one of Waugh's closest friends, said of him: "He liked life to be full of disturbance."[5]

Turning to his fiction, the body of work for which he must be evaluated, one would be hard pressed to find any celebrations of the Permanent Things. His few novels which deal directly with Christian themes, for example, are often considered his weakest, even by sympathetic critics. Of his famous Catholic novel, *Brideshead Revisited*, one correspondent wrote to Waugh: "Your *Brideshead Revisited* is a strange way to show that Catholicism is an answer to anything. Seems more like the kiss of Death."[6] In his purely satirical novels, the most consistently engaging and delightful characters are the amoral, anarchic frauds, while the representatives of authority and tradition are, with few exceptions, shown to be corrupt, hypocritical, and fatuous.

In fact, it seems to me that Waugh is just the sort of writer who

---

3. John Carey, "Evelyn Waugh: Who Needs Thought?" *Sunday Times*, London, 12 February 1984, 43.

4. *The Letters of Evelyn Waugh* (Harmondsworth: Penguin, 1982), 451.

5. Quoted in Martin Stannard, *Evelyn Waugh: The Early Years, 1903-1939*, (London: Dent, 1986), 3.

6. "Fan-Fare," *Essays*, 304.

ought to appeal to the new school of literary criticism known as deconstruction. The deconstructionists, who claim to be able to find contradictions at the heart of any literary work, reducing it to either sheer nonsense or the opposite of what it appears to be, could have a field day with Waugh. They would show that Waugh's sympathies clearly lie with the forces of chaos. William Blake's famous comment on Milton's *Paradise Lost*, that Milton "was of the Devil's party without knowing it," could well be applied to Evelyn Waugh.

It is a tribute to Waugh that he recognized in himself this anarchic temperament. But if he was willing to admit his own strange attraction to chaos, Waugh held that all men are barbarians beneath the thin layers of clothing which make up the fabric of civilization.

> Civilization [he wrote] has no force of its own beyond what is given to it from within. It is under constant assault and it takes most of the energies of civilized man to keep it going at all. . . . Barbarism is never finally defeated; given propitious circumstances, men and women who seem quite orderly will commit every conceivable atrocity. The danger does not merely come from habitual hooligans; we are all potential recruits for anarchy.[7]

These words, written in 1935, have in hindsight an eerily prophetic ring in the light of the Third Reich and the Gulag Archipelago. The theme of the fragility of civilization, however, is central to our literary heritage, from Homer and Virgil down to Dante and Shakespeare. Waugh's peculiar imaginative gift was his vivid awareness of the absurd, his ability to see the irrational and bizarre tendencies of human nature.

Waugh, like all artists, possessed an imaginative sensibility that left him susceptible to what he portrayed. Though this fact helps to mitigate somewhat our suspicions of Waugh's misanthropy, the issue cannot be so easily resolved. The missing piece to the puzzle can be found, I think, in an essay Waugh published in *Life* magazine in 1946. Entitled "Fan-Fare," the article is, on the surface, a fairly light and ironic reflection on the fame that *Brideshead Revisited* brought him, along with the inevitable letters from readers. In the course of the article he deals with a number of the most frequent questions he is asked. Among these is the question: "Are your books meant to be satirical?" Waugh answers, flatly, no.

7. "Conservative Manifesto," *Essays*, 161-62.

Satire is a matter of period. It flourishes in a stable society and presupposes homogeneous moral standards — the early Roman Empire and eighteenth-century Europe. It is aimed at inconsistency and hypocrisy. It exposes polite cruelty and folly by exaggerating them. It seeks to produce shame. All this has no place in the Century of the Common Man where vice no longer pays lip service to virtue. The artist's only service to the disintegrated society of today is to create little independent systems of order of his own. I foresee in the dark age opening that the scribes may play the part of the monks after the first barbarian victories. They were not satirists.[8]

There is no doubt that even here Waugh is being playfully ironic, evading the label of satirist with a rather pedantic display of his knowledge of literary history. But in this dense and suggestive paragraph Waugh also provides several important clues for penetrating to the core of his vision and understanding the unique nature of the *form* his fiction took.

Certainly one of the main functions of satire in the West has been to "correct and elevate" tastes and morals. By showing various ideas and forms of behavior to be abnormal through caricature and exaggeration, it has pointed the way back to society's norms. In this sense Waugh's term "shame" is not inappropriate, for shame is what one feels when one is shown to be a deviant, someone who literally deviates from the norms of the community. Waugh's definition clearly fits the genial satire of Horace and Pope, but it also applies to an extent to the harsher satire of Juvenal and Swift.

The centerpiece of Waugh's argument about satire is his claim that in the modern world there no longer exists a homogeneous and universal set of moral standards. In such a fragmented society, the artist cannot appeal to norms; even the most fantastic caricature may end up on the evening news as a meaningful "alternative lifestyle." Without a society based on shared norms, the artist must create order within the work of art itself: these are the "little independent systems of order." The form of the work must be self-contained, relying on its own internal logic.

Ironically, it is in Waugh's aesthetic of the novel as a little system of order that he comes extremely close to the aesthetic of high mod-

8. "Fan-Fare," *Essays*, 304.

ernism, represented by such artists as Picasso, Stravinsky, James Joyce, Ezra Pound, and T. S. Eliot. I say ironic because for much of his career Waugh affected a withering contempt for "modern art." (There is the famous line in *Brideshead Revisited* when Cordelia asks Charles Ryder whether modern art isn't really all "bosh." "Yes, Cordelia, great bosh," he answers.) But if one reads Waugh's letters and diaries, it is evident that as a young man he had read and admired Joyce's *Ulysses* as well as Eliot's poems. The modernists were also aware of the fragmented nature of modern society and modern sensibilities. The tremendous disruptive force of technology, with its shattering of older patterns of perception, was only one dimension of contemporary experience which the modernists incorporated into their works. A cubist painting by Picasso does not rely on shared perceptions of the "real world," but breaks up the picture plane in order to show objects from a variety of angles, simultaneously. Eliot's *Waste Land* does not fit into any traditional genre, and can only "make sense" when its fragments are compared and contrasted with each other.

The modernist work of art stresses the disjointedness of our daily experiences and rejects any neat organization of them in some alleged form of "realism." But, contrary to popular belief, modern art, at least in the hands of its early masters, does not necessarily deny that we can know reality. Instead, we are presented with a distorted and reconstituted reality that we as readers, viewers, and listeners must help to put back together. Our participation and cooperation is necessary; we have to locate and discover meaning. *The Waste Land* will only yield its meaning if we look up the allusions, and compare their meaning in the sources against Eliot's use of them. The tremendous advantage of this form is that it avoids any hint of *imposed* meaning, or didacticism, and requires the reader to make his or her own judgments.

Waugh firmly repudiated the obvious fragmentations of literary modernism; his prose style, however brilliant, is syntactically traditional. But Waugh did adapt the modernist aesthetic to his own use.[9] In writing novels filled with chaotic and frequently absurd activity, shorn of any

---

9. I reached this conclusion independently of George McCartney's recently published *Confused Roaring: Evelyn Waugh and the Modernist Tradition* (Bloomington: Indiana University Press, 1989). McCartney, it seems to me, has made a major contribution to the study of Waugh's fiction.

authority figures or established norms against which that activity can be measured, Waugh was quintessentially modern. Within the mayhem lies the little system of order we must puzzle out for ourselves. This is why Waugh's dominant technique is a pervasive irony. Believing as he did that the modern world had lost ready access to the norms of a traditional society, his novels all revolve around this very absence. Ultimately, Waugh would say, human life *is* absurd in the absence of God, but the absence is not immediately obvious, and so Waugh's ironic art proceeds by way of indirection.

Here too we have an insight into the nature of Waugh's humor. For there is no question that Waugh's novels are excruciatingly funny — in a very literal sense. The essence of Waugh's comic genius is his ability to cause the reader to feel both pleasure *and* pain. No sooner are you laughing at some bizarre caricature or energetic tableau of madcap farce than Waugh suddenly inserts the stiletto between your ribs. The comedy gives way, if not to tragedy, at least to something horrifying. But Waugh's narrative voice is always impassive, conveying even the horrifying events in an utterly restrained manner. The cursory reader may not dwell on the pain for more than a moment; Waugh will continue to entertain him. But for the more persistent reader, the horror may well remind him of a lost moral standard, faded only to the merest instinct, but real nonetheless, and appealing to something deep within human nature.

The protagonists (one hesitates to say heroes) of Waugh's novels are essential to his technique. Nearly all of them could be described as decent chaps, middle class, Oxford-educated, apparently civilized human beings. But they are also passive, without identity; they lack moral intuition and will. Typically, they drift through the crashing waves of lunacy breaking all around them, occasionally getting caught in the undertow, but eventually surfacing and floating off into the indefinite future. Seldom do they appear to have learned much from their adventures. Acted upon rather than acting, they are the perfect foil for the craziness they encounter.

The most engaging and dynamic characters in the novels, of course, are the crooks and shysters. In those figures, Waugh's attraction to the anarchic is most keenly felt. They illustrate the somber opinion of William Butler Yeats, stated in "The Second Coming," his apocalyptic poem about the modern age, that "the best lack all conviction while the worst are full of passionate intensity." One of Waugh's best critics has spoken of the theme of displacement in his novels: the right thing in the wrong place.[10] The undirected or misdirected energy of his villains, when compared to the passivity of his protagonists, is a striking illustration of Waugh's belief that the civilization has lost the force necessary for its maintenance. Paradoxically, Waugh never fails to show some latent sympathy for those who would break rather than build. As an example of this, listen to Waugh's description of a short story by Arthur Calder-Marshall concerning a group of striking coal miners.

> The mood of rebellion is brilliantly treated — the background of five weeks' boredom, of a nagging wife, of the camaraderie found only among fellow unfortunates, of the physical itch to hit something in an idle body accustomed to hewing coal. The whispered agitation before the outbreak of violence, the sudden sense of liberation in finding that bosses can be knocked about, that policeman's skulls can be cracked, the symbolism and futility of pushing the safe down the mine shaft, the exultance of manslaughter — all excellent.[11]

The very tone and diction of this passage reveal something of Waugh's relish for "disturbance." Despite Calder-Marshall's left-leaning politics, Waugh found himself admiring the concreteness of his stories, which were not marred by the reduction of characters into abstractions. "If this is Marxist fiction," Waugh concluded, "I have no quarrel with it."

We are perhaps now in a position to agree with Waugh's most recent biographer, who holds that Waugh's writings constitute "an anarchic defence of order, at first similar in form to that of some of the *avant garde* in France and America, but profoundly different in its implications."[12] It is also time to turn from broad generalizations about his fiction to a reading of two of his novels, *Decline and Fall* and *A Handful of Dust*, in order to discover how these "little independent systems of order" work their magic on us.

And what better place to begin than the beginning? Waugh's first novel, *Decline and Fall*, published in 1928 and written when he was only twenty-five, is a full-fledged work, carefully crafted and informed by a

---

10. Ann Pasternak Slater, "Waugh's *A Handful of Dust*: Right Things in Wrong Places," *Essays in Criticism* 32 (1982): 48-68. For this idea and for much of my interpretation of *Decline and Fall*, I am indebted to Ms. Slater, whose Oxford University lectures on Waugh I attended in 1982.

11. "Art From Anarchy," *Essays*, 205.

12. Stannard, 3.

remarkably mature vision. The plot is simple enough. Paul Pennyfeather, a student at Scone College, Oxford, is in his final year studying theology when a prank pulled by some drunken young aristocrats leads to his expulsion on grounds of "indecent behavior." He seeks employment at a third-rate and rather seedy public school, Llanabba Castle in Wales. While there he meets and falls in love with the mother of one of his students, the recently widowed Margot Beste-Chetwynde, a glamorous and fabulously wealthy socialite. After leaving the school, he and Margot become engaged. But on the eve of their wedding, she sends him to arrange a business deal for her, which turns out to involve an international prostitution ring. Paul is arrested and sent to prison, while Margot goes scot-free. Eventually Margot, who now plans to marry Viscount Metroland, manages to stage Paul's "death," and he returns to Scone College, unrecognized by the college authorities, in order to once again pursue his studies in theology.

The plot is plainly circular, for Waugh is portraying a world of futility, going around in circles. The novel begins with the sound of "confused roaring," as the drunken members of the Bollinger Club approach and proceed to remove the clothes of an innocent bystander, in this case, Paul Pennyfeather. As the novel ends, Paul can once again hear the "confused roaring" of the Club, as he calmly goes to sleep. In between these two moments, Paul is sucked into the vortex of an anarchic world of confusion and noise, the modern Babel which is all that remains of Western civilization.

It is not hard to see that a character named Pennyfeather is something of a lightweight. Paul is one of Waugh's typically decent, passive protagonists. Sent down for something he was not responsible for, Paul takes the first opportunity that comes his way. Llanabba Castle is run by a quack named Augustus Fagan, whose name is reminiscent of a certain character in Dickens who also had a group of children under his care. As one might imagine, very little education takes place at Llanabba. Paul's colleagues consist of Mr. Prendergast, a feckless ex-minister, and the unforgettable Captain Grimes, directly modeled on a man Waugh met on one of his own youthful stints as a schoolmaster.

One of Waugh's key techniques in creating his little system of order is present in *Decline and Fall:* it has been called the "submerged narrative."[13] This involves one or more minor characters who are en-

---

13. Slater, in her Oxford lectures on Waugh.

tirely tangential to the main plot. But throughout the novel, they reappear briefly; their ministry is to be a faint reminder of the main themes of the novel. In *Decline and Fall,* there are two submerged narratives, both dealing with students at Llanabba. One is associated with a vile brat named Clutterbuck, and the other with a tyke named, appropriately enough, Lord Tangent, son of Lady Circumference.

We first hear of Lord Tangent when Paul teaches his first class. In calling the roll, every student claims to be Tangent, and this naturally sets Paul's blood boiling. We next hear of Tangent at Llanabba's disastrous Annual School Sports Day. Mr. Prendergast, firing a revolver as a starting pistol, manages to graze Tangent's foot with a bullet. Twenty pages later, we discover that "Tangent's foot has swollen up and turned black." Then: "Poor Tangent's still laid up I hear." A little later: "Everybody was there except little Lord Tangent, whose foot was being amputated at a local nursing-home." Finally, Lady Circumference, in one of her fits of ill-temper, blurts out: "It's maddenin' Tangent having died at just this time." The hapless youth is tangential not only to the narrative, but to the callously self-obsessed lives around him. His progressive decline and ultimate fall echo that of the novel's title.

The submerged narrative of Clutterbuck oddly coincides with Captain Grimes. Clutterbuck is first seen looking for Grimes. He also seems to go for walks with Grimes and receive special treatment from him, including the gift of cigars. The only clue to their relationship comes out when Grimes admits that he never seems to last out an entire term at any school due to his problems with "temperament and sex." For it turns out that Grimes is a pederast and Clutterbuck is his partner in sin. Waugh had good reason for making this a submerged narrative in 1928, even though Grimes is modeled on a certain Mr. Young, whom Waugh had met and befriended.

Captain Grimes is one of those loveable rogues in Waugh's fiction, such as the homosexual Anthony Blanche in *Brideshead Revisited,* who threatens to run away with the novel. Unlike Paul, who is buffeted about by the winds of fortune, Grimes has an endless capacity to escape and resurrect himself in another place, to float above the confused roaring of the world. As a former public school student himself, Grimes is mysteriously protected by the British class system; he is eternally employable, no matter what scandals he may stir up.

The other who skates pirouettes over the cracking ice of modern

England is the voluptuous and desirable Margot Beste-Chetwynde, who has risen from a mysterious past, and uses her immense wealth to enter the social circle of the British aristocracy. Paul is smitten by her; he cannot see anything but the glamourous lady whose photogenic figure appears daily in the gossip columns of the tabloids. Characteristically, Margot buys an ancient and venerable Tudor stately home only to have it demolished and rebuilt in the style of the Bauhaus in glass and ferro-concrete. The architect, a young German nihilist named Otto Silenus, is one of Margot's camp followers. Here, in his first novel, Waugh introduces the symbol of architecture as a register of the moral health of the social order. Despite the complaints of a few preservationists, Margot continues her rise into the upper echelons of the British class system. Her wealth is a welcome addition to an impoverished and doddering class of well-educated idiots.

Ironically, Paul meets his nemesis in the figure of his former college friend, Arthur Potts. Paul and Potts had been conscientious members of the Oxford League of Nations Club, and Potts, as it turns out, goes on to work for the League in a rather nebulous position. While teaching at Llanabba, Paul had received a letter form Potts which contains this significant passage:

> It seems to me that the great problem of education is to help train moral perceptions, not merely to discipline the appetites. I cannot help thinking, that it is in greater fastidiousness rather than in greater self-control that the future progress of the race lies.[14]

Potts, like the earnest young friends of Charles Ryder's Oxford days in *Brideshead Revisited*, is a half-educated man who would reduce morality, which in the West has always involved the discipline of the will, to a matter of taste. It is Potts, in his amorphous role as an employee of the League of Nations, who is responsible for Paul's arrest. But the League, Waugh wants us to see, far from being the engine of progress, is in fact one of the forces unraveling the ancient moral and spiritual order of Europe. The puritanical fastidiousness of Potts is an anile reduction of the Judeo-Christian heritage.

When he enters prison, Paul takes the bath required by regulations, in the prescribed nine inches of water, a pseudo-baptism which

14. Evelyn Waugh, *Decline and Fall* (Harmondsworth: Penguin, 1981), 43.

will not regenerate his soul a whit. There he meets up again with Mr.
Prendergast, who has discovered that a type of minister known as a
Modern Churchman does not have to believe in the faith, so he has
returned to the ministry as a prison chaplain. But Mr. Prendergast, who
is more of a lost soul than a malicious barbarian, is fated to be another
victim of the modern world. The governor of the prison, Sir William
Lucas-Dorkery, is a former sociologist bent on humane reform of the
penal system. One of the prisoners he decides to rehabilitate is a religious
fanatic who believes that he is God's agent in ridding the earth of the
devil's minions, even though this seems to include just about everyone
on the planet. Sir William's diagnosis is that the fanatic is suffering from
a stifled creative urge. So the prisoner is given a mallet and a saw in
order to encourage carpentry. When Paul does not see Mr. Prendergast
the next day at chapel he is curious. The only way the prisoners can
gossip, it seems, is by rewording the hymns they sing. The following
exchange ensues:

> "O God, our help in ages past," sang Paul,
>   "Where's Prendergast to-day?"
> "What, ain't you 'eard 'e's been done in."
>   "And our eternal home."
> "Old Prendy went to see a chap
>   What said he'd seen a ghost;
> Well, he was dippy, and he'd got
>   A mallet and a saw."
> "Who let the madman have the things?"
>   "The Governor; who d'you think?
> He asked to be a carpenter,
>   He sawed off Prendy's head." . . .
> "Time, like an ever-rolling stream,
>   Bears all its sons away."
> "Poor Prendy 'ollered fit to kill
>   For nearly 'alf an hour."[15]

In the midst of the unreality of the Governor's psychological pipe
dreams, the fanatic's grisly murder of Mr. Prendergast has the odd effect
of being an almost healthy, old-fashioned sin. Mr. Prendergast's death

---

15. Ibid., 183-84.

provides the quintessentially painful laugh that Waugh inflicts on his reader.

Waugh's system is constructed out of submerged narratives and parallels that never state the answer; rather, they invite the reader to form his or her own judgment. The circular futility of the modern world, echoed in the narrative framework, finds its thematic exposition near the end. Just before he is arrested, Paul raises a toast to "Fortune, a much maligned lady!" But Fortune, in the Western tradition, is always a fickle mistress, and Paul finds that her wheel turns quickly. Fortune, as one encounters it in the works of Boethius, Dante, and Chaucer, symbolizes "the way of the world," the purely secular chain of events divorced from God's grace and providence. Waugh takes the concept of the Wheel of Fortune and ingeniously updates it. He allows the architect Silenus to state the theme. Fortune, he says, is like the merry-go-round at Luna Park (Luna being moon, another symbol of mutability and madness).

> You see, the nearer you can get to the hub of the wheel the slower it is moving and the easier it is to stay on. . . . Lots of people just enjoy scrambling on and being whisked off and scrambling on again. How they all shriek and giggle! Then there are others, like Margot, who sit as far out as they can and hold on for dear life and enjoy that. But the whole point about the wheel is that you needn't get on it at all, if you don't want to. People get hold of ideas about life, and that makes them think they've got to join the game, even if they don't enjoy it. It doesn't suit everyone.[16]

Silenus goes on to characterize people as either static or dynamic. These are the choices in the modern world: either you stay off the wheel, as Paul eventually chooses, or you keep scrambling on, and remain subject to the fickleness of Fortune. But as it turns out, Paul's choice of being a static man does not imply anything like T. S. Eliot's famous image of the "still point of the turning world," a contemplative attunement to transcendent being. That is the realm of grace, and it is not an option modern man even knows how to choose. Rather, Paul's retreat to his theological studies is an opting out of life altogether. His theology is as static as he is. Paul goes back to the beginning, no wiser than he began. He finds a substitute for his former nemesis, Potts, by the name of

16. Ibid., 208.

Stubbs; they are model members of the League of Nations Society. Paul's death and resurrection have no spiritual efficacy. The wheel will continue to turn, and civilization will slowly give way to the barbarians in business suits.

Many critics consider Waugh's fourth novel, A *Handful of Dust*, his best. It is a bleaker novel than the more jaunty *Decline and Fall*, for it contains Waugh's anguished emotional reactions to his own failed first marriage. Here, Waugh is less dependent on submerged narratives, concentrating more on key images and ironic parallels. The conflict between civilization and barbarism is heightened in A *Handful of Dust*, and the barbarians are singularly lacking in the vitality which radiates from the immortal Captain Grimes. But the later novel gains depth because there is more at stake. It achieves the status of a true tragicomedy, perhaps the most perfect aesthetic whole Evelyn Waugh ever created.

We meet Tony and Brenda Last seven years into their marriage. They live at Hetton Abbey, a Victorian neo-Gothic stately home in the countryside outside London. Tony is utterly content in his role as country squire; he loves Hetton with a passion and never wants to leave it. But Brenda is restless, pining for the social life of the smart set in London. When a penniless young sponger named John Beaver comes for a weekend visit, Brenda finds herself being drawn into an affair with him. She successfully hides the affair from Tony until their son, John Andrew, is killed in an accident during a fox hunt. With the boy's death, Brenda announces that she wants to divorce Tony in order to marry Beaver. Tony at first goes along with the plan, but later changes his mind. Then, on impulse, he decides to accompany an explorer to the jungles of South America in search of El Dorado, the lost golden city. When the explorer meets an untimely end, Tony is taken in by an eccentric half-breed, Mr. Todd. Todd forces Tony to read the complete works of Charles Dickens aloud — not just once, but over and over until one of them dies. Back in England, Tony is presumed dead. Hetton reverts to his nearest relatives, without a penny going to Brenda — whereupon Beaver drops her and leaves for California.

As his name would indicate, Tony is the last representative of the English aristocracy. But he is so cut off from the spiritual underpinnings of the tradition he represents that it no longer forms his personality in any significant way. As in so many of Waugh's books, architecture provides the central image which incarnates the novel's themes. The current Hetton Abbey stems only from the Victorian era, when the

Romantic movement had glorified the Middle Ages. It is thus mock medieval, a romantic extravaganza, seen through the eyes of an age which knew only the barbaric values of wealth and power. No contact with the original abbey, a place of monastic worship and preservation of civilization, remains. The rooms of the house are given names from Malory's version of the Arthurian legend. Tony's dressing room is named after the enchantress Morgan le Fay, and Brenda's is ominously named for Guinevere. The novel will end with Tony's participation in a quest for the ideal city, but he will not find the Holy Grail, much less the New Jerusalem, only an aging lunatic whose only grasp of culture stems from another limited nineteenth-century figure, Charles Dickens.

Tony's ignorance of the nature of the world around him is hardly blissful. England in the twentieth century is a harsher and less hospitable jungle than that of the Amazon. John Beaver's mother is an interior designer, a vulgar middle-class woman who lives parasitically on the upper classes by stripping their ancestral mansions and installing anti-septic, metallic wall-coverings. When she visits Hetton, she suggests that the walls be covered with "white chromium plating" and the floors laid out in "natural sheepskin." Mrs. Beaver is the figure who opens *A Handful of Dust*, an opening so brilliant that it begs to be quoted.

> "Was anyone hurt?"
>
> "No one I am thankful to say," said Mrs. Beaver, "except two housemaids who lost their heads and jumped through a glass roof into the paved court. They were in no danger. The fire never properly reached the bedrooms I am afraid. Still they are bound to need doing up, everything black with smoke and drenched in water and luckily they had that old-fashioned sort of extinguisher that ruins *everything*. One really cannot complain. The chief rooms were *completely* gutted and everything was insured. Sylvia Newport knows the people. I must get on to them this morning before that ghoul Mrs. Shutter snaps them up."
>
> Mrs. Beaver stood with her back to the fire, eating her morning yoghort. She held the carton close under chin and gobbled with a spoon.[17]

Mrs. Beaver possesses the energy and determination of her namesake in the animal kingdom, but not his capacity for building. She is really

---

17. Evelyn Waugh, *A Handful of Dust* (Boston: Little, Brown, 1934), 3.

more of a scavenger, ready to gobble up the carcasses of a decayed social order. She thrives on ruin. Her son's initial question, in a novel about the breakdown of a marriage and the death of a young boy ("Was anyone hurt?"), becomes wrenchingly ironic by the story's conclusion. The housemaids don't count as anyone, of course. Their hysterical act is without reason, because in an age without reason, human action can only be arbitrary and meaningless.

The death of John Andrew provides the moral crisis of the novel. When Tony sends a friend up to London to inform Brenda, the ambiguity of his phrasing leads her to believe that Beaver has been killed — he had flown the same weekend to France. When she realizes that it is her son instead, she cries out in relief: "Oh thank God . . . ," and then, realizing the horror of her reaction, she bursts into tears. But the words have been spoken and cannot be taken back. Brenda Last is not an evil woman; she and Beaver know only the law of the jungle: use whatever comes to hand for the immediate craving of hunger, then discard the rest.

The figure of Lady Fortune shows up again in *A Handful of Dust* in the form of Mrs. Rattery, an American millionairess. A visitor at Hetton when John Andrew meets his untimely end, she tries to comfort Tony. As she speaks with him, she silently plays solitaire, which the English call "patience," which one can almost win. "It's a heartbreaking game," she says, and the phrase applies equally to the immanent logic of a world without grace. When she asks Tony to play a card game with her, the only one he knows is the children's game, "animal snap."[18]

Tony's decision to go to South America with Dr. Messinger is not the result of a deliberate quest for ultimate truth, but an impulsive desire to escape; it is as arbitrary as the housemaids' leap through the glass roof. Messinger's attitude toward the native Indians is typical of the modern scientist: they are nothing more than children, their religion nothing but fear of lightning and thunder and other loud noises. As it turns out, his mishandling of these natives leads to his death and Tony's perpetual imprisonment with Mr. Todd. The natives may live by a fairly harsh code, but their efficiency and commitment to the needs of their community offer a sharp contrast with the rapacious individualism of Europe.

With Dr. Messinger dead, Tony is left in the middle of the jungle, delirious with fever, no closer to the mythical city of El Dorado. Some of the most suggestive and powerful passages of the novel record the

18. Ibid., 151.

phantasmagoria of Tony's mind under the sway of the fever. The hallucinations and ironic parallels draw the novel's themes and images into a tightly compact frame.

> You would hear better and it would be more polite if you stood still when I addressed you instead of walking around in a circle. . . . I know you are friends of my wife and that is why you will not listen to me. But be careful. She will say nothing cruel, she will not raise her voice, there will be no hard words. She hopes you will be great friends afterwards as before. But she will leave you. She will go away quietly during the night. She will take her hammock and her rations of farine. . . . Listen to me. I know I am not clever but that is no reason why we should forget courtesy. Let us kill in the gentlest manner. I will tell you what I have learned in the forest, where time is different. There is no City. Mrs. Beaver has covered it with chromium plating and converted it into flats. . . .[19]

Mr. Todd's name means "death." His hut in the jungle, with its Dickens novels, is the dead end to which Tony has been tending all along. Waugh, though he admired Dicken's imaginative energy, nonetheless felt that he too was limited by the sentimental romanticism of the nineteenth century. The first book which Mr. Todd asks Tony to read, it should come as no surprise, is *Bleak House*.

In creating his "little systems of order," Evelyn Waugh intended to be more than a polite satirist, an improver of tastes and habits. His novels are Modernist constructions which invite the reader to supply the missing elements, and to render judgment on the actions set forth. If carefully read, these ingeniously crafted silhouettes create an outline whose shape is that of the Permanent Things. Through indirection Waugh hoped to restore a sense of the tremendous loss that has afflicted the West in the modern era. The tragicomic twentieth century is filled with absurdity, with anarchic eccentrics who scamper over the ruins. But our laughter at these antics is balanced by the kidney punch which Waugh delivers to our moral consciences. To bear witness to the spiritual truths that order human life is indeed the work of the scribe who seeks to keep the candle of culture burning. And that is a greater and more enduring task than the writing of satires.

19. Ibid., 288.

C. S. Lewis Celebrates "Patches of Godlight"

George Musacchio

In chapter 17 of *Letters to Malcolm* C. S. Lewis talks about the adoration of God that often accompanies his ordinary daily experiences of God's creation. In cool water on a hot day, in the sweetness of an apple tasted, in the song of a bird, he experiences what he calls "patches of Godlight." As a patch of sunlight in the woods shows us something about the sun, so a patch of Godlight shows Lewis something about God.[1] As our "mind runs back up the sunbeam to the sun," so Lewis experiences a "tiny theophany" in a patch of Godlight.[2] It provides for him pleasure and produces in him gratitude, adoration, and worship.[3] It is Lewis's celebration of these "patches of Godlight" that I wish to explore.

These "patches" have characteristics that include the ordinary, the homely, the small quotidian detail. Key words in Lewis's descriptions are "simple," "ordinary," "everyday," "homely," "domestic," even "stodgy." He finds these pleasing patches in nature and in books. They are like the "splendor in the ordinary" that Thomas Howard wrote about in his 1976 book by that title.[4] To the student of theology, they constitute a sacramental view of the material world. To the student of literature, they are one facet of English romanticism.

---

1. C. S. Lewis, *Letters to Malcolm: Chiefly on Prayer* (New York: Harvest-Harcourt, 1964), 91.
2. Ibid., 90.
3. Ibid., 89-91.
4. Thomas Howard, *Splendor in the Ordinary*, reprinted as *Hallowed Be This House* (Wheaton, Ill.: Harold Shaw, 1979).

82

As the term "patches" connotes, these "tiny theophanies" are in the small, ordinary, everyday objects and experiences that, for most people, do not inspire adoration of the Creator. Mrs. Beaver's "frying-pan . . . nicely hissing,"[5] the snowball in Jill's face as she emerges into Narnia from the stifling Underworld,[6] the garden at St. Anne's where Jane Studdock confronts Ultimate Reality[7] — these are more than the concrete details of an excellent writer. They are little patches of Godlight, everyday symbols of God's goodness and mercy and love.

The sources of this concept are various. In as far as it constitutes "sacramental mysticism," Father Ian Boyd would point to Chesterton and George MacDonald.[8] As a philosophical concept that Lewis came to with difficulty, it owes much to Owen Barfield.[9] But I want to explore an additional important source.

Lewis's delight in the ordinary, which he credits to the fictional "Malcolm,"[10] developed to a large extent during the years 1914-1917. It was a concept he derived from Arthur Greeves, his longtime friend in Northern Ireland. In *Surprised by Joy* he tells how Arthur helped him enjoy novels by Dickens, the Bröntes, and Jane Austen:

> What I would have called their "stodginess" or "ordinariness" he called "Homeliness" — a key word in his imagination. He did not mean merely Domesticity, though that came into it. He meant the rooted quality which attaches them to all our simple experiences, to weather, food, the family, the neighborhood. . . . This love of the "Homely" was not confined to literature; he looked for it in out-of-door scenes as well and taught me to do the same.[11]

5. C. S. Lewis, *The Lion, the Witch, and the Wardrobe* (London: Geoffrey Bles, 1950), 72.

6. C. S. Lewis, *The Silver Chair* (London: Geoffrey Bles, 1953), 196.

7. C. S. Lewis, *That Hideous Strength: A Modern Fairy-Tale for Grown-Ups* (New York: Macmillan, 1965), 318.

8. Ian Boyd, "Sacramental Mysticism in Chesterton and Lewis," *CSL: The Bulletin of the New York C. S. Lewis Society* 21, no. 1 (November 1989): 1-2.

9. R. J. Reilly, *Romantic Religion: A Study of Barfield, Lewis, Williams, and Tolkien* (Athens: University of Georgia Press, 1971), 105-107.

10. *Letters to Malcolm: Chiefly on Prayer*, 88-89, 91.

11. C. S. Lewis, *Surprised by Joy: The Shape of My Early Life* (New York: Harvest-Harcourt, 1956), 152.

Lewis contrasts this enjoyment of ordinary nature with his previous "romantic" enjoyment of awe-inspiring landscapes.[12] Arthur, with his artist's eye, taught Lewis "to see other things as well":

> But for him I should never have known the beauty of the ordinary vegetables that we destine to the pot. "Drills," he used to say. "Just ordinary drills of cabbages — what can be better?" And he was right. Often he recalled my eyes from the horizon just to look through a hole in a hedge, to see nothing more than a farmyard in its mid-morning solitude, and perhaps a gray cat squeezing its way under a barn door, or a bent old woman with a wrinkled, motherly face coming back with an empty bucket from the pigsty.[13]

Also in *Surprised by Joy* Lewis says that Arthur "could get endless enjoyment out of the opening sentence of *Jane Eyre,* or that other opening sentence in one of Hans Andersen's stories, 'How it did rain, to be sure'."[14] George Sayer testifies that Lewis also acquired this "habit of gloating over a single sentence, often the first in a novel. He once surprised me by his delight in the very domestic opening of Charlotte Yonge's *The Trial.* 'Richard? That's right! Here's a tea-cup waiting for you.'"[15]

The young Lewis described his growing perception of splendor in the ordinary in his letters to Greeves from 1914 to 1917, while Lewis was in Surrey being tutored by W. T. Kirkpatrick. In July 1915, Lewis says he reads few novels, unlike Greeves, and has read none by George Eliot,[16] and later he warns Greeves that too much Trollope and Austen will give him "a very stodgy mind."[17] But by September of 1916 he is praising "good, stodgy books like Scott,"[18] and the next month he says, ". . . it is nice to get more & more into each other's style of reading, is it not — you with poetry and I with classical novels?"[19] In May 1916 he shows a developing appreciation for ordinary natural scenery: "The

12. Ibid., 152-57.

13. Ibid., 157.

14. Ibid., 152.

15. George Sayer, *Jack: C. S. Lewis and His Times* (San Francisco: Harper & Row, 1988), 53.

16. C. S. Lewis, *They Stand Together: The Letters of C. S. Lewis to Arthur Greeves (1914-1963),* ed. Walter Hooper (New York: Macmillan, 1979), 80.

17. Lewis to Greeves, 14 March 1916, *They Stand Together,* 95.

18. Lewis to Greeves, 27 September 1916, *They Stand Together,* 130.

19. *They Stand Together,* 136.

country round here is looking absolutely lovely: not with the stern beauty we like of course: but still, the sunny fields full of buttercups and nice clean cows, the great century old shady trees, and the quaint steeples and tiled roofs . . . — all these are nice too, in their humble way."[20] Throughout these years he uses "homely" in approbation of natural and literary details.[21] It is his appreciation of homeliness, we remember, that he credits to Greeves when he comes to write *Surprised by Joy.* Kirkpatrick wasn't his only teacher during the Surrey years.

But coming while Lewis was an avowed atheist, this new perceptiveness fell short of theophany; the pleasure was there, but not yet the recognition of a Creator-God as the source of that pleasure. As the psychologists tell us, our expectations that constitute our "perceptual set" determine our interpretation of what we perceive.[22] Or as some theologians say, natural theology has its limits; we depend upon revelation for an adequate interpretation of God. The heavens do declare His glory,[23] but the natural human does not heed the declaration. Spiritual things are spiritually discerned.[24] That Godlight shines through ordinary things is a "secret doctrine," says Lewis to Malcolm.[25]

Pilgrim's Regress is Lewis's allegorical and *Surprised by Joy* his expository account of how he came to recognize one special flood of Godlight, the kind that prompts one's desire for something not of this world, the longing that nothing in this world fulfills. The desire, his readers will remember, is triggered by some tangible thing, or often, by the memory of a tangible thing in nature or in a book: a miniature garden in a cookie-can lid, Beatrix Potter's depiction of autumn, Longfellow's translation of *Tegner's Drapa.*[26] But no tangible thing turns out to be the object of the *Sehnsucht.* After his conversion to Christianity these experiences of joy continued, he tells us, but they ceased to be as important to him; he now knew them for signposts pointing toward the eminently important Celestial City.[27] At this point in his life, he was

20. Ibid., 99.

21. Ibid., 103, 108, 129, 166, 169, 176.

22. David G. Myers and Malcolm A. Jeeves, *Psychology Through the Eyes of Faith* (New York: Harper & Row, 1987), 57-58.

23. Ps. 19:1.

24. 1 Cor. 2:13-14.

25. *Letters to Malcolm: Chiefly on Prayer,* 89.

26. *Surprised by Joy: The Shape of My Early Life,* 16-17.

27. Ibid., 238.

now in a position to appreciate lesser patches of Godlight, the spiritual splendors in ordinary sights and sounds and smells.

Indeed, it is in the very letter to Greeves in which he first tells of his conversion that he credits Arthur with having taught him the "homeliness" he will later elaborate on in *Surprised by Joy*. On October 1, 1931, he has been rereading his letters to Arthur (returned for Warnie to type up for the family papers), and he has enjoyed "the glorious memories they call up." He continues:

> I think I have got over *wishing* for the past back again. I look at it this way. The delights of the past were given to lure us into the world of the Spirit, as sexual rapture is there to lead to offspring and family life. They were nuptial ardours. To ask that they should return, or should remain, is like wishing to prolong the honeymoon at an age when a man should rather be interested in the careers of his growing sons. They have done their work, those days, and led on to better things. All the "homeliness" (wh. was your chief lesson to me) was the introduction to the Christian virtue of charity or love. I sometimes manage now to get into a state in wh. I think of all my enemies and can honestly say that I find something lovable (even if it is only an oddity) in them all: and your conception of "homeliness" is largely the route by wh. I have reached this.[28]

In the next paragraph he says that he has "just passed on from believing in god to definitely believing in Christ — in "Christianity."[29]

Does not this passage from 1931 contain the seeds of both Lewis's concept of *Sehnsucht* (the delights given "to lure us into the world of the Spirit") and his concept of patches of Godlight, the divine glory to be enjoyed in the "homely"? Lewis was learning to celebrate the splendor of the ordinary; or to put it another way, he was learning that there are no "ordinary" creatures.[30]

Two years after his conversion Lewis published *The Pilgrim's Regress*, depicting, among other things, the yearnings for God brought on by sense experiences. In his later preface to this work (1943), he mixes the ordinary with the strange as he exemplifies these catalysts

28. *They Stand Together*, 424-25.
29. Ibid., 425.
30. See C. S. Lewis, "The Weight of Glory," *Transposition and Other Addresses* (London: Geoffrey Bles, 1949), 33.

of *Sehnsucht,* "that unnameable something, desire for which pierces us like a rapier at the smell of a bonfire, the sound of wild ducks flying overhead, the title of *The Well at the World's End,* the opening lines of *Kubla Khan,* the morning cobwebs in late summer, or the noise of falling waves."[31]

With Lewis's Christian conversion, then, came the ability to celebrate God in the ordinary objects and experiences of daily life. The pleasures of the ordinary that he had earlier learned from Greeves now became specifically spiritual pleasures. The transformation was probably gradual, even partly preceding the experience on the road to the Whipsnade Zoo. I cannot trace it precisely. But by the mid-1940s, as we shall see shortly, Lewis was practicing the presence of God in the ordinary, the practice he would recommend in fictional letters to Malcolm in the last year of his life.[32]

The speaker in *Letters to Malcolm,* then, is the mature Christian, enlightened about the Creator behind all creation. Of course, he does not claim perfection in his adoration of God through ordinary pleasures. "I don't always achieve it," he says, but "[i]f I could always be what I aim at being, no pleasure would be too ordinary or too usual for such reception; from the first taste of the air when I look out of the window — one's whole cheek becomes a sort of palate — down to one's soft slippers at bed-time."[33]

After his conversion Lewis practiced utilizing his new insight. He speaks of training himself to celebrate God in ordinary daily experiences. Since the day Malcolm cooled his "face and hands in the little waterfall," "I have tried," says Lewis, "to make every pleasure into a channel of adoration."[34] It is, he admits, "a somewhat arduous discipline."[35] Through the eyes of his Christian faith, and then through conscious practice, Lewis came to experience God habitually in the patches of Godlight that appeared in the woods of his daily experience.

31. C. S. Lewis, *The Pilgrim's Regress: An Allegorical Apology for Christianity, Reason and Romanticism* (Toronto: Bantam, 1981), xii.

32. In *Reflections on the Psalms* (London: Fontana-Collins, 1961), 69-71, Lewis discusses the ancient Hebraic shift to seeing God reflected in His creation, a perception that came with difficulty in Lewis's own life, as I suggested above.

33. *Letters to Malcolm,* 90.

34. Ibid., 88-89.

35. Ibid., 90-91.

Two examples from the mid-1940s will conclude my exploration. First, this practice is the key to our appreciating "Hedonics," a little essay published in *Time and Tide* in June of 1945 (reprinted in *Present Concerns*). It recounts the pleasure Lewis experienced on a train ride from London's Paddington Station through the city's suburbs, where he saw the homes of many of his fellow passengers. I think this essay must puzzle many readers, for Lewis is generally vague in his description of the pleasure he is commending. Indeed, his opening sentence is "There are some pleasures which are almost impossible to account for and very difficult to describe."[36] A casual reader might accuse him of sentimentality when he describes the sense data of his train ride as offering him an "invitation into Eden."[37] Eden in the suburbs of London, near the end of World War II, at rush hour?

The antidote to sentimentality here is Lewis's concept of splendor in the ordinary. As we have seen, to him the everyday "domesticities"[38] of people are patches of Godlight, "shafts" of God's glory striking our senses pleasurably, if we are sensitive to them. Then "we know we are being touched by a finger of that right hand at which there are pleasures for evermore," he tells Malcolm, alluding to Psalm 16.[39] In "Hedonics" he offers this principle as a means of knocking down the "Jailer" of modern psychology, the jailer who imprisons us in a reductive dungeon of materialism and behaviorism, teaching us to ignore or explain away the other voice within that invites us to celebrate patches of Godlight.[40] "Hedonics" is not one of Lewis's best essays; it is not self-contained enough for clarity and force. But in the light of *Letters to Malcolm*, it is a nourishing example of this cultivated row of cabbages in the garden of Lewis's Romantic religion.

The other example is a poem, "On Being Human," published in 1946, the year following "Hedonics." Interesting in itself, the poem radiates shafts of brilliance when read in the context of patches of Godlight, the context that says our human senses bring us God's splendor through his creation. The first lines praise the angels, with

---

36. C. S. Lewis, "Hedonics," *Present Concerns*, ed. Walter Hooper (San Diego: Harvest-Harcourt, 1986), 50.

37. Ibid., 54.

38. Ibid., 52, 54.

39. *Letters to Malcolm*, 89-90.

40. "Hedonics," 54-55.

their intuitive intelligence that grasps the very Forms and Archetypes of things, beyond human grasp. Angels know quiddities and meanings, "all the verities / Which mortals lack or indirectly learn" (lines 3-4).

> But never an angel knows the knife-edged severance
> Of sun from shadow where the trees begin,
> The blessed cool at every pore caressing us
>   — An angel has no skin.
>
> They see the Form of Air; but mortals breathing it
> Drink the whole summer down into the breast.
> The lavish pinks, the field new-mown, the ravishing
> Sea-smell, the wood-fire smoke that whispers *Rest*.
> The tremor on the rippled pool of memory
> That from each smell in widening circles goes,
> The pleasure and the pang — can angels measure it?
>   An angel has no nose.
>
> The nourishing of life, and how it flourishes
> On death, and why, they utterly know; but not
> The hill-born, earthy spring, the dark cold bilberries[,]
> The ripe peach from the southern wall still hot,
> Full-bellied tankards foamy-topped, the delicate
> Half-lyric lamb, a new loaf's billowy curves,
> Nor porridge, nor the tingling taste of oranges —
>   An angel has no nerves.
>
> Far richer they! I know the senses' witchery
> Guards us, like air, from heavens too big to see;
> Imminent death to man that barb'd sublimity
> And dazzling edge of beauty unsheathed would be.
> Yet here, within this tiny, charm'd interior,
> This parlour of the brain, their Maker shares
> With living men some secrets in a privacy
>   Forever ours, not theirs.[41]

41. C. S. Lewis, *Poems*, ed. Walter Hooper (New York: Harvest-Harcourt, 1977), 34-35. Cf. Lewis, "Scraps," first published Dec. 1945: " 'The angels', he said, 'have no senses; their experience is purely intellectual and spiritual. That is why we know something about God which they don't. There are particular aspects of His love and joy which can be communicated to a created being only by sensuous

To celebrate God's splendor in ordinary sensory experiences is neither an original nor a surprising idea. Many have given God the glory for dappled things. But C. S. Lewis might never have come to do so without the help of Arthur Greeves. Greeves taught him to enjoy homely, ordinary things. The pursuit of joy led him to the Permanent Things behind them. And his disciplined practice of experiencing the presence of God in everyday pleasures made that very practice an act of worship and adoration. It is his celebration of the permanent behind the masks of this temporal stage.

---

experience. Something of God which the Seraphim can never quite understand flows into us from the blue of the sky, the taste of honey, the delicious embrace of water whether cold or hot, and even from sleep itself.' " *God in the Dock,* ed. Walter Hooper (Grand Rapids, Mich.: Eerdmans, 1970), 216.

The Permanent Things
in the Public Square

Chesterton, Democracy and the Permanent Things

Kent R. Hill

Few writers can compare with T. S. Eliot for capturing the despair and rootlessness of so much of twentieth-century culture. Yet it was Eliot who pointed a way out of the cul-de-sac of modern relativism by embracing religious faith and championing what he called the Permanent Things.

When G. K. Chesterton, one of the great Christian journalists and apologists of our time, died in 1936, Eliot's obituary declared that Chesterton had done "more than any man of his time . . . to maintain the existence of the important [Christian] minority in the modern world."[1] This is high praise indeed coming from one defender of the Permanent Things to another.

Does the debate over political and economic arrangements in society have anything to do with the Permanent Things? In 1917, Chesterton quipped that politics was left to politicians because they were "the only people too dull to be bored by it."[2] Despite Chesterton's more than half-serious jab, there is a connection between the Permanent Things and political arrangements, though it is one which is frequently misunderstood. My focus here will be on democracy and its relation to transcendent truths.

It must be noted at the outset that democracy, whatever its virtues

---

1. Quoted in Alzina Stone Dale, *The Outline of Sanity* (Grand Rapids, Mich.: Eerdmans, 1982), 262.
2. Quoted in George J. Marlin, et al., eds., *More Quotable Chesterton* (San Francisco: Ignatius Press, 1988), 122.

or vices, is *not* one of the Permanent Things. As Chesterton put it in 1931: "Nothing so much threatens the safety of democracy as assuming that democracy is safe."[3] In fact, when seen against the backdrop of human history, democracy is but a fragile flower, and in its distinctive modern form, a rather recent one at that. Nor, it must be added, is there the slightest certainty that it will long exist on this earth.

Furthermore, it would behoove partisans of democracy to recognize and embrace the glorious truth that Christianity can and has survived under all sorts of political systems — good ones and bad ones alike. Enlightened monarchs and aristocracies, for example, have affirmed Christianity and carried out liberal reforms that have enhanced human dignity. And fiercely anti-religious totalitarian regimes on both the Right and the Left have crippled churches as institutions, but repeatedly failed to extinguish religious faith among the people.

Surely one of the chronic weaknesses of our age is that we increasingly confuse "temporary things" with Permanent Things; that we mistake contingent political judgments for timeless creedal affirmations. We make idols out of democracy or monarchy, or capitalism or socialism, and forget the command to put no other gods before Him.

As important as it is to avoid idolizing our contingent political and economic judgments, it is also essential that we not succumb to the gnostic temptation. The Gnostics feared and hated the material world, and were scandalized by the idea that God would become incarnate in human flesh, among a particular people, at a particular moment in human history. But all orthodox Christian peoples — Catholic, Eastern Orthodox, and Protestant — have insisted for centuries that in the fullness of time in Bethlehem God became man in Christ Jesus.

Hence, Christians in particular ought to understand that the infinite intimately mingles with the finite, the sacred does deign to interact with the profane. Heaven does touch earth. There is a vital connection between Permanent Things and temporary things. Indeed, contact with the finite, profane, and temporary is not just permitted, it is mandated. To seek by human means and divine grace to bring eternal values to bear on earthly realities is the essence of the Christian walk. To presume to remain pristinely above the political and economic struggles of our time, as if all human options are somehow equally flawed because they are all imperfect and temporal, is moral muddle, an escapist idealism.

3. Ibid., 124.

Hence, to be merely worldly or merely otherworldly are both moral failures for the Christian community.

Few people in the twentieth century have been as eloquent in their defense of the Permanent Things as has G. K. Chesterton.[4] An integral part of his genius is his ability to communicate how the Permanent Things manifest themselves and are reflected in the everyday and the mundane, in the simple pleasures of average people carving out for themselves and their families a unique place of sovereignty and joy far from the intrusive arm of the state. If democracy is understood as that system which particularly guards against the all-powerful and ever-expanding state, then G. K. Chesterton is one of its greatest exponents.

My objective here is to think about what democracy and, to a somewhat lesser extent, what capitalism means in the modern world from the standpoint of the Permanent Things. Before we attempt to make contingent political or economic judgments, we need some notion of an eternal landscape against which we can measure our temporal options. Chesterton rarely lost touch with that eternal backdrop as he roamed from topic to topic with his journalistic eye. As one of his publishers once put it: "You may tap any subject you like, he will find a theme on which to hang all the mystery of time and eternity."[5]

Chesterton was a man deeply centered on the Permanent Things. As his good friend Hilaire Belloc put it:

> He produced the shock of illumination. He *taught*. He made men see what they had not seen before. He made them *know*. He was an architect of certitude. . . .[6]

Most of his life was spent not in the quest to discover, but in the passion to communicate eternal verities and apply them to the time in which he lived. While many of his contemporaries measured intellectual progress by how many dogmas had been abandoned, he reveled in how many could be recovered. As he put it:

4. Elsewhere I have written about the "sweet grace of reason," or what I have called Chesterton's "common sense" apologetics. See Michael H. Macdonald and Andrew A. Tadie, eds., *The Riddle of Joy* (Grand Rapids, Mich.: Eerdmans, 1989), 226-45.

5. Quoted in Dale, 78.

6. Quoted in Michael Finch, G. K. *Chesterton: A Biography* (San Francisco: Harper & Row, 1986), 88.

> I am proud of being fettered by antiquated dogmas and enslaved by dead creeds . . . , for I know very well that it is the heretical creeds that are dead, and that it is only the reasonable dogma that lives long enough to be called antiquated.[7]

In *Heretics* (1905) Chesterton insisted that when a person

> drops one doctrine after another in a refined skepticism, when he declines to tie himself to a system, when he says that he has outgrown definitions, when he says that he disbelieves in finality, when, in his own imagination, he sits as God, holding no form of creed but contemplating all, then he is by that very process sinking slowly backwards into the vagueness of the vagrant animals and the unconsciousness of the grass. Trees have no dogmas. Turnips are singularly broadminded.[8]

In his *Autobiography*, three decades later, Chesterton noted that his old intellectual sparring partner H. G. Wells believed

> that the object of opening the mind is simply opening the mind. Whereas I am incurably convinced that the object of opening the mind, as of opening the mouth, is to shut it again on something solid.[9]

The challenge for Chesterton was not to invent new truths, but to recover timeless ones and to align one's life with them.

Implicit within this epistemological starting place, this certainty that there is such a thing as Truth and that it is rooted fundamentally in a reality beyond the individual human being, is the core of everything Chesterton believed about God and man. For Chesterton, the first Permanent Thing is God — the transcendent Creator and sustainer of this world, the source of all truth.

Chesterton was at his best in revealing the consequences of nonbelief. Without an anchor, the twentieth-century sailor was bound to be awash in moral relativism, cancerous skepticism, and final despair. According to Chesterton,

---

7. G. K. Chesterton, *Collected Works* (San Francisco: Ignatius Press), 16: 85.
8. Ibid., 1: 196-197.
9. Ibid., 16: 212.

atheism is abnormality. It is not merely the denial of a dogma. It is the reversal of a subconscious assumption in the soul; the sense that there is a meaning and a direction in the world it sees.[10]

It was inevitable that Chesterton's unflinching affirmation of this primary truth would put him in tenacious and perpetual conflict with all that was militantly secular, with all that would arrogantly place the Creature and the state at the center of the universe.

For Chesterton, "It is the idea of the fatherhood that makes the whole world one. And the converse is also true."[11] The modern, secular world, with its refusal to recognize the authority of the Father, cannot produce anything but orphans alienated from each other as well as from God.

Yet, there is another vital dimension to affirming the existence and sovereignty of the Creator God besides one of submission to realities and authority beyond oneself. This is the dimension of gratitude, which in turn was a direct product for Chesterton of a sense of wonder at the beautiful and amazing world in which he so mysteriously found himself.

For many, the tortured entrée into the world of theological inquiry is the problem of evil. How can an allegedly omnipotent, good God allow so much evil to exist? But logic and a grateful heart can force another question onto the theological stage: what is the origin of so much good and is there really no one to thank?

To read Chesterton is to be bathed with the joy of the second question. Somewhere I read or heard that for Chesterton the origin of theology was gratitude. I have been unable to locate such a quotation, but I am confident that if he didn't say it, he thought it. Near the end of his life, in fact, he described his youth as a troubled time when he "hung on to the remains of religion by one thin thread of thanks."[12] He continued:

> No man knows how much he is an optimist, even when he calls himself a pessimist, because he has not really measured the depths of his debt to whatever created him and enabled him to call himself anything. At the back of our brains, so to speak, there was a forgotten blaze or burst of astonishment at our own existence.[13]

10. Ibid., 2: 294.
11. Ibid., 2: 227.
12. Ibid., 16: 97.
13. Ibid.

In *Orthodoxy* he mused, "We thank people for birthday presents of cigars and slippers. Can I thank no one for the birthday present of birth?"[14]

Chesterton rather looked with disdain on the arrogant tendency of the contemporary world to wrap itself in "rights" and "demands." As Chesterton saw it,

> in that ultimate sense uncreated man, man merely in the position of the babe unborn, has no right even to see a dandelion; for he could not himself have invented either the dandelion or the eyesight.[15]

He goes on to answer an imaginary critic.

> What nonsense all this is; do you mean that a poet cannot be thankful for grass and wild flowers without connecting it with theology; let alone your theology? To which I answer, "Yes; I mean he cannot do it without connecting it with theology, unless he can do it without connecting it with thought. If he can manage to be thankful when there is nobody to be thankful to, and no good intentions to be thankful for, then he is simply taking refuge in being thoughtless in order to avoid being thankless.[16]

A second Permanent Thing which Chesterton was sure of was the reality of human sin. He considered it "a fact as practical as potatoes." In contrast to "certain new theologians" who "dispute original sin," Chesterton insisted that original sin was "the only part of Christian theology which can really be proved."[17] It was a reality which presented itself to him quite vividly in his youth. At the end of his life Chesterton recalled this troubling discovery in the following way.

> I deal here with the darkest and most difficult part of my task; the period of youth which is full of doubts and morbidities and temptations; and which, though in my case mainly subjective, has left in my mind for ever a certitude upon the objective solidity of Sin. . . . I could at this time imagine the worst and wildest disproportions and distortions of more normal passion. . . . I dug quite

14. Ibid., 1: 258.
15. Ibid., 16: 325.
16. Ibid.
17. Ibid., 1: 217.

low enough to discover the devil; and even in some dim way to recognize the devil.[18]

In *The Everlasting Man* Chesterton asserted that

> whatever else men have believed, they have all believed that there is something the matter with mankind. This sense of sin has made it impossible to be natural and have no laws.[19]

Chesterton was convinced that the modern thinker had things very much backward. In *Orthodoxy* he commented:

> A man was meant to be doubtful about himself, but undoubting about the truth; this has been exactly reversed. Nowadays the part of a man that a man does assert is exactly the part he ought not to assert — himself. The part he doubts is exactly the part he ought not to doubt — the Divine Reason.[20]

As for handling sin, Chesterton had two responses. First, since at its most fundamental level sin involved an offense of the child against the Father, a theological answer was required. That solution can be best described as absolution, and it is facilitated by divine grace, confession, and the sacraments. Chesterton captures the utter joy which permeates the Church's teaching on sin.

> When people ask me, or indeed anybody else, "Why did you join the Church of Rome?" the first essential answer . . . is, "To get rid of my sins."
> . . . The Church deduces that sin confessed and adequately repented is actually abolished; and that the sinner does really begin again as if he had never sinned. . . . When a Catholic comes from Confession, he does truly, by definition, step out again into that dawn of his own beginning and look with new eyes across the world to a Crystal Palace that is really of crystal. He believes that in that dim corner, and in that brief ritual, God has really remade him in His own image.[21]

Second, since sin is a continuing reality in the here and now on the temporal plane, then its existence and consequences ought to be faced

18. Ibid., 16: 85, 96.
19. Ibid., 2: 185.
20. Ibid., 1: 234-35.
21. Ibid., 16: 319.

squarely. Much of what Chesterton wrote was clearly aimed at a modern world which failed, in his estimation, to take seriously the reality of sin. In contrast, Chesterton's Father Brown perceived accurately the human condition, and as a result he could solve the mysteries that his "worldly-wise" contemporaries could not.

A third Permanent Thing in which Chesterton believed was the dignity of human beings. He constantly attacked the modern tendency, particularly found among many Darwinians, to turn a human being into just another member of the animal kingdom. Chesterton particularly ridicules the allegedly scientific discussion of the cavemen or reindeer men.

> When all is said, the main fact that the record of the reindeer men attests, along with all other records, is that the reindeer men could draw and the reindeer could not. If the reindeer man was as much an animal as the reindeer, it was all the more extraordinary that he could do what all other animals could not.[22]

In another passage, Chesterton argues:

> His body may have been evolved from the brutes; but we know nothing of any such transition that throws the smallest light upon his soul as it has shown itself in history.[23]

Such passages reveal an unswerving commitment to defend the uniqueness of God's creation of human beings. The Scriptural warrant for doing so is to be found in Genesis 1:27: "So God created man in his own image, in the image of God he created him: male and female he created them."

Perhaps the best way to sum up G. K. Chesterton's sense of the Permanent Things is to cite the Apostles' Creed. In 1908 he told his readers that this ancient Christian creedal affirmation was what he meant when he talked about "orthodoxy." He went on to assert that the Apostles' Creed "is the best root of energy and sound ethics":[24]

> I believe in God the Father Almighty, Maker of heaven and earth: And in Jesus Christ his only Son our Lord: Who was conceived by

22. Ibid., 2: 166.
23. Ibid., 2: 174.
24. Ibid., 1: 215.

the Holy Ghost, Born of the Virgin Mary: Suffered under Pontius Pilate, Was crucified, dead, and buried: He descended into hell: The third day he rose again from the dead: He ascended into heaven, And sitteth on the right hand of God the Father Almighty: From thence he shall come to judge the quick and the dead. I believe in the Holy Ghost: the holy Catholic Church: the Communion of Saints: The Forgiveness of sins: The Resurrection of the body: And the Life everlasting. Amen.[25]

When combined with Scripture, it is all there: the sovereignty of God; the creation of human beings in God's own image; the Fall; and, the Incarnation of Christ as a means to provide salvation for human beings lost in sin. This set of core beliefs is what the Church has believed for two millennia, and it is what unites Catholics, Eastern Orthodox, and Protestants. As a faithful child of the Church universal, and later as a convert to Catholicism, Chesterton sought to use these beliefs, these Permanent Things, as the key reference points for his commentary on the modern world.

With this as a backdrop, let us now turn our attention to things which are not "permanent" — judgments about how best to organize human societies in ways that are consistent with and supportive of the Permanent Things. In particular, let us consider democracy, and, to a somewhat lesser extent, the economic system which in modern times has frequently existed to some degree with it: capitalism.

The first lesson in high school debate is the importance of defining one's terms before setting out one's position. Sadly, much of our public discourse takes place without any concerted effort to determine how we are even using the terms around which passionate wars of words are being waged. And therein lies the problem. "When *I* use a word," Humpty Dumpty scornfully exclaimed to Alice, "it means just what I choose it to mean — neither more nor less."[26]

To a liberal, being a liberal probably means being concerned about the unemployed, the homeless, and the disenfranchised. But when a conservative thinks of a liberal he or she probably has visions of a peace

---

25. Hugh T. Kerr, ed., *Readings in Christian Thought* (Nashville: Abingdon Press, 1966), 75.

26. Lewis Carroll, *Through the Looking-Glass* (New York: New American Library, 1960), 186.

activist who is soft on communists and naively thinks that domestic problems can be solved by throwing money at them.

To a conservative, being a conservative probably means defending the family, the country, and the faith. But when a liberal thinks of a conservative there may well be visions of intolerant, narrow-minded reactionaries who don't care about the environment, the poor, or the possibility of nuclear war.

To be sure, each group resents being excluded from what the other considers to be its own virtues, while being blamed for vices it does not believe it has. The net result is that discussions between liberals and conservatives often go nowhere because we are not talking about the same things, although we use the same terms.

What complicates the matter even further is that terms like liberal and conservative have meant radically different things at different moments in history. A liberal in nineteenth-century England had libertarian economic ideas. Today such a position would probably be identified with one narrow slice of the conservative perspective. John F. Kennedy, usually viewed as a moderate or liberal Democrat, followed foreign policy initiatives which, by the 1980s, seemed more in keeping with today's conservative Republicans.

Is a religious fundamentalist a defender of orthodox Christian truths or a narrow, sectarian conservative? Is an oldline Protestant a compassionate Christian activist or a muddle-headed, theological liberal? It all depends on one's perspective. People clearly use these terms in all these different ways and many more besides.

Does liberation theology mean a recognition that there is a social dimension to the gospel, that Christians are mandated to be passionately concerned about the poor of this world? If so, then I am a liberation theologian. But if it means an attempt to combine Christian commitments with Marxist (or even socialist) social and economic analysis, then I am not a liberation theologian. What kind of communication is possible when a proponent of liberation theology who has the first definition in mind debates with someone who says he is opposed to liberation theology because he has in mind only the second definition?

Even though real differences exist between liberals and conservatives, between fundamentalists and oldline Protestants, and between defenders and critics of liberation theology, too often these people fail to communicate accurately and fairly what those differences are. No one need fear that there will be nothing left to argue about after terms have been clarified; there will be plenty to discuss. We must "achieve" what the American Jesuit thinker John Courtney Murray called true "disagreement," that is, talking with one another long enough to know truly how we differ. We must get well beyond the "misunderstanding" which so often passes for "disagreement" today.

Many seem more interested in ideological warfare than in honest disagreement, and thus terms are used in deliberately sloppy ways so as to discredit or misrepresent an opponent. This situation is regrettable, but there are people in all parts of the religious and political spectrum, including the middle, who do this. The good news is that there are people of good will and integrity who run the entire gamut from conservative to liberal, who have strong opinions, but who are nevertheless committed to honest disagreement.

The problem of understanding terms is made more difficult by the fact that some terms seem to be desirable to people of radically different opinions. After all, few will say they are against peace, democracy, and the family. To be sure, there are some who prefer monarchy or aristocracy to plebeian democracy, and will say so, but most will not endorse nondemocratic positions. The problem with terms that seem to be coveted by folks with widely different perspectives is that in time the terms are in danger of losing any precise meaning.

The word *democracy* no longer has a precise meaning. In the nineteenth century Alexis de Tocqueville observed:

> It is our way of using the words "democracy" and "democratic government" that brings about the greatest confusion. Unless these words are clearly defined and their definition agreed upon, people will live in an inextricable confusion of ideas, much to the advantage of demagogues and despots.[27]

Democracy is one of those words most seek to endorse. As Chesterton put it in 1919, democracy "is employed anywhere because it is employed to mean anything."[28] Five years later he commented, "When a word can be adopted by all parties, it means that it has ceased to be anything except a word."[29] In the past many people were surprised to

27. Quoted in Giovanni Sartori, *The Theory of Democracy Revisited* (Chatham, N.J.: Chatham House Publishers, 1987), 3.
28. Quoted in *More Quotable Chesterton*, 123.
29. Ibid.

learn that the German Democratic Republic referred to East Germany, rather than West. In fact, throughout Eastern Europe, that is, before the dramatic events of 1989 and 1990, communist countries described themselves as "people's democracies." Though there may have been some sympathizers in the West who actually believed these countries were "democratic," the peoples of these countries in question have made it abundantly clear in recent months that they believe that the term "democracy" was but a cynical travesty for the reality under which they had been compelled to live.

But even among many who were not naive about the realities of the communist world, their definition of democracy was woefully inadequate. "Majority rule" is often tossed out as the quick definition of democracy. And what if the majority wants to kill Jews or discriminate against blacks? Is that democracy? If it is, then I am opposed to democracy. In fact, such a definition makes democracy indistinguishable from despotism or fascism.

A significant difference exists between what was meant by democracy in fifth-century Greece and what is usually understood by it today. The older reference was to direct, participatory democracy in a small "city-community" (*polis*).[30]

It comes as a shock to some to learn that our American forefathers were not fond of the term democracy. James Madison always talked of a "representative republic," not a "democracy." He associated the latter with the ancient, direct democracies of the past. He did not believe they had been very successful.

> Democracies have ever been spectacles of turbulence and contention; have ever been found incompatible with personal security or the rights

---

30. Sartori is insistent that "city-state" is an improper definition for *polis,* since the modern notion of the state — as an impersonal, distant authority — was still foreign to the Greeks. Hence, the notion of a "democratic state" would have been for them a contradiction in terms (278-79). See 278-97 for an excellent treatment of the differences between the Greek and modern understandings of democracy. Today democracies invariably depend on indirect representation and the number of people involved is many, many times greater than in the ancient past. It follows quite naturally that the possibility of alienation within large modern democracies, even when "the people" rule, is ever present. And yet, Sartori makes a very compelling case that "direct democracies" are not practical today, and furthermore the "liberal democracies" of today represent a significant improvement over Greek democracy in terms of the security and freedom enjoyed by the individual — a freedom which would have been inconceivable to most ancient Greeks (283).

of property; and have in general been as short in their lives as they have been violent in their deaths.[31]

Alexander Hamilton, like Madison, would have agreed with Immanuel Kant's 1795 view that every government was either "republican or despotic" and that democracy "is necessarily a despotism."[32] Though Chesterton was usually willing to use the term democracy in a positive way, there are passages when he seems to be much more at home in the late eighteenth-century tradition. For example, in his *Autobiography* he asserts that "there is a thin difference between good despotism and good democracy. . . ."[33]

The negative view of democracy is in large part due to the fact that its definition does not rule out the possibility of either despotic collective action or an evolution towards plutocracy — the rule of the wealthy. A government which institutionally seeks to guard against these dangers might be called a republic, or depending on one's definition, a modern, liberal democracy.

It is not my purpose here to analyze all the diverse ways in which the term democracy has been or is being used or misused. For the purposes of discussion, however, I will set out a definition of democracy that will allow us to consider its relation to the values and thought of Chesterton. It is not an arbitrary definition and I believe it is quite consistent with Western democratic systems as they have actually evolved in practice.

What I mean by democracy is a system that allows the majority of citizens to determine their own fate, which strives to protect the rights of minorities against majorities, and which institutionally limits the power of the state to interfere with the basic human rights of its citizens.

The definition implies that democracies seek to protect individuals and groups from state power. John Courtney Murray addressed this implication:

> . . . The political substance of democracy consists in the admission of an order of rights antecedent to the state, the political form of society. These are the rights of the person, the family, the church, the

31. *The Federalist*, no. 10; quoted in Sartori, 288.
32. Sartori, 287-88.
33. Chesterton, *Collected Works*, 16: 279.

associations men freely form for economic, cultural, social, and religious ends. In the admission of this prior order of rights — inviolable as well by democratic majorities as by absolute monarchs — consists the most distinctive assertion of the service-character of the democratic state.[34]

The only logical way to affirm "an order of rights antecedent to the state" is by reference to a transcendent moral authority — God.

The political framework of democracy does not exist in a cultural or economic vacuum. It is therefore useful to make some observations about the environment in which democracy is usually found and which seems to nurture it best.

There seems to be a strong correlation between free, democratic societies and capitalism, or market-driven, competitive, free-market economies. In addition, democracies allow and even encourage the creation and maintenance of what have been called mediating institutions — churches and other private, voluntary associations of individuals. The latter serve as a check not only on the tendency of the state to gain more and more power, but upon the unbridled excesses which can tempt the powerful in a capitalist economy.

The contemporary Catholic thinker Michael Novak has coined the term "democratic capitalism" to describe this combination of political, economic, and cultural factors:

> I mean three systems in one: a predominantly market economy; a polity respectful of the rights of the individual to life, liberty, and the pursuit of happiness; and a system of cultural institutions moved by ideals of liberty and justice for all. In short, three dynamic and converging systems functioning as one: a democratic polity, an economy based on markets and incentives, and a moral-cultural system which is pluralistic and, in the largest sense, liberal. Social systems like those of the United States, West Germany, and Japan (with perhaps a score of others among the world's nations) illustrate the type.[35]

Novak is not shy about singing the praises of democratic capitalism:

34. John Courtney Murray, *We Hold These Truths* (Kansas City, Mo.: Sheed and Ward, 1960), 325.
35. Michael Novak, *The Spirit of Democratic Capitalism* (New York: Simon and Schuster, 1982), 14.

Of all the systems of political economy which have shaped our history, none has so revolutionized ordinary expectations of human life — lengthened the life span, made the elimination of poverty and famine thinkable, enlarged the range of human choice — as democratic capitalism.[36]

Nor does he shirk from acknowledging that it is not perfect:

Democratic capitalism is neither the Kingdom of God nor without sin. Yet all other known systems of political economy are worse. Such hope as we have for alleviating poverty and for removing oppressive tyranny — perhaps our last, best hope — lies in this much despised system.[37]

It was Churchill who observed that democracy was the worst possible form of government, except for all the others that have been tried. Or as Chesterton put it in 1917, "though all governments are faulty, that is least faulty in which the commonest sort of men can ask more directly for what they want and get it."[38]

Chesterton was an ardent foe of early twentieth-century British imperialism. Yet he could be extremely hard on democracy in practice, as he observed it in his native England, because he believed that democracy had given way to plutocracy. He did not mince words:

We may say, with some truth, that Democracy has failed; but we shall only mean that Democracy has failed to exist. . . . It is nonsense to say that the complicated but centralized Capitalist States of the last hundred years have suffered from an extravagant sense of the equality of men or the theory has provided a sort of legal fiction, behind which a rich man could rule a civilization where he could once rule a city; or a usurer throw his net over six nations, where he once threw it over one village. But there is no stronger proof of the fact that it emphatically is plutocracy, and most emphatically is not democracy, that has caused popular institutions to become unpopular, than this example of the pull of the Pacifists upon the Liberal Government just before the Great War. It is only necessary to ask exactly how much

36. Ibid., 13.
37. Ibid., 28.
38. Quoted in *More Quotable Chesterton*, 122.

such extreme Pacifists counted in the Party Fund, and how much they counted in the Party.[39]

Chesterton even went so far as to charge that during World War I Parliament came "to mean only a secret government by the rich."[40] It should be noted, however, that the England of today is far more egalitarian than it was during Chesterton's lifetime.

Despite Chesterton's objections to certain elements of "democracies" in practice, he was one of their defenders in theory. In *Orthodoxy* Chesterton declares, "I was brought up a Liberal, and have always believed in democracy, in the elementary liberal doctrine of self-governing humanity."[41] He goes on to identify two propositions central to his understanding of democracy. "The first is this: that the things common to all men are more important than the things peculiar to any men. . . . The second principle is merely this: that the political instinct or desire is one of these things which they hold in common."[42]

Chesterton's first principle is a strong endorsement of the value of community. He would be greatly disturbed by the strong impulse towards selfish individualism which is increasingly common in Western democracies today. His second principle affirms the old Aristotelian idea that human beings are indeed "political" beings, whose natural state is to want to interact with each other.

There is a strong, anti-big-state sentiment which infuses virtually everything Chesterton wrote. He possessed, as he put it, a "fancy for having things on a smaller and smaller scale," which is why he was uncomfortable with both socialism and imperialism.[43] A few years later, Chesterton commented:

> The democratic faith is this: that the most terribly important things must be left to ordinary men themselves — the mating of the sexes, the rearing of the young, the laws of the state. This is democracy; and in this I have always believed.[44]

39. Chesterton, *Collected Works*, 16: 200.
40. Ibid., 16: 201.
41. Ibid., 1: 249.
42. Ibid., 1: 249-50.
43. Ibid., 16: 112. His novel *The Napoleon of Notting Hill* is a hilarious defense of the independence of a London borough against the London municipal authorities.
44. Ibid., 1: 250.

The freshness and originality of Chesterton's thought is illustrated well by his firm belief that there was a strong connection between the democracy of the living and tradition.

> Tradition means giving votes to the most obscure of all classes, our ancestors. It is the democracy of the dead. Tradition refuses to submit to the small and arrogant oligarchy of those who merely happen to be walking about. All democrats object to men being disqualified by the accident of birth; tradition objects to their being disqualified by the accident of death. Democracy tells us not to neglect a good man's opinion, even if he is our groom; tradition asks us not to neglect a good man's opinion, even if he is our father. I, at any rate, cannot separate the two ideas of democracy and tradition. . . .[45]

Chesterton's strong endorsement of tradition here is firm evidence that he would never have sanctioned a narrow definition of democracy as meaning what the majority at any given moment happened to want. He meant by tradition the values and wisdom which we inherit through our Judaeo-Christian roots. Those roots are interwoven with the Permanent Things: the sovereignty of God and the dignity of human beings. It follows quite naturally that a full-orbed definition of democracy would have to include limits on majorities and on the power of the state if it were in any way to be consistent with the thought of G. K. Chesterton.

Though Chesterton's basic values and his strong affirmation of the Permanent Things are fully consistent with the definition of democracy used in this essay, he seems not to have recognized the importance of establishing institutional structures to prevent democracies from becoming despotisms. As a result, he did not appreciate, as much as he ought to have, an essential ingredient in the genius of the American political experiment.

The fundamental political problem for James Madison, and other of the founders, was how to guard against tyranny. The system of checks and balances and the Bill of Rights were responses in an institutional form to that problem. Chesterton's romantic attachment to the earlier "direct" form of democracy missed two fundamental points. First, the early form of democracy did *not* protect the individual from the arbitrary will of either a majority or subsequent plutocratic leaders. Second, an indirect vote is

---

45. Ibid., 1: 251.

indeed an improvement in some respects. It is not just a question of the size of the political group necessitating an end to direct and immediate control by citizens of their corporate policies, but the desirability of con-structing an additional barrier against precipitous, passionate, and often unwise collective action. It would not be an improvement to devise a means whereby American citizens could simply press a button on their wrist after viewing the evening news to decide the country's policies.

Chesterton's writings contain references to both democracy and capitalism; however the phrase "democratic capitalism" did not exist when he was writing. Once we have sorted through the way he used the terms, it may prove interesting, even instructive, to consider to what degree his ideas and analyses support free-market economies. My sense is that they do. True, there is a certain romantic flourish in Chesterton whenever he talks of medieval rural communities. His romanticism is a bit surreal, but hyperbole is a technique he frequently employs.

Before discussing Chesterton's use of the term "capitalism," it is important that we first have a clear understanding of what economic system he did advocate: "Distributism." Long before the Distributist League was founded in 1926, with Chesterton as its first president, Chesterton was obsessed with the importance of private property dis-tributed in small parcels over the great majority of the population. He once commented that property, like manure, was best if it was spread around.[46] Edward Shapiro summarizes the key components of Distributism well:

> The Distributist movement opposed big business, economic central-ization, socialism and government bureaucracy, while favoring a re-turn to the soil and the strengthening of small business.[47]

Chesterton viewed Distributism as an alternative to capitalism and communism, both of which he identified with industrialized economic systems which he believed strongly tended towards collectivization. In a column in 1919, Chesterton commented:

> Modern capitalism is a curse — not because some men have capital, but because some have not. A modern city can be a nightmare — not because its houses belong to those who own them, but because

46. Quoted by Edward S. Shapiro, "Postscript: A Distributist Society," in *Collected Works*, 5: 211.
47. Ibid., 5: 211.

they do not belong to those who live in them. This is the real case against modern capitalism; and it is also the case against modern collectivism, or socialism, which is its child.[48]

Although Chesterton frequently criticized the policies and practices of his native England, he was usually positive about the term "democracy." With respect to capitalism, this is not the case, he invariably used it in a pejorative sense. For example, in 1922 he wrote,

> The nineteenth century was the very reverse of normal. . . . Capitalism was not a normalcy but an abnormalcy. Property is normal, and is more normal in proportion as it is universal. Slavery may be normal and even natural, in the sense that a bad habit may be a second nature. But Capitalism was never anything so human as a habit; we may say it was never anything so good as a bad habit. . . . It was from the first a problem; and those who will not even admit the Capitalist problem deserve to get the Bolshevist solution.[49]

Or consider this attack:

> A wise man's attitude towards industrial capitalism will be very like Lincoln's attitude towards slavery. That is, he will manage to endure capitalism; but he will not endure a defence of capitalism.[50]

In fact, Chesterton was aware that the definition of capitalism was a matter of some dispute. The following passage is quite helpful to get to the bottom of what he meant by the term.

> I assure the reader that I use words in quite a definite sense, but it is possible that he may use them in a different sense; and a muddle and misunderstanding of that sort does not even rise to the dignity of a difference of opinion.
>   For instance, Capitalism is really a very unpleasant word. It is also a very unpleasant thing. Yet the thing I have in mind, when I say so, is quite definite and definable; only the name is a very unworkable word for it. But obviously we must have some word for it. When I say "Capitalism," I commonly mean something that may be stated

48. Quoted in *More Quotable Chesterton*, 65.
49. Chesterton, *Collected Works*, 21: 130.
50. Ibid., 21: 204.

thus: "That economic condition in which there is a class of capitalists roughly recognizable and relatively small, in whose possession so much of the capital is concentrated as to necessitate a very large majority of the citizens serving those capitalists for a wage." This particular state of things can and does exist, and we must have some word for it, and some way of discussing it. But this is undoubtedly a very bad word, because it is used by other people to mean quite other things.[51]

What Chesterton was quite clearly attacking was the threat to private property which the growth of monopoly represented. He even goes so far as to concede that "if capitalism means private property, I am capitalist. . . . The truth is that what we call Capitalism ought to be called Proletarianism."[52]

In contrast to his rather unique use of the term "capitalism," his definition of socialism is a bit closer to the usual understanding of the term.

Socialism is a system which makes the corporate unity of society responsible for all its economic processes, or all those affecting life and essential living. If anything important is sold, the Government has sold it; if anything important is given, the Government has given it; if anything important is even tolerated, the Government is responsible for tolerating it. This is the very reverse of anarchy; it is an extreme enthusiasm for authority. . . . A Socialist Government is one which in its nature does not tolerate any true and real opposition. For there the Government provides everything; and it is absurd to ask a Government to *provide* an opposition.[53]

What he has described here seems quite close to what the Marxist version of socialism (or communism) has been in practice. Whatever noble ideals the socialists may have (Chesterton acknowledged that at one time he considered himself one), in practice, they have usually ended up as supporting an ever bigger state. And this, of course, is precisely what disturbed Chesterton the most.

Chesterton was extremely supportive of the thesis of Hilaire Belloc's book, *The Servile State* (1912), which, according to Chesterton, was that

51. Ibid., 5: 42-43.
52. Ibid., 5: 43.
53. Ibid., 5: 44.

the Socialist movement does not lead to Socialism. This is partly because of compromise and cowardice; but partly also because men have a dim indestructible respect for property, even in its disgusting disguise of modern monopoly. Therefore, instead of the internal result, Socialism, we shall have the unintentional resultant: Slavery.[54]

There is quite a spectrum of people today who call themselves capitalist, ranging from a rather small group of *laissez-faire* libertarians to a much larger group who also defend private property, a market economy, and entrepreneurship, but believe in some government intervention to preserve competition (and thus restrict the uncontrolled growth of monopolies). This latter group has also come to accept the importance of establishing and maintaining some sort of "social net" for those in need. Chesterton would quite clearly identify much more with the latter group than the former. A staunch defender of "democratic capitalism," such as Michael Novak, (though he does not agree with Chesterton at every point), still argues that the values and economic judgments made by Chesterton are in general far more an endorsement of "democratic capitalism" than a critique of it. He does concede, however, that Chesterton's "salvoes against 'capitalism'," bearing in mind of course his peculiar use of the term, are "warning shots well-fired."[55]

What is distressing is that some commentaries on Chesterton quote him out of context or in sloppy ways which pay little or no attention to exploring the realities behind undefined terms. For example, Garry Wills in a recent *Christian Century* article declares that there is in Chesterton a "deep and omnipresent opposition to capitalism," and that the "right-wing celebrants behind the Ignatius Press edition" of Chesterton's *Collected Works* have been "highlighting the worst aspects" of his work.[56] Apparently, Wills believes that the editors of *Collected Works* are guilty of ideological bias because they did not purge passages Wills considers to be "militarism, anti-feminism and anti-Semitism."[57] In fairness to Chesterton it should be noted that Wills

---

54. Ibid., 16: 284.

55. Michael Novak, "Introduction: Saving Distributism," in *Collected Works*, 5:15.

56. Garry Wills, "A Chesterton for the Religious Right," *Christian Century*, 16-23 May 1990, 532.

57. Ibid.

provides no evidence, analysis, or definition of these terms in his sweeping judgments. He goes on to dismiss the eleven volumes of Chesterton's essays from the *Illustrated London News* as "formulaic trash."[58] In contrast, C. S. Lewis laments that for the scoffers "or critics who think Chesterton frivolous or paradoxical I have to work hard to feel even pity. Sympathy is out of the question."[59] Some might argue that the phrase "Collected Works" might need to be redefined somewhat if editors were allowed to leave out what Wills considers Chesterton's "tawdrier work."[60] It would appear that Wills really is angry about the fact that Novak was allowed to write an introduction to Chesterton's *Outline of Sanity*, which in part deals with the English writer's unique economic theory of Distributism.

There is no problem in Wills disliking Novak, or, for that matter, Chesterton, but to have not even gone to the trouble of reading Novak or Chesterton closely enough to see clearly what they mean when they employ terms under discussion is indeed lamentable.

In spite of the weaknesses of Wills' argument, there are at least two problems in Chesterton's economic analysis. First, his analysis does not provide a workable blueprint for achieving his Distributist ideal. His romantic talk about a more agrarian, pre-industrial world is not of much use in dealing practically with the world as it is. Second, though he understood well why the socialist ideal tended towards collectivism, he seriously misjudged the degree to which freer economies and more democratic societies could escape or at least minimize the drift towards the dreaded collectivism and monopoly that he so deplored. Chesterton's comments on industrial capitalism have proven to be just as inaccurate in some respects as those of Friedrich Engels. In contrast to Engels, however, Chesterton did not propose a system that was worse than the one he critiqued.

Both Chesterton and Belloc were concerned that, since the United States was primarily Protestant, it would likely be less prone to realize the Distributist ideals than Catholic areas, which they considered to be the most fertile soil for their views. In this they were wrong. As Edward Shapiro has pointed out, Distributist principles have been more valued and practiced in the United States than in Europe, despite the fact that

58. Ibid.
59. C. S. Lewis quoted in the preface to *More Quotable Chesterton*, 9.
60. *Christian Century*, 533.

America became the world's greatest industrial power. In other words, large-scale industrialization developed side-by-side with the continuation of numerous and vibrant small-scale businesses, and the continued widespread private property holdings for tens of millions of average people.[61]

Monopolies in the U.S. have often been deliberately broken up or have failed. According to U.S. Bureau of Census statistics for 1982-83, of the 100 million people in the American work force, only sixteen million work for one of the Fortune 500 companies, another sixteen million work for federal, state, or local government, while the significant majority work for small business or are self-employed.[62]

Michael Novak concludes his introduction to Chesterton's defense of Distributism, the *Outline of Sanity* (1926), with the following words.

> Granted that Chesterton means by Capitalism what I do not, I would nonetheless say that whoever loves democracy and liberty must love Capitalism. For Capitalism is today their necessary, although not their sufficient, condition. In the world as it is, there is no democracy without it.
>
> In the long run, Keynes said, we are all dead. So Chesterton, alas, is dead. But Distributism lives, in the land which the builders of Distributism rejected. It is a paradox at which Chesterton would have laughed heartily.[63]

Regardless of whether one agrees with Novak's definition or evaluation of capitalism, there ought to be far less debate among Christians regarding his view that capitalism is not a "sufficient" condition. And this brings us back to the Permanent Things. If democracy loses sight of the Permanent Things, then it will not survive.

James Madison was right two centuries ago when he observed: "To suppose that any form of government will secure liberty or happiness without any virtue in the people is a chimerical idea." Virtues are best cultivated and most logically sustained where transcendent religious truths are consciously affirmed. In short, the future of democracy will be decided in part by whether a significant-enough portion of the citizenry possesses virtues which are derived from a mature religious

61. Shapiro, in Chesterton, *Collected Works*, 5: 213-21.
62. Novak, in introduction to *Collected Works*, 5: 30-31.
63. Ibid., 5: 33.

faith. To assert that democracy has an Achilles heel, that its future is tied to the virtues of its citizens, is not to deprecate it, but simply to note that it is not a Permanent Thing. It is a decidedly impermanent thing whose very existence is dependent on mortals acting responsibly.

In 1922, following a trip across the Atlantic the previous year, Chesterton published his intriguing book *What I Saw in America*. The final chapter of this work, entitled "The Future of Democracy," includes the following remarkable observation:

> There is no basis for democracy except in a dogma about the divine origin of man. That is a perfectly simple fact which the modern world will find out more and more to be a fact. Every other basis is a sort of sentimental confusion, full of merely verbal echoes of the older creeds.[64]

The view that there is such a thing as "inalienable" human rights depends on the dignity and value of the individual which ultimately derives from the Creator, not from the state. The view that the power of the state ought to be limited follows naturally from a theologically informed understanding of human sinfulness and from empirical evidence from history. Thus, American democracy has been based on the assumption that no man or woman can be trusted with total power. To this assumption should be added that the virtues of responsibility mandated by Christian faith are necessary if democracy is not to devolve into the anarchy of excessive individualism, special-interest politics, and apathy.

Speaking of the American democratic experiment, Chesterton prophesied,

> So far as that democracy becomes or remains Catholic and Christian, that democracy will remain democratic. In so far it does not, it will become wildly and wickedly undemocratic.[65]

Though Chesterton was unashamedly Catholic, there is no doubt that he understood the term Christian to embrace the extended Orthodox and Protestant bodies as well.

For more than half a century since Chesterton's death, there has

---

64. Ibid., 21: 261.
65. Ibid., 21: 263.

been a growing temptation for many in democratic societies, particularly among the cultural elite, to succumb to the notion that society can and ought to be value-neutral. Yet, presently, in a strange sort of reversal of roles, formerly communist societies seem to be more open to the positive role that religious faith can play in shaping and preserving society.

In the West, a secular and increasingly antireligious bias is taking its toll. Traditional family values are eroding. The virtues of responsible citizenship are either derided or ignored. Rampant individualism and consumerism threaten community cohesion. On a more basic philosophical level, there is a growing cynicism about the very notion of truth as something existing beyond the illusions of the "inescapably subjective" individual.

To be sure, religion has proven to be a stubborn reality in American life. In fact, while secularism is growing in some places in America, religion is gaining influence in others. Tension between the two perspectives is definitely on the rise. Almost seventy years ago Chesterton predicted optimistically that

> men will more and more realise that there is no meaning in democracy if there is no meaning in anything; and that there is no meaning in anything if the universe has not a centre of significance and an authority that is the author of our rights.[66]

Democracy, in the best sense of the term, is consistent with and sustained by eternal values and truths. Apart from them, it will not, indeed, cannot long endure.

66. Ibid.

G. K. Chesterton and the Science of Economics

William F. Campbell

G. K. Chesterton's approach to economics was light-hearted and rooted in common sense. Yet his thought is extremely pertinent to an assessment of the modern science of economics. He did not illuminate the details of our analytical apparatus, but he touched profoundly on the basic assumptions of our discipline. Such concepts as utility, efficiency, progress, free choice, and goods were clarified in the cold light of everyday usage and purged of misleading policy implications.

Why then is Chesterton seldom referred to in economic discussion? Occasional references are made to Chesterbelloc Distributism as a social movement or policy-oriented model. General treatments of Chesterton usually cover the Distributist period. Chesterton's policy model has appealed to such non-economists as Michael Novak and James Schall. Recently Chesterton's name has surfaced in discussions of Schumacher's *Small is Beautiful.* But most mainstream economists dismiss Schumacher as much as they do Chesterton. The Chesterbelloc Distributism, which in fact was an important source of inspiration for Schumacher, is usually dismissed as a piece of medieval nostalgia.

But even among professional economists there are exceptions. In a recent essay, Milton and Rose Friedman point to the antisocialist currents which were "kept alive in Britain by G. K. Chesterton, Lionel Robbins, Friedrich Hayek, and some of their colleagues at the London School of Economics."[1] Certainly this is one of the few times when these names were strung together.

1. Milton Friedman and Rose Friedman, "The Tide in the Affairs of Men" in

118

More important exceptions were Colin Clark and Wilhelm Roepke, two recognized professional economists who admired Chesterton. Clark was a well-known Roman Catholic economist who wrote about Chesterton in the *Chesterton Review*.[2] Roepke was one of the few economists who was rooted in the moral and spiritual traditions of the Permanent Things. He mentions Chesterton in several essays and books; the title of one of his books in the 1930s, *What's Wrong With the World*, was the same as Chesterton's best exposition of his social and economic thought originally published in 1910.

But Roepke did not go much beyond recognizing in Chesterton a kindred spirit to his Third Way Program. He did not attempt to plumb Chesterton's metaphysical and religious perspective to get at the roots of economic science.

Chesterton would be unappealing to modern theoretical economists. In terms of method, no equations, models, statistical facts, or even rigorous scholarship appear in his books. Chesterton was never known as a systematic thinker in the sense of building a logical structure. Do not look for a treatise comparable to Ludwig von Mises's *Human Action*. His thoughts and insights are expressed in passing and in paradox, parceled out over many books and essays.

Although Chesterton could never be called a "man of system," he was neither antirational nor antilogical. In fact, his paradoxes entail the use of logic. Chesterton's complaint about modern thinkers is not their appeal to logic, but either their first premises or their lack of logic which results in metaphorical fuzziness: "Mysticism and common sense alike consist in a sense of the dominance of certain truths and tendencies which cannot be formally demonstrated or even formally named. Mysticism and common sense are alike appeals to realities that we all know to be real, but which have no place in argument except as postulates."[3]

The clarifications of some of the basic concepts of economics are rooted in a deeper level of substance. The texture of Chesterton's thought is found in grace, gratitude, and a deep respect for the objective

---

Thinking About America: The United States in the 1990's (Stanford: Hoover Institution Press, 1988), 463.

2. Colin Clark, "An Economist's View of Chesterton," *The Chesterton Review* 2, no. 2 (Spring-Summer 1976): 149-157.

3. G. K. Chesterton, "Thomas Carlyle," in *The Twelve Types* (London: Arthur L. Humphreyes, 1910), 131.

nature of things. These are the opposite of the economist's normal assumptions of ingratitude or subjectivism. Ingratitude was found in both the classical and Marxian tendency to a labor theory of value (whether source or measure) which stems from the Lockean escape from the state of nature. For these God or Nature provided only paltry materials to be manipulated by a self-sufficient man. In later neoclassical thought the labor theory of value is discarded for the marginal utility theory where the emphasis is on the subjective theory of value. Man is either the sovereign arbiter of his own tastes or even the creator of his own values.

The moral impetus behind mainstream economics, both classical and to a lesser extent neoclassical, is the devotion to peace, conflict resolution, and individual liberty. This is the "old" laissez-faire liberalism which believed in material progress and individual responsibility. Classical liberalism of this sort is still alive today.

Chesterton's work included numerous references, usually critical, to classical economic thinkers. He explicitly discussed Adam Smith, Malthus, and Ricardo in a manner reminiscent of Charles Dickens' *Hard Times*. However, he did not show any real familiarity with the basic texts. But as is often the case with Chesterton, one should read him for Chesterton and not for the authors he criticizes.

In making a sharp attack against classical economists and utilitarians, Chesterton committed the common mistake of lumping them together when they should be kept separate. His strictures were more appropriate to the utilitarians than to the classical economists.

Chesterton correctly understood that Adam Smith was no Calvinist. Instead of being Calvinists, the "uncommon men" of the eighteenth century were a

> dry sort of Deists drying up more and more like Atheists; and they are no longer pessimists but the reverse; only their optimism is often more depressing than pessimism. There were the Benthamites, the Utilitarians, the servants of the Economic Man; the first Free-Traders. They have the credit of having first made clear the economic theories of the modern state; and the calculations on which were mainly based the politics of the nineteenth century. It was they who taught these things scientifically and systematically to the public, and even to the populace. But what were the things, and what were the theories? Perhaps the best and broadest of them was a most monstrous and

mythical superstition of Adam Smith; a theological theory that providence had so made the world that men might be happy through their selfishness; or, in other words, that God would overrule everything for good, if only men would buy and sell freely, lend or borrow freely, sweat or sack freely, and in practice, steal or swindle freely, humanity would be happy. The Common Man soon found out how happy; in the Slums where they left him and in the Slump to which they led him.[4]

Smith's theory is, however, much more subtle than this statement would imply. Self-interest should not be equated with selfishness. Furthermore, Smith was not exclusively concerned even with self-interest.

Certain Malthusianisms — birth control and abortion — also come in for withering attacks. Chesterton's strictures are perhaps not fully applicable to Malthus who still called the preventive checks "vice," but he is on target in discussing a classical economist like John Stuart Mill. In the 1820s John Stuart Mill was arrested for distributing pamphlets explaining the techniques of a primitive birth control device.[5]

The onslaught on childhood is most startlingly seen in abortion, but preceding abortion is the contraceptive mind. Chesterton called it "birth prevention" rather than birth control.

My contempt boils over into bad behaviour when I hear the common suggestion that a birth is avoided because people want to be 'free' to go to the cinema or buy a gramophone or a loud-speaker. What makes me want to walk over such people like doormats is that they use the word 'free.' By every act of that sort they chain themselves to the most servile and mechanical system yet tolerated by men. . . . For a child is the very sign and sacrament of personal freedom. He is a fresh free will added to the wills of the world; he is something that his parents have freely chosen to produce and which they freely agree to protect. . . . He has been born without the intervention of any master or lord. He is a creation and a contribution. . . . People who prefer the mechanical pleasures to such a miracle are jaded and enslaved. They are preferring the last, crooked, indirect, borrowed, repeated and exhausted things of our dying Capitalist civilization, to the reality which is the only rejuvenation of all civilisation.

4. G. K. Chesterton, *The Common Man* (New York: Sheed & Ward, 1950), 8.
5. Torsten Gardlund, *The Life of Knut Wicksell* (Stockholm: Almquit & Wiksell, 1958), 55.

It is they who are hugging the chains of their old slavery; it is the child who is ready for the new world.[6]

Rather ironically Chesterton claims that the Common Man is not so much interested in the liberty to found a sect, but "to found a family. And it is exactly *there* that the modern emancipators are quite likely to frustrate him; in the name of Malthusianism or Eugenics or Sterilization or at a more advanced stage of progress, probably, Infanticide. It would be a model of modern liberty to tell him that he might preach anything, however wild, about the Virgin Birth, so long as he avoided anything like a natural birth. . . ."[7] One might think that Chesterton had the later neo-Malthusian economist, Knut Wicksell, explicitly in mind. Wicksell served a jail sentence for blasphemy connected with his remarks on the Virgin Birth at age 59; he used this time to write up his ideas on population which included advocacy of birth control.[8]

> Chesterton continued his argument that the Common Man was welcome to build a tin chapel to preach a twopenny creed, entirely based on the text, "Enoch begat Methuselah," so long as he himself is forbidden to beget anybody. And, as a matter of historical fact, the sects which enjoyed this sectarian freedom, in the seventeenth or eighteenth centuries, were generally founded by merchants or manufacturers of the comfortable, and sometimes of the luxurious classes. On the other hand, it is strictly to the lower classes, to use the liberal modern title for the poor, that such schemes as Sterilization are commonly directed and applied.[9]

Chesterton's most systemic attack on Malthus was his pamphlet *Social Reform versus Birth Control* (1927). Here in Cobbett-like fashion he attacks Malthus as the lackey of the old oligarchs against the new democrats Godwin and Shelley. He even refers to the "fantastically mathematical formula about geometrical progression."

Chesterton's treatment of David Ricardo is perhaps even less informed by confrontation with the text than his treatment of Malthus. He views Ricardo simply as an orthodox, laissez-faire theorist. In spite

6. G. K. Chesterton, *The Well and the Shallows* (London: Sheed & Ward, 1937), 145ff.

7. *The Common Man*, 1.

8. Gardlund, 249ff.

9. *The Common Man*, 1-2.

of this, Chesterton still gets to the essence of Ricardo's thought, that political economy is a humanistic substitute for God. In a brief essay, "God and Goods" Chesterton attacks Rousseau's primitivism, Ricardo's progressivism, and Bolshevism along with the Industrial Revolution:

> Then after the political revolution came the industrial revolution; and with it an enormous new importance attached to science. The amiable atheists went back to the people, smiled at them, coughed slightly, and explained that it was still necessary to burn down churches, but that a slight error had been made about the substitute for churches. The second atheist philosophy was founded, not on the fact that nature is kind, but on the fact that Nature is cruel; not that fields are free and beautiful, but that scientific men and industrialists are so energetic, that they will soon cover all the fields with factories and warehouses. Now there was a new substitute for God; which was gas and coal and iron and the privilege of turning wheels in order to work these substances. It was now positively stated that economic liberty, the freedom to buy and sell and hire and exploit, would make people so blissfully happy that they would forget all their dreams of the fields of heaven; or for that matter of the fields of earth. And somehow that also has been a little disappointing.[10]

Much more interesting to Chesterton than village atheists are the believers in cruel mother nature or the tyrannical God who must be destroyed or overcome!

He goes on to argue that Rousseau and Ricardo are both guilty of attempting to "immanentize the eschaton" to use the phrase of Eric Voegelin: "Two Earthly Paradises had collapsed. The first was the natural paradise of Rousseau; the second the economic paradise of Ricardo. Men did not become perfect through being free to live and love; men did not become perfect through being free to buy and sell."[11] Even though it is not clear that Ricardo was that optimistic, the description is very apt for the later Manchester School of Cobden and Bright who waved millenarian and pacifist banners.

In his summing up of the Victorian age in 1913, Chesterton pointed out two mistakes from which we could learn: "They thought that commerce outside a country must extend peace: it has certainly

10. Ibid., 75.
11. Ibid.

often extended war. They thought that commerce inside a country must certainly promote prosperity; it has largely promoted poverty. But for them these were experiments; for us they ought to be lessons."[12] These words were written in 1913, a year before the German "Ideas of 1914" were to unleash Sombart's Heroes of the German imagination on the Huckster Englishmen. In the light of Chesterton's hatred of Prussian Germany and in the light of economic history since 1913 we might be inclined to draw different lessons. Commerce and free trade are more connected with peace and prosperity than Chesterton thought.

We should take Chesterton's criticisms of the classical economists with a grain of salt; he saw them through the lens of utilitarianism which is not always an accurate way to understand these economists. But there were familiar slogans and fudge words of nineteenth-century liberalism which are still used by social scientists and reformers today.

Chesterton's scathing critique of these popular slogans which obscured any objective discussion of good and evil is still relevant:

> Every one of the modern popular phrases and ideals is a dodge in order to shirk the problem of what is good. We are fond of talking about "liberty"; that, as we talk of it, is a dodge to avoid discussing what is good. We are fond of talking about "progress"; that is a dodge to avoid discussing what is good. We are fond of talking about "education"; that is a dodge to avoid discussing what is good. The modern man says, "Let us leave all these arbitrary standards and embrace liberty." This is logically rendered, "Let us not decide what is good, but let it be considered good not to decide it." He says, "Away with your old moral formulae; I am for progress." This, logically stated, means, "Let us not settle what is good; but let us settle whether we are getting more of it." He says, "Neither in religion nor morality, my friend, lie the hopes of the race, but in education." This, clearly expressed, means, "We cannot decide what is good, but let us give it to our children."[13]

At the end of the nineteenth century the classical economists and their supporters (the "old economists") were under attack from the "new economists." There was a major confict between the "old school"

12. G. K. Chesterton, *The Victorian Age in Literature* (1913; reprint, London: Oxford University Press, 1961), 153.

13. G. K. Chesterton, *Heretics* (London: John Lane, 1905), 33.

who were the preservers of classical liberalism and laissez faire and the "new school" prophets of interventionism, protectionism, and socialist planning. It is here where we find the transition from nineteenth-century liberalism to the twentieth-century understanding of liberalism.

The "new liberalism" believed in a much more positive role for the state, it tended to deny individual responsibility, and it added welfare and egalitarian impulses which often wreaked havoc with the goal of individual liberty. If the "old liberalism" attempted to homogenize the privileged class structure of society in the name of the individual, then the "new liberalism" simply homogenized the individual further in the name of equality; in the "new liberalism" the state was to be made out of the pasteurized individuals reconstituted into the milk of human kindness. These are the analogies appropriate to the welfare state; stronger analogies are necessary for the totalitarian regimes. As Wilhelm Roepke has stressed in many places, the "pulverization" into the "dust bowl" of society or the "termite state" is the final result of the march into equality.

The "new school" was a term which amalgamated together all the non-orthodox opponents of laissez-faire. Chesterton often personally engaged these non-orthodox economists and social commentators such as the Webbs, Bernard Shaw, and Bertrand Russell; many explicit references to their writings appear in his works. He was a lifelong critic of the "experts" of social design theory.

Chesterton explicitly referred to this conflict between the "old economists" and the "new economists" in a discussion of H. G. Wells:

> The old economists, he [H. G. Wells] says, made generalizations, and they were (in Mr. Wells's view) mostly wrong. But the new economists, he says, seem to have lost the power of making any generalizations at all. And they cover this incapacity with a general claim to be, in specific cases, regarded as "experts," a claim "proper enough in a hair-dresser or a fashionable physician, but indecent in a philosopher or a man of science."[14]

One is reminded here of Keynes's wish that economists would come to be thought of as expert dentists.

Two occurrences in nineteenth-century England aided the transition from the "old" to the "new" economics. The first was a change of theological perspective, the second a change in social perspective.

14. *Heretics*, 34.

For many intellectuals in the nineteenth century the traditional idea of sin and God's judgment could not really be true. Hell was a scandal. The experience of sin and Last Judgment was replaced first by ideas of universal salvation. During the nineteenth century, unwillingness to believe in the finality of the Last Judgment characterized both clergyman economists, such as Malthus, and secular liberals, such as the Mills. In the later nineteenth century the Christian Socialist F. D. Maurice with his ideas of universal salvation appealed to many, including Alfred Marshall who had rejected his earlier religious inclinations. According to Koot, Maurice "rejected the reality of eternal damnation and taught instead a religion of love, in which Christians would subordinate their wills to the will of God, as expressed in the personal example of Jesus and as taught by the Church of England."[15]

Parallel to this theological atrophy was a flowering of the social science movement with its practical reform-oriented side. The reform was not to be personal, but social and institutional. The social science movement was a secular counterpart to the practical concerns of the churches. In effect, there was a transition from the ideal of a saint imitating Christ to the secularized social worker. The final denouement was the secularized social scientist. This is not meant to deny that in all periods there have been saints, social workers, and social scientists, but their role models have changed over time. Saints, priests, and ministers were the ultimate methodological personalists (as distinct from the methodological individualists) concerned with the art of arts, the health of souls. They were fully preoccupied with the concrete reality of each individual person. They did not overly concern themselves with material conditions; they did not concern themselves at all with a generic problem of scarcity. By contrast, the social worker and the early social-science movement in the nineteenth century were both concerned with practical results. They wished to alleviate the "social problem." But social problems like poverty, alcoholism, and drugs are notoriously difficult to solve and it is frustrating to engage in these concrete realities.

An important step in the secularization process was to collectivize the individual sense of sin and guilt. This was effectively accomplished by late nineteenth-century liberalism. The Webbs in particular tried to replace the old-fashioned idea of personal sin with

15. Gerard M. Koot, *English Historical Economics, 1870-1926* (Cambridge: Cambridge University Press, 1987), 136.

collective sin or collective guilt. Whatever sin remained was duly collectivized. Guilt was no longer to be felt on the individual level, but on the social level; collective guilt was to be assuaged through liberal social programs and institutional transformation. The Oxford emphasis on "conscious corporate action" replacing "individual impulsive action" defined the "new" liberalism which came to replace laissez-faire liberalism.[16] Beatrice Webb, for example, points out that "This class-consciousness of sin was usually accompanied by devoted personal service, sometimes by open confession and a deliberate dedication of means and strength to the reorganization of society on a more equalitarian basis."[17]

Although Chesterton flirted with Fabian Socialism, he was a lifelong critic of Bernard Shaw and the Webbs. In a single sentence, Chesterton captured the maternalistic atmosphere of Fabian socialism as exemplified in the thought of Beatrice Webb: "Nor can I at this moment think of a single modern woman writing on politics or abstract things, whose work is of undisputed importance; except perhaps Mrs. Sidney Webb, who settles things by the simple process of ordering about the citizens of a state, as she might the servants in a kitchen."[18]

The "burnout" of people dealing with real-world social problems probably also fed into the positivistic growth of abstract social science. When the "economic problem" is defined as an abstract scarcity, economics appears to be cooler, more abstract, and more susceptible to mathematical formulations. Economics becomes modeled on the physical sciences or on engineering, and economists become "experts." New economists became more likely to be considered experts as economics began to be viewed as a "profession." This fact was certainly the most important movement defining the modern nature of economics, a movement that took place mainly in the latter part of the nineteenth century and the early part of the twentieth century.

The strident policy differences between the laissez-faire, free trade, hard money, private property rights "old school" and the protectionist, interventionist/socialist, soft money "new schools" threatened the

16. Alon Kadish, *The Oxford Economists in the Late Nineteenth Century* (Oxford: Clarendon Press, 1982).

17. Beatrice Webb, *My Apprenticeship* (London: Longmans, Green, and Co.), 1926.

18. *The Victorian Age*, 58.

claims of economists to be thought of as "experts."[19] These differences had to be transmuted to non-rational, non-examinable differences in tastes and preferences. Neoclassical economists stressed their continuity with classical economics rather than their discontinuities. But to make their claims to professional competence, they had to surrender their claims to the liberalism component of classical liberalism. No one has ever heard of the concept of "neoclassical liberalism."

On the level of theory, the alchemy which produced the scientific economic expert was the fact-value distinction deriving from the positivist tradition and cemented into the social sciences by Max Weber. On the level of organization, it was accomplished by the transformation of the American Economic Association from its original reform-oriented Christian Socialist, German historicist purposes to a neutral, sanitized economic science. To my knowledge Chesterton never mentioned by name the British developers of neoclassical economics, Alfred Marshall and W. S. Jevons. Nor did he mention the market-failure theorists such as A. C. Pigou and John Maynard Keynes. In spite of this, Chesterton's thought is still relevant to the essential presuppositions of neoclassical economic thought. Chesterton saw the flaws in both the cosmopolitan liberals and the social imperialists contending for the economists' allegiance at the turn of the century. Both of them argued in terms of the concept of efficiency. The classical economists' concern with individual liberty was to be replaced by a more neutral concept of "efficiency." As good and evil had been earlier replaced by freedom and liberty, so they in their turn were replaced by the mainstream economists to a neutral efficiency. In the case of the social imperialist and neomercantilists, "efficiency" came to mean organic preparedness for war and the strains of empire.

Chesterton would have been unhappy with both the open-ended efficiency of neoclassical economics and the social imperialistic efficiency of the Coefficients, the group of Fabians and Liberal Imperialists who met in the first decade of the twentieth century. The latter were devoted to "rearing an Imperial race."[20] If the cosmopolitan liberals

19. The change in titles of books is important. Alfred Marshall wrote the first *Principles of Economics* in 1890 which replaced the older *Principles of Political Economy*. The science of economics was flexing its muscles against "political economy" whether interpreted as laissez-faire liberalism or socialist interventionism.

20. Bernard Semmel, *Imperialism and Social Reform: English Social-Imperial Thought 1895-1914* (Garden City, N.Y.: Doubleday & Company, 1968), 63.

refused to examine tastes and utility functions in the name of tolerance, then the social imperialists and neomercantilists too often uncritically sanctioned national power.

Chesterton pointed out that the debate between the cosmopolitans and the nationalists obscured the fact that neither part was willing to examine preferences in a rational manner:

> For instance, two men will argue about whether patriotism is a good thing and never discover until the end, if at all, that the cosmopolitan is basing his whole case upon the idea that man should, if he can, become as God, with equal sympathies and no prejudices, while the nationalist denies any such duty at the very start, and regards man as an animal who has preferences, as a bird has feathers.[21]

Although Chesterton is explicitly attacking the social imperialist's concept of efficiency, his insight is also appropriate to economists who are tempted to use a tautological definition of efficiency which finds efficiency everywhere:

> A school, of which Lord Rosebery is representative, has endeavoured to substitute for the moral or social ideals which have hitherto been the motives of politics a general coherency or completeness in the social system which has gained the nickname of "efficiency." I am not very certain of the secret doctrine of this sect in the matter. But as far as I can make out, "efficiency" means that we ought to discover everything about a machine except what it is for.[22]

He hammers home on the difficulties of using efficiency in the social sciences:

> "Efficiency," of course, is futile for the same reason that "strong men," "will power" and the superman are futile. That is, it is futile because it only deals with actions after they have been performed. It has no philosophy for incidents before they happen; therefore it has no power of choice.[23]

21. *Twelve Types*, 128-29.
22. Ibid., 9.
23. Ibid.

It is the capability of choice between good and evil that defines man for Chesterton.

Modern economics does lay some claim to being a science based on choice. The view of the individual as one who maximizes his utility is what lies behind the "pure logic of choice." Indifference curves are the skeleton's bones on which modern demand theory is laid. However, there is no good and evil to be seen in indifference curves; there is no good and evil in utility functions; there is no good and evil in the modern economist's treatment of value judgments. These are simply preferences. Paradoxically, the draining of all idea of rational judgment from "value judgments" — the core of positivism in all its many varieties — probably stems from a fear of objective good and evil. Value judgements are still treated today as arbitrary emotions, tastes, or feelings which have no objective referent. In modern social science experts cannot be authorities in matters of morals. The only "good" is agreement between consenting persons. Paretian welfare economics simply elaborates on the paradigm of voluntary exchange.[24]

If Chesterton rejects modern social science in almost all its manifestations, with what does he plan to replace it? For him the core of much modern social thought is at bottom a sour ingratitude or a sullen treason, attitudes which have replaced the experience of loyalty. If one wishes to call this experience "medieval" in order to dismiss it, then one has perhaps established a benchmark to measure modern decline and decay. Insofar as the stamp of modernity is distrust and treason, then there are good grounds for rejecting modernity.

Chesterton's idea of loyalty is multifaceted. The concept includes the person, material goods, property, family, country, the cosmos, and God. All of these loyalties share the very long-run perspective of eternity. Economists are best at the short-run, occasionally illuminating on the long-run, but totally inept at the longest run of eternity.

If the Catholic principle of subsidiary runs down to the individual, it still recognizes a hierarchical structure of authority which relates the

---

24. If we stop to think about it, modern welfare economics is simply childish in the derogatory sense of that word. The exhilaration of experiencing gains from trade or consumer's surplus are real experiences, but one should not try to make a complete social philosophy out of them. Consumer's surplus is the thrill of making a good deal — paying less for something than you would be willing to pay. Pareto-optimality, requiring unanimous consent, is simply the systematic extension of the petulance of childhood: wanting everything one's own way. If I may be excused a contemporary pun, it is as if we made "Let's make a deal" a Trump card for social policy.

130

individual all the way back to God. If the negative side of the person is the possibility of damnation, the positive side is freedom, responsibility, and possible salvation. With respect to the draining of the sense of individual sin and its replacement with a secularized collective guilt, Chesterton continually comes back to the main point which still needs to be reaffirmed. Chesterton will not allow the reality of eternal damnation to be lost no matter how much he affirms the religion of love:

> The same process of thought that has prevented nationalities disappearing in Christendom has prevented the complete appearance of Pantheism. All Christian men instinctively resist the idea of being absorbed into an Empire; an Austrian, a Spanish, a British, or a Turkish Empire. But there is one empire, much larger and much more tyrannical, which free men will resist with even stronger passion. The free man violently resists being absorbed into the empire which is called the Universe. He demands Home Rule for his nationality, but still more Home Rule for his home. Most of all he demands Home Rule for himself. He claims the right to be damned in spite of theosophical optimism.[25]

Defending man's right to be damned is the essence of Chesterton's thought. Chesterton saw the individual person poised between good and evil. His individualism is neither the isolated individual of libertarian fancy nor the narcissistic self.

Chesterton's description of Henri Massis could very well stand for Chesterton's own position:

> M. Massis stands in all his works . . . for the idea of a certain dignity and independence in the human soul, such as is expressed in the idea of free will and of a final choice between good and evil. In this he is equally opposed to all that type of materialism which makes the mind mechanical, and also to all that type of transcendentalism which would merely melt it into everything or into nothing. It is true that some of the German and other transcendentalists whom he attacks with so much vigour, have themselves talked a great deal about the Will. But in them it is so anarchic that it might more properly be called the Wish. It is not a command of conscious choice; but rather a surrender to the drive of unconscious desire. In the philosophy of

---

25. G. K. Chesterton, "The Separatist," in *A Miscellany of Men* (New York: Dodd, Mead & Co., 1912).

M. Massis the Will is wedded to the Reason; and it is his whole point to protest against either sceptics or mystics putting asunder those whom God has joined to make Man. It is this sane tradition of a reasonable and responsible dignity in the Will which he here defends against all the vast intellectual invasion from Asia.[26]

There is a sense of a story, of meaningful drama, to the Christian view of history. Both ideas and actions have consequences. The drama of the Last Judgment and man's responsibility to his Creator is certainly more dramatic than the last whimper of the last man clinging to the fact of his existence.

There is also a positive side to Chesterton's critique of utility and efficiency. Although Chesterton had no formal demand theory, he had quite decided views on the nature of pleasure, enjoyment, and consumption. There was a sympathy with the old-style utilitarian who would really talk about pain-pleasure as a test or criterion. That is far superior to the subjectivization of utility which is often encountered in modern economics. Modern subjectivism allows us to talk about the man in the gutter maximizing his utility by having another bottle of wine. Yes, he does what he does, but that is to simply enshrine the will and deny man's reason. I am not certain that Chesterton would be delighted with Pareto's desire to quit talking about utility, but I am sure that he would respect Pareto's "ophelimity" which is a technical term meaning desiredness having no common-sense overtones of usefulness. G. K. Chesterton emphasized the distinction between use and enjoyment in a little essay on "Music with Meals":

> I think it was a great medieval philosopher who said that all evil comes from enjoying what we ought to use and using what we ought to enjoy. A great many modern philosophers never do anything else. Thus they will sacrifice what they admit to be happiness to what they claim to be progress; though it could have no rational meaning except progress to greater happiness. Or they will subordinate goodness to efficiency; though the very name of good implies an end, and the very name of efficiency implies only a means to an end. Progress and efficiency by their very titles are only tools. Goodness and happiness by their very titles are a fruition; the fruits that are to be produced by the tools.[27]

26. G. K. Chesterton, "Defending the West" in *The Chesterton Review* (double issue) 15, no. 4 (1989); 16, no. 1 (1990): 432. Originally the preface to Henri Massis, *Defense of the West*, 1927.

27. G. K. Chesterton, "Music with Meals," reprinted in Jacques Barzun, ed.,

Chesterton's appreciation of material things delighted in their presence and materiality. But at the same time they could be symbols of the spiritual life:

> . . . the Christmas pudding, though substantial enough, is itself an allegory and a sign. The little boy expects to find sixpences in the pudding; and this is right enough, so long as the sixpences are secondary to the pudding. Now the change from the medieval to the modern world might be very truly described under that image. It is all the difference between putting sixpences in a Christmas pudding and erecting a Christmas pudding around sixpences. There was money in the old days of Christmas and Christendom; there was merchandise; there were merchants. But the moral scheme of all the old order, whatever its other vices and diseases, always assumed that money was secondary to substance; that the merchant was secondary to the maker. Windfalls of money came to this man and that, as shillings and sixpences are extracted excitedly from Christmas puddings. But the idea of normal ownership or enjoying preponderated over the idea of accidental or adventurous gain. With the rise of the merchant adventurers the whole world gradually changed, until the preponderance was all the other way. The world was dominated by what the late Lord Birkenhead described as "the glittering prizes," without which, as he appeared to believe, men could not be really moved to any healthy or humane activity. And it is true that men came to think too much about prizes, and too little about pudding. This, in connexion with ordinary pudding is a fallacy; in connexion with Christmas pudding it is a blasphemy. For there is truly something of perversity, not unmixed with profanity, about the notion of trade completely transforming a tradition of such sacred origin. Millions of perfectly healthy and worthy men and women still keep Christmas, and do in all sincerity keep it holy as well as happy. But there are some, profiting by such natural schemes of play and pleasure-seeking, who have used it for things far baser than either pleasure-seeking or play. They have betrayed Christmas. For them the substance of Christmas, like the substance of Christmas pudding, has become stale stuff in which their

---

Pleasures of Music (New York: Viking Press, 1951), 163-64. I have long been working on an article with a Chestertonian title, "Let's put utility back in the closet." Mops and brooms help bring out the "incarnational" nature of Chesterton's thought. Nowhere is this more obvious than in his treatment of material goods.

133

own treasure is buried; and they have only multiplied the sixpences into thirty pieces of silver.[28]

The theme of private property is continually stressed in Chesterton's writing. But it is never treated in the individualistic/libertarian way that the economics of property rights would do. Chesterton's views on private property are very similar to those of Richard Weaver. Property is cherished for its potentiality in providing creativity to ordinary persons; it is cherished for nurturing character. He does not defend corporate capitalism or unrestricted freedom of contract. According to Chesterton:

> I am well aware that the word "property" has been defiled in our time by the corruption of great capitalists. One would think, to hear people talk, that the Rothschilds and the Rockefellers were on the side of property. But obviously they are the enemies of property; because they are the enemies of their own limitations. They do not want their own land; but other people's. When they remove their neighbour's landmark, they also remove their own. A man who loves a little triangular field ought to love it because it is triangular; anyone who destroys the shape, by giving him more land, is a thief who has stolen a triangle. A man with the true poetry of possession wishes to see the wall where his garden meets Smith's garden; the hedge where his farm touches Brown's. He cannot see the shape of his own land unless he sees the edges of his neighbour's. It is the negation of property that the Duke of Sutherland should have all the farms in one estate; just as it would be the negation of marriage if he had all our wives in one harem.[29]

Chesterton constantly combines the ideas of creation with limits.[30]

The idea of property ownership permeated Chesterton's defense of Distributism. It was the ideal of ownership of the means of production in the hands of the workers and farmers that inspired him. His flirtations with syndicalism and guilds were based on this understanding. Furthermore, guilds required loyalty and vows. The virtues of altruism, charity, and self-sacrifice allows a defense of unions as industrial democracies where the worker had progressed to sacrifice his own narrow interests in favor of corporate interests.

28. G. K. Chesterton, "On Christmas that is Coming," in *Avowals and Denials* (London: Methuen & Co. Ltd., 1934), 7-12.
29. *What's Wrong*, 36.
30. Ibid., 35-36.

Now, this view can be attacked in the name of the "old" liberalism because it allows an antisocial conspiracy against the consumer. In fact, the Scholastic tradition was really not very far from classical liberalism in its distrust of combinations and conspiracies in restraint of trade. What's more clubby than a cartel? If there are errors here, perhaps they result from the fact that Chesterton did not pay sufficient attention to the Scholastics of the Middle Ages.

We now move from Chesterton's ideas about the individual good to his view of the social good. There is no question that proper ideas about marriage and the family were central concerns of Chesterton's Distributism. When writing to Maurice Baring explaining the importance of *G. K.'s Weekly* in the fight for "Catholic ethics and economics," he stressed that "There is nobody to say a single word for the family, or the true case for property, or the proper understanding of the religious peasantries, while the whole press is full of every sort of sophistry to smooth the way of divorce, of birth control, of mere State expediency and all the rest."[31]

The key concept for understanding social arrangements in Chesterton is again the importance of vows. Vows are intermediary between status and contract. They are voluntary like contract and permanent like status. In a sense they are voluntary subordination or submission of will to something greater than the individual. Chesterton's concern for vows is made clear in his *St. Francis of Assisi:* "Family life as much as feudal life is in its nature a system of dependence."[32] In the modern world the vows of marriage are replaced by a fleeting contract at best; patriotism is replaced by Pareto optimality. Morality, the family, and the state are "withered away." They are dissolved by analysis into temporary mutual gains from exchange.

Chesterton's concept of family and marriage are crucial to understanding his ideas of the spiritual life. Dependence and independence in Chesterton's thought are kept in a state of tension so that he avoids the extremes of slavery and absolute freedom. A beautiful passage from G. K. Chesterton captures the reality of eternity for the most important human things:

> . . . all the noble necessities of man talk the language of eternity. When man is doing the three or four things that he was sent on this

31. Jay P. Corrin, *G. K. Chesterton and Hilaire Belloc: The Battle Against Modernity* (Athens: Ohio University Press, 1981), 104.

32. G. K. Chesterton, *St. Francis of Assisi* (1924; reprint, Garden City, N.Y.: Doubleday & Company, Inc., 1957), 102.

earth to do, then he speaks like one who shall live for ever. A man dying for his country does not talk as if local preferences could change. Leonidas does not say, "In my present mood, I prefer Sparta to Persia." William Tell does not remark, "The Swiss civilization, so far as I can yet see, is superior to the Austrian." When men are making commonwealths, they talk in terms of the absolute, and so they do when they are making (however unconsciously) those smaller commonwealths which are called families.[33]

How different all this is from the language and rhetorical appeal of modern economists! Gary Becker on the household and James Buchanan on the state talk a totally different language. Their language is expediency: utility, temporary contract, and agreement of wills. The language of Chesterton is substantive morality, obligation, and eternity.

Let me conclude by saying that Chesterton will not allow the economist to forget that man is a creature poised between good and evil as well as between the neutral language of utility and the technical apparatus of indifference curves. The realm of the useful means something conducive to the good. The realm of the indifferent things (the *adiaphora*) only makes sense as a contrast to the choice between good and evil. Efficiency should mean something efficacious in achieving a good. But the good in all these cases cannot simply mean desiredness or an object of will. Families, nations, and constitutions have inescapably moral foundations, and as such are Permanent Things.

Economics as a profession does not like being put between a rock and a hard place. We turn our rocks into bread, sand into gold, and soften the hard places by infinite substitutability. By going with the flow, we refuse to cast the first stone, not because we are sinless, but because we have rejected the idea of sin. Sins are merely subjective tastes or preferences. It is the great glory of Chesterton to remind us that the fundamental equality of all men is grounded in original sin: "Carlyle says, for instance, that most men are fools — that was his great mistake. Christianity with much sounder wisdom says that they are all fools. That principle may be called the doctrine of original sin, or the doctrine of the equality of man — it comes out the same thing."[34]

33. G. K. Chesterton, "Questions of Divorce," in *The Uses of Diversity* (New York: Dodd, Mead & Company, 1921), 180-81.

34. G. K. Chesterton, "'Vox Populi, Vox Dei,'" *The Chesterton Review* 11, no. 3 (1985): 264. Originally given as a lecture to the Christian Social Union, 16 March 1905.

Finding the Permanent in the Political:
C. S. Lewis as a Political Thinker

John G. West, Jr.

The year was 1951, and England was embroiled in a bitter general election campaign. Six years earlier the Conservative Party of Winston Churchill had been thrown out of power. Now the same party, still led by the same indomitable Churchill, was attempting a comeback. The conventional wisdom was that the attempt would fail. The conventional wisdom was wrong. Voters went to the polls on October 25, and the next morning the whole world knew that the Conservative Party had recaptured control of Parliament and Churchill had regained the post of prime minister.

Within a few weeks of the change of power, Churchill's office sent a letter to C. S. Lewis, inviting him to receive the honorary title "Commander of the British Empire." One can only guess what Lewis thought when he first read the letter, but one suspects that he appreciated it, for he greatly admired Churchill.[1]

Despite his admiration, however, Lewis declined the proposed honor. He wrote back to Churchill's secretary that he was grateful for the recognition, but he worried about the political repercussions: "There are always . . . knaves who say, and fools who believe, that my religious writings are all covert anti-Leftist propaganda, and my appearance in the Honours List wd. of course strengthen their hands. It is therefore better that I shd. not appear there."[2] The letter is characteristic of Lewis,

1. See C. S. Lewis, "Private Bates," in *Present Concerns* (New York: Harcourt Brace Jovanovich, 1986), 46.
2. C. S. Lewis, *Letters of C. S. Lewis,* ed. with a memoir by W. H. Lewis (New York: Harcourt, Brace and World, 1966), 235.

for it shows how diligently he tried to steer clear of partisan entangle-
ments. He was never a party hack like John Milton; he never founded
a political movement like G. K. Chesterton and Hillaire Belloc; he even
shunned giving money to political causes. Prior to World War II, one
of Lewis's students informed him of his work on behalf of the Com-
munist-backed loyalists in the Spanish Civil War. Lewis quickly told the
student that he had a rule about not donating money "to anything that
had a directly political implication."[3] After the War, Lewis continued
to keep his distance from politics. According to stepson David Gresham,
Lewis was skeptical of politicians and not really interested in current
events.[4] Lewis's own writings seem to bear this out. His wry poem "Lines
During a General Election," for instance, presents the following rather
bleak assessment of politicians: "Their threats are terrible enough, but
we could bear/All that; it is their promises that bring despair."[5] And as
far as caring about the "great issues" of his day, Lewis wrote his brother
in 1940:

> Lord! how I loathe great issues. . . . "Dynamic" I think is one of the
> words invented by this age which sums up what it likes and I abom-
> inate. Could one start a Stagnation Party — which at General Elec-
> tions would boast that during its term of office no event of the least
> importance had taken place?[6]

Paradoxically, none of this means that Lewis never said anything
important about politics. In fact, he said a great deal — more than most
people probably realize. It is startling to note just how many political
topics Lewis broached in his writings: crime, obscenity, capital punishment, conscription, communism, fascism, socialism, war, vivisection, the
welfare state, the atomic bomb.[7] When Lewis talked about these mat-

---

3. Lewis, quoted in William Griffin, *Clives Staples Lewis: A Dramatic Life* (San
Francisco: Harper & Row, 1986), 137.

4. Gresham's views as recounted by Chad Walsh in *The Literary Legacy of C. S.
Lewis* (New York: Harcourt Brace Jovanovich, 1979), 15.

5. C. S. Lewis, "Lines During a General Election," in *Poems* (London: Geoffrey
Bles, 1964), 62.

6. Lewis, *Letters*, 179.

7. See, for example, "The Pains of Animals," "Dangers of National Repentance,"
"Vivisection," "The Humanitarian Theory of Punishment," "Delinquents in the Snow,"
"Is Progress Possible? Willing Slaves of the Welfare State," in *God in the Dock: Essays
on Theology and Ethics,* ed. Walter Hooper (Grand Rapids, Mich.: Eerdmans, 1970),

ters, however, it was not in the way most politicians do. He was wholly unconcerned with what political scientists today like to call "public policy," that conglomeration of compromise, convention, and self-interest that forms the staple of much of our own political diet. If you expect to find a prescription for solving air pollution or advice on how to win an election, don't bother reading Lewis. He has nothing to tell you. His concern was not policy but principle; political problems of the day were interesting to him only insofar as they involved matters that endured, the Permanent Things. Looked at in this light, Lewis's penchant for writing about politics and his simultaneous detachment from the political arena seem perfectly explicable. It is precisely because Lewis was so uninterested in ordinary political affairs that he has so much to tell us about politics in the broad sense of the term. By avoiding the partisan strife of his own time, he was able to articulate enduring political standards for all time. Nowhere is this clearer than in Lewis's writings on tyranny and morality.

Fascism and communism were the two most obvious manifestations of tyranny about which Lewis wrote, but they were far from the only kinds of tyranny with which he was concerned.[8] Tyranny comes in many forms, most of which are more subtle than Stalin's gulag or Hitler's death camps. Lewis knew this, and his most compelling writings on tyranny focus on these more subtle forms of oppression. In particular, Lewis was concerned about the tyranny that could result from the union of modern science and the modern state.

To understand the dangers of a scientific state, one must first understand something about modern science. Modern science is premised on the notion that all things are determined by material causes. It proposes strict laws that explain natural phenomena in terms of physical,

---

161-71, 189-92, 287-300, 306-10, 311-16; "Why I Am Not a Pacifist," "The Inner Ring," in *The Weight of Glory and Other Addresses,* rev. edition, ed. Walter Hooper (New York: Macmillan, 1980), 33-53, 93-105; "A Reply to Professor Haldane," in *C. S. Lewis on Stories and Other Essays on Literature,* ed. Walter Hooper (New York: Harcourt Brace Jovanovich, 1982), 69-72; all the essays in *Present Concerns.*

8. For Lewis's view of both the extreme right and the extreme left see "To the Author of *Flowering Rifle,*" in *Poems,* 65; and Stuart Barton Babbage, "To the Royal Air Force," in Carolyn Keefe, *C. S. Lewis: Speaker and Teacher* (Grand Rapids, Mich.: Zondervan, 1971), 67. Also noteworthy is a letter Lewis wrote in 1933 condemning Hitler's persecution of the Jews. See *They Stand Together: The Letters of C. S. Lewis to Arthur Greeves (1914-1963),* ed. Walter Hooper (New York: Macmillan, 1979), 468.

environmental or hereditary necessities: for example, the ball falls when dropped because of the law of gravity; the dog salivates at the sound of the bell because of environmental conditioning; the mosquito generates other mosquitoes because of its genetic code. Now, no matter how necessary such materialistic determinism may be in the study of the natural world, it cannot be applied indiscriminately to humans without destroying the very possibility of knowledge and virtue. Such determinism destroys the possibility of knowledge, according to Lewis, because it undermines the validity of human reasoning;[9] it destroys the possibility of virtue because it denies the free choice upon which all virtue depends.

If modern science is correct that human thought and conduct are functions of nonrational causes, then the nature of politics changes fundamentally. Under the old order, politics involved serious reflection about justice and the common good. But the more man thinks he is determined by nonrational causes, the less important serious reflection becomes. Under the new order, all that matters is achieving the end result. The only deliberation is among social science bureaucrats, and the only question is not "What is just?" but "What works?" Moreover, since the new order has dispensed with the notion of man as a moral agent, "what works" will almost inevitably be intrusive. As long as man was regarded as accountable for his actions, there were certain limits beyond which the state was not supposed to tread. Laws promulgated under the old system promised punishment, but they could not compel obedience. This is because the very idea of punishment presupposes free choice: one can only be punished *after* one has done something meriting punishment. If a person is willing to face the consequences of his actions, he can still break the law. His ability to choose is left intact.

If people act only because of environmental and biological necessities, however, the government no longer need deal with them as free moral agents. Under the new system, preemption replaces punishment as the preferred method of social control. Instead of inflicting punishment for making the wrong choice, the state simply eliminates the possibility of choice. So, instead of laws telling us to wear seat belts, we have passive restraints that automatically strap us into our car seats. Instead of simply being told to pay our taxes, our taxes are automatically deducted from our paychecks.

9. For Lewis's reasoning, see C. S. Lewis, *Miracles: A Preliminary Study* (New York: Macmillan, 1960), 14-15.

In this brave new world, the relationship between citizen and state begins to resemble the relationship between master and slave, as Lewis pointed out so perceptively in his essay, "Willing Slaves of the Welfare State." The cardinal difficulty with this type of scientific paternalism is that it undercuts that which makes us human; in the name of saving man from his problems, it abolishes man:

> The question . . . has become . . . whether we can discover any way of submitting to the worldwide paternalism of a technocracy without losing all personal privacy and independence. Is there any possibility of getting the super Welfare State's honey and avoiding the sting?
>
> Let us make no mistake about the sting. The Swedish sadness is only a foretaste. To live his life in his own way, to call his house his castle, to enjoy the fruits of his own labour, to educate his children as his conscience directs, to save for their prosperity after his death — these are wishes deeply ingrained in . . . civilised man.[10]

Lewis's most haunting portrait of this kind of despotism came in his novel *That Hideous Strength*.[11] There the spirit of modern social science becomes incarnate in the National Institute for Coordinated Experiments — NICE, for short. Of course, there is nothing nice about NICE; its social scientists are exactly the type of bureaucratic manipulators that Lewis attacked in nonfiction works like *The Abolition of Man*.[12]

At this point one can anticipate several objections: Isn't Lewis being unfair to science by implying that it inevitably leads to tyranny? And isn't he being unfair to scientists by implying that all they want is power to enslave others? And don't many modern problems — from air pollution to congestion on our freeways — require technological solutions that can be provided only by scientific experts?

Lewis was aware of such objections and replied that he wasn't against scientists *per se* and that of course he did not think that science would necessarily lead to tyranny of the sort depicted in *That Hideous Strength*.[13]

---

10. "Is Progress Possible? Willing Slaves of the Welfare State," 316.

11. C. S. Lewis, *That Hideous Strength: A Modern Fairy-Tale for Grown-Ups* (New York: Macmillan, 1965).

12. C. S. Lewis, *The Abolition of Man* (New York: Macmillan, 1955), see in particular, 65-91.

13. See *The Abolition of Man*, 86-87; "A Reply to Professor Haldane," 72-74.

One might be tempted to conclude from this that Lewis's objection to science was narrow — that all he really opposed was the abuse of science. But such a conclusion would be misleading. For when Lewis said he wasn't attacking "science" or "scientists," he seems to have had a very specific meaning in mind. He was not attacking science insofar as it was the quest for greater knowledge; he *was* attacking it insofar as it was a quest for power, in particular for power over man. In practice this meant that while Lewis accepted the legitimacy of natural science, he rejected much of the social sciences. Learning about chemistry or biology was acceptable, if not honorable; trying to use chemical or biological maxims to understand the nature of man was not. A glimpse of this view can be found in the character of William Hingest in *That Hideous Strength*. Hingest is Lewis's prototype for the "good scientist," a brilliant and crusty physical chemist who thinks more highly of his family tree than of his scientific prowess. Hingest is interested in science for the sake of knowledge rather than power, and he takes a dim view of those who want to use science to control man.[14] Indeed, he does not regard as science at all those disciplines that try to use the scientific approach to analyze man. When Mark Studdock talks to him about "sciences like Sociology," Hingest coldly replies: "There *are* no sciences like Sociology."[15]

As for the objection that we must rely on the advice of scientists, because only they have the answers to today's complicated problems, Lewis could not agree. He does not dispute that scientists have plenty of knowledge; the problem is that most of it is irrelevant. Political problems are preeminently moral problems, and scientists are not equipped to function as moralists. Said Lewis:

> I dread specialists in power because they are specialists speaking outside their special subjects. Let scientists tell us about sciences. But government involves questions about the good for man, and justice, and what things are worth having at what price; and on these a scientific training gives a man's opinion no added value.[16]

The cardinal danger of depending on science for political solutions, then, is that science is divorced from those permanent principles of morality upon which all just political solutions depend. Indeed, words

14. *That Hideous Strength*, 71.
15. Ibid., 70.
16. "Is Progress Possible? Willing Slaves of the Welfare State," 315.

like "justice," "virtue," "mercy," and "duty," are terms without meaning within the scientific framework. And so while science is not necessarily tyrannical, it can easily become a tool for tyrants because it has no firm grounding in morality. The same goes for politics: without a firm grounding in a firm morality, politics easily slides into tyranny.

But if morality is what we need, how do we go about achieving it? Lewis's answer to this query is far more controversial than one might suppose.

Many Christians today argue that morality must be founded upon the Bible. The extent to which this belief holds sway can be seen in the catchwords Christians use when they become involved in politics; most argue for a return to "biblical values," "Christian values," "transcendent religious truths," or (to use the dominant phrase) "traditional values" based on the "Judeo-Christian tradition." The terms differ slightly, but the bottom line remains the same: the only real source of morality is Christian revelation.[17]

Lewis was aware of this view, but rejected it. As he wrote in his posthumously published essay on ethics:

> It is often asserted . . . that the world must return to Christian ethics in order to preserve civilization. . . . Though I am myself a Christian, and even a dogmatic Christian untinged with Modernist reservations and committed to supernaturalism in its full rigour, I find myself quite unable to take my place beside the upholders of . . . [this] view. . . .
>
> It is far from my intention to deny that we find in Christian ethics a deepening, an internalization, a few changes of emphasis in the moral code. But only serious ignorance of Jewish and Pagan culture would lead anyone to the conclusion that it is a radically new thing.[18]

17. For examples of this view, see Carl F. H. Henry, *God, Revelation and Authority* (Waco: Word Books, 1976-83), 6: 423-27; Francis A. Schaeffer, *He Is There and He Is Not Silent*, in *Complete Works of Francis A. Schaeffer* (Westchester, Ill.: Crossway Books, 1982), 1: 295; Greg L. Bahnsen, *By the Standard: The Authority of God's Law Today* (Tyler, Tex.: Institute for Christian Economics, 1985), 2-4, 12-28, but note concessions on 141, 171; John W. Whitehead, "The Dangers in Natural Law," *Action: A Monthly Publication of The Rutherford Institute*, November 1991, 3, 7; Bryce J. Christensen, "Against the Wall: Why Character Education Is Failing in American Schools," in *School Based Clinics and Other Critical Issues in Public Education*, ed. Barrett L. Mosbacker (Westchester, Ill.: Crossway Books, 1987), 122-23; Barrett L. Mosbacker, "The Christian, Morality, and Public Policy," in *School Based Clinics*, 181-214.

18. C. S. Lewis, "On Ethics," in *Christian Reflections* (Grand Rapids, Mich.: Eerdmans, 1967), 44 and 46.

Rejecting the notion of a peculiarly "Christian" morality, Lewis argued for the existence of a natural moral law known by all through human reason. This natural moral code is the source from which all moral judgments come. Its fundamental truths — maxims like "good should be done and evil avoided," "caring for others is a good thing," "dying for a righteous cause is a noble thing" — are known independent of experience. They are grasped in the same way that we know $2 + 2 = 4$.

Lewis was certainly not the first to articulate the idea of natural law. As any good medievalist could tell you, "It's all in Aquinas." It is also in Paul, Augustine, Cicero, Grotius, Blackstone, and the Declaration of Independence. But this idea of natural law is precisely what many modern Christians reject, even some who cite Lewis. Unintended ironies often result. In an essay on "Law and Nature" written by one prominent evangelical, for example, extensive favorable citations of Lewis's *Abolition of Man* appear on one page, while the following denunciation of natural law appears on another:

> Even if man can treat the so-called natural laws as absolutes for society and government, the consequence is cruelty to man. Without the reference point in the Bible, there is no basis to judge which laws of nature are applicable to government and man. Depending upon the man or elitist group in power, many different things can be perpetrated and can be justified on the basis of natural law.[19]

Lewis regarded this point of view as the cobelligerent of modern philosophy. For just as modern philosophy denied the ability of reason to discern an objective moral law, this sort of Christianity considered reason to be too corrupted by sin to know objective morality apart from the Bible. Lewis found this belief disheartening, as he wrote his brother:

> Did you fondly believe — I did — that where you got among Christians, there at least you would escape from the horrible ferocity and grimness of modern thought? Not a bit of it. I blundered into it all, imagining that I was the upholder of the old, stern doctrines against modern quasi-Christian slush; only to find that *my* sternness was *their* slush. . . . They all talk like Covenantors or Old Testament prophets. They don't think human reason or human conscience of any value at all. . . .[20]

19. John W. Whitehead, "Law and Nature," in *The Second American Revolution* (Elgin, Ill.: David C. Cook, 1982), 185.
20. Lewis, *Letters*, 177.

As far as I know, Lewis never directly addressed the political difficulties of this rejection of natural law by Christians; yet these difficulties must be understood in order to grasp fully the importance of Lewis's natural law teaching. The problem with tying all morality to the Bible is that it implies that those who don't believe in the Bible cannot really be good citizens. After all, if only believers can have access to true morality through the Bible, perhaps only they can be trusted to make the laws. What has been called the theological-political problem resurfaces with a vengeance, for in this situation there exists no common ground on which believers and nonbelievers can meet for debate and joint action in the political arena. The natural law rescues us from this quagmire by articulating a morality shared by believer and unbeliever alike. This is not to say that the only justification for natural law is political. The overarching reason for Christians to believe in natural law is because it is demanded by revelation itself. Lewis knew this with full force, but before examining his comments we would do well to refer to the apostle Paul. In chapter two of Romans, Paul argues that

> when Gentiles . . . do by nature things required by law, they are a law for themselves, even though they do not have the law, since they show that the requirements of the law are written on their hearts, their consciences also bearing witness, and their thoughts now accusing, now even defending them.[21]

Now according to Paul, the Gentiles have a knowledge of morality even without having Old Testament revelation. They do that which is right "by nature." "By nature" does not mean "by instinct" because Paul describes the process by which the Gentiles come to moral knowledge as a rational one. It consists of the inner mental dialogue of the conscience with "thoughts now accusing, now even defending them." Nor does Paul diminish the rationality of this knowledge by the phrase "written on [or "in"] their hearts." As Lewis argued in *The Discarded Image*, Paul's statement here is in complete harmony with the ancient view that morality is dictated by "right reason" — and more particularly, with the Stoic conception of natural law:

> The Stoics believed in a Natural Law which all rational men, in virtue of their rationality, saw to be binding on them. St. Paul['s] . . . state-

21. Romans 2:14-15 (NIV).

ment in Romans (ii 14 sq.) that there is a law "written in the hearts" even of Gentiles who do not know "the law" is in full conformity with the Stoic conception, and would for centuries be so understood. Nor, during those centuries, would the word hearts have had merely emotional associations. The Hebrew word which St. Paul represents by *kardia* would be more nearly translated "Mind."[22]

Though Romans 2:14-15 is the single explicit reference in the New Testament to natural law theory, its importance should not be minimized on that account. In the immediate context of the passage, Paul is trying to explain how a just God can condemn wicked Gentiles who have not had the benefit of the Mosaic law. Paul argues that the Gentiles have "no excuse" because they themselves recognize the substance of the moral law by nature.

In the broader context of Pauline theology, the necessity of a natural law becomes even more evident once one focuses on the proper function of Old Testament law. Paul emphasized that Old Testament law was worthless as a method to save people from their sins because no one could ever hope to fulfill it perfectly. All the Old Testament law did was make the Jews conscious of sin so that they would know that they needed a savior; the law demonstrated their need for repentance before God.[23] But Christ died to save Gentiles as well as Jews. Because God never promulgated the moral law to them through revelation, Gentiles must have been conscious of their sin through some other route, or they never would have known of their need to repent. This "other route" is natural law. Without it, Gentiles could never understand their need to be saved.

Viewed in this way, it does not matter that the letter to the Romans is the only place where Paul explicitly delineates the natural law for the Gentiles, because the need for a natural law is presupposed by the very

---

22. C. S. Lewis, *The Discarded Image: An Introduction to Medieval and Renaissance Literature* (New York: Cambridge University Press, 1964), 160.

23. "Now we know that whatever the law says, it says to those who are under the law, so that every mouth may be silenced and the whole world held accountable to God. Therefore no one will be declared righteous in his sight by observing the law; rather, through the law we become conscious of sin" (Romans 3:19-20, NIV). Paul implicitly includes the natural law in his discussion here. The "whole world" obviously includes the Gentiles as well as the Jews; and the only "law" they know (and the only law that they are "under") is the one "by nature."

preaching of the gospel of repentance to anyone who is not a Jew. As Lewis noted in his essay on ethics:

> The convert accept[s] . . . forgiveness of sins. But of sins against what Law? Some new law promulgated by the Christians? But that is nonsensical. It would be the mockery of a tyrant to forgive a man for doing what had never been forbidden until the very moment at which the forgiveness was announced. . . . Essentially, Christianity is not the promulgation of a moral discovery. It is addressed only to penitents, only to those who admit their disobedience to the known moral law.[24]

Lewis made this same argument somewhat more fully in *The Problem of Pain*,[25] where he cited Luke 12:57 and Jeremiah 2:5 to show how the Bible itself appears to our natural moral judgments as authoritative.

The Bible, then, does attest to the existence of a natural law. But this does not mean that natural law is a cure-all. Natural law provides a basis for Christian political action, but it does not supply simple-minded solutions to specific political problems. Nor did Lewis claim that it would. As he more than once explained (echoing Aristotle's *Ethics*): "[M]oral decisions do not admit of mathematical certainty."[26] Natural law only supplies general moral precepts; prudence is required for precepts to be applied correctly in particular situations. Hence there is always the chance that one's political decision will be wrong.[27]

Contrary to those Christians who reject natural law, however, this problem of uncertainty cannot be solved by replacing the law of nature with the law of revelation as expressed in the Bible, because the Bible rarely gives particular advice on specific political issues. The Scriptures invariably require interpretation if they are to be used as a political guidebook, and interpretation opens the door for misconstruction. The Bible can be abused and misused as much as natural law.

Now I am not arguing — and I know Lewis would not argue — that the Bible has no role in the area of morality. But in a society that

24. C. S. Lewis, "On Ethics," 46-47.

25. C. S. Lewis, *The Problem of Pain* (New York: Macmillan, 1962), 39; also see Lewis's argument in "The Poison of Subjectivism," in *Christian Reflections*, particularly 78-80.

26. C. S. Lewis, "Why I Am Not a Pacifist," in *The Weight of Glory*, 53. The passage in Aristotle which Lewis is recalling can be found in the *Nicomachean Ethics*, 1094b. Lewis explicitly refers to this passage in "A Reply to Professor Haldane," 76.

27. "A Reply to Professor Haldane," 76.

is not a theocracy the Bible can never be the primary *political* standard of morality. The Christians who lived during the American Founding recognized this fact, and their political rhetoric was fashioned accordingly. They spoke regularly of the "Laws of Nature and Nature's God" and of acting in accord with *both* "reason and revelation."[28] They saw natural law as the necessary meeting point for citizens of all religious beliefs.[29] Like the early American Christians, Lewis recognized the inescapable truth of natural law. Christians today would do well to heed Lewis's advice.

28. See, for example, John Witherspoon, *Annotated Edition of Lectures on Moral Philosophy,* ed. Jack Scott (Newark, N.J.: University of Delaware Press, 1982), 64-65; "John Jay to John Murray," April 15, 1818, in *Correspondence and Public Papers of John Jay,* ed. Henry Johnston (New York: G. P. Putnam's Sons, 1890-1893), IV: 403, 407-8; James Wilson, *Lectures on Law* in *Works of James Wilson,* ed. Robert Green McCloskey (Cambridge, Mass.: Belknap Press, 1967), 1: 123-25, 143-44.

29. For a development of this idea, see Thomas G. West, "Comment on Richard John Neuhaus's 'Religion and the Enlightenments: Joshing Mr. Rorty.'" Prepared for the conference on "The Ambiguous Legacy of the Enlightenment," sponsored by the Clarement Institute, Claremont, California, January 27, 1990; also see Harry V. Jaffa, *The American Founding as the Best Regime: The Banding of Civil and Religious Liberty* (Montclair, Calif.: Claremont Institute, 1990).

Of Golden Threads:
Poets "Set on the
Marble of Exchange"

What Dorothy L. Sayers Found Permanent in Dante

Barbara Reynolds

An American reader of my recent book *The Passionate Intellect: Dorothy L. Sayers's Encounter with Dante* wrote a letter to me saying, "From *Gaudy Night* to the Penguin Dante, to *The Mind of the Maker*, Dorothy L. Sayers has been one of my Virgils." She says that she had previously tried someone else's translation of the *Inferno*, but could not get through it. Later on she found the Sayers translation and got on much better. She says: "What I like best about the commentary is that she insists on dealing with the *content* of the poem; my impression is that this is rather out of fashion in contemporary scholarship. . . . Miss Sayers starts with the premise that Dante has something valuable and pertinent to say to us *now*, and that, for me, is what makes her edition so good." She tells me her age: it is thirty-three.

I find her observation very striking. Here is a young person, born the year Dorothy Sayers died, finding, more than forty years after the first publication of the Penguin translation of *Inferno*, that what Sayers stressed then as valuable and pertinent in Dante is still valuable and pertinent now.

Dorothy Sayers read Dante in the midst of World War II, in 1944. She began in an air-raid shelter in her garden, with the noise of Hitler's guided missiles screeching down from the skies. I remember the time very well. My aunt and my cousin were in a block of flats in London which received a direct hit. Most of the residents were killed, but my relatives escaped with minor injuries and took refuge with me in Cambridge, their faces grey with the shock, their backs lacerated by the fall of a ceiling on them. No one at that time could avoid the impact of the immediate, and Dorothy Sayers's reaction to Dante could not help but be influenced by

151

what was going on all around her. When she looked for a publisher for her translation of *Inferno*, she chose that quite new venture, Penguin Classics, originally designed for wartime readers, for whom books were becoming a rarity. She had, therefore, a specific public in mind. In writing her plays on the life of Christ, *The Man Born to be King*, she had a wartime audience — envisaged first by the BBC as the scattered, evacuated children. Just so, in presenting Dante anew to the British public she was vividly aware of the conditions in which they would be reading, and of their lack of understanding, even of knowledge, of basic Christian beliefs (no wartime casualty, this, but the result of declining educational standards). Nevertheless, in these compelling and specific circumstances, and separated by six and a half centuries, she seized on what was permanent in Dante.

In my book I have described Dorothy Sayers's first delighted reaction to her discovery of Dante as a superb craftsman and storyteller. I go on to examine what she considered important and permanently relevant in Dante's picture of the world as he knew it in the late thirteenth and early fourteenth centuries. In chapter 7 of my book, entitled "The City of Dis," I speak of the connection Sayers made between belief and behavior. What we believe, or do not believe, is not a matter of purely private concern: it will issue in deeds, which may have far-reaching consequences. The war had brought sharply into focus for her the religious issue underlying the conflict. In the talk entitled "Creed or Chaos?" which she gave in May 1940, she begins:

> Something is happening to us today which has not happened for a very long time. We are waging a war of religion. Not a civil war between adherents of the same religion, but a life-and-death struggle between Christian and pagan.[1]

She undertook as her war work the emphasis of this, in lectures and in articles. As Ralph E. Hone has said in *Dorothy L. Sayers: A Literary Biography*, her publishing record during World War II was amazing: "She lectured widely and participated in numerous conferences and committee meetings. She spoke on radio. She traveled up and down the island. . . . With a Pauline glare, she reproved, she corrected, she instructed in righteousness."[2]

1. Dorothy L. Sayers, *Creed or Chaos?* (London: Methuen, 1947), 25.
2. Ralph E. Hone, *Dorothy L. Sayers, A Literary Biography* (Ohio: Kent State University Press, 1979), 102.

And then, in August 1944 Sayers began to read Dante. What did she find? Nothing less than the greatest Christian poet saying for her, in a master's powerful voice, what she had been trying to tell people through five years of war. Her mind leapt in creative response. There-after she would be Dante's spokesman and interpreter.

I have described in my book the circumstances in which she trans-lated the *Divina Commedia,* and the nature and function of her commen-tary and annotations. I have also described the occasion of her first lecture on Dante, delivered in 1946 to the first postwar summer school organized by the Society for Italian Studies. This was the magnificent lecture on canto 26 of *Inferno,* the Ulysses canto. I have not, however, done justice in my book to her later lectures, which were subsequently published in three volumes, *Introductory Papers on Dante, Further Papers on Dante* and, after her death, *The Poetry of Search and the Poetry of Statement.* All these three volumes are out of print and it is time that they be made available again. There, particularly in the first volume, *Introductory Papers,* you will find the "golden thread" of Permanent Things.

In writing these lectures, Dorothy Sayers was addressing a much smaller audience than the reading public of the Penguin Classics — between two and three hundred on each occasion. Yet, paradoxically, she was aiming at much wider and deeper issues, suitable for a more lasting public. She overestimated our capacity to follow all that she was saying — thank goodness she did, for if she was often over our heads then, as we listened, we have the benefit now of being able to read and contemplate what she said, taking our own necessary time over it. For the purpose of this paper I have recently reread all of Dorothy Sayers's lectures on Dante. I heard nearly all of them and can remember the tone of her voice, the expression of her face, sometimes the gesture of her hand, the reaction of the audience, and my own sense of being in the presence of something beyond my capacity, yet which I was deter-mined to come to grips with if I could. The most original, the most profound, and, with reference to the theme of Permanent Things, the most relevant of these lectures are: "Dante's Imagery: Symbolic," "Dante's Imagery: Pictorial," "The Meaning of Heaven and Hell," "The Paradoxes of the *Comedy* (in *Introductory Papers*) and "The Poetry of the Image in Dante and Charles Williams" (in *Further Papers*). In these five lectures, plus the introduction to the first volume, is found a defi-nition of the enduring standards, the continuity, the essence of our civilization, that which is permanent in a time of change.

153

When Dorothy Sayers pounced with a shock of awareness on the *Divina Commedia* in 1944, it was not merely because she saw it as relevant to the state of the world as it was then. That was only part of the story. When she undertook to translate the work, she must have been prepared to dedicate the rest of her creative life to the task. (It did not work out like that actually, because during those last thirteen years, as well as translating the *Commedia,* she wrote two dramas, *The Just Vengeance* and *The Emperor Constantine* and translated the *Chanson de Roland.*) However, to give the major part of her time and energy to Dante's poem, she must have been convinced of the "permanence" of it.

In what, for Dorothy Sayers, did the permanence of the *Commedia* consist? First, it proclaims the truth of the Christian faith. But so do many other works. It asserts the existence of good and evil, the freedom of the will to choose between them, and consequently the responsibility for that choice. But so do many other works: *Paradise Lost,* for instance, and *The Pilgrim's Progress.* What, for her, was so special about Dante? I think it was the fact that she found him *buried,* buried under misinterpretation, misleading translation, misunderstanding of his theology, hidden away behind a "historical perspective," locked in a cupboard to which only scholars were allowed the key. She says as much in the introduction to her first volume of lectures. First, she quotes Etienne Gilson:

> As for the vast literature on Dante, I cannot think of it without experiencing a kind of dizziness. One cannot open an Italian review without saying to one's self: "Another book, another article that I ought to have read before expressing my opinion on this question!"[3]

Then she goes on:

> To ignore the work of innumerable conflicting authorities is to expose one's self to the imputation of ignorance and presumption; to take them all into account (supposing one could possibly do so) is to bury Dante and his poem under a cairn so heavy that nothing can issue from it except the faint voice of his protesting ghost.[4]

Then comes one of her most important statements:

3. Etienne Gilson, *Dante the Philosopher* (London: Ward and Sheed, 1948), x.
4. Dorothy L. Sayers, *Introductory Papers on Dante* (London: Methuen, 1954), 10.

Yet Dante wrote to be read by the common man and woman, and to distribute the bread of angels among those who had no leisure to be learned.[5]

And she continues:

> I have . . . tried to show how the great poem . . . is relevant, not merely to fourteenth-century man, but to twentieth-century man, and indeed to man in all ages and all places. . . . [Dante's] poem is as public and universal as the Christian faith itself.[6]

This, I think, is the fuel that powers Sayers. She is like an archaeologist who discovers an ancient monument, let us say, a fountain, intended originally for public use. She cleans and restores it and refuses to allow it to be shut up in a museum, but cajoles the town council into putting it in order and providing new apparatus so that people can again draw water from it. By cleaning and restoring, we can understand the art of translating; by cajoling the town council, we can understand persuading the editor of Penguin Classics to agree to substantial introductions to each volume and long, explanatory notes, and maps and diagrams, all of which constituted the most expensive apparatus Penguin Classics had allowed to date!

Let us now go through those five lectures to which I have referred, looking for the "golden threads" which link Dante with readers of all ages. The first two, "Dante's Imagery: Symbolic" and "Dante's Imagery: Pictorial" stress the visual nature of Dante's poem. He lived at a time when it was natural to think and write in allegorical terms; and allegory is a visual art. As T. S. Eliot had pointed out in his essay on Dante, "Speech varies, but our eyes are all the same."[7] (Eliot agreed, partly for this reason, that Dante was the most universal of poets in the modern languages.) Dante's allegory was even more vivid and imaginable than the traditional kind, because, instead of using personified abstractions, or, as Dorothy Sayers called them, "perambulating labels," he peopled his poem with real characters who in themselves symbolized the various sins and virtues without losing anything of their humanity. These are what Charles Williams and Dorothy Sayers termed "natural symbols."

5. Ibid.
6. Ibid., xiv, xv.
7. T. S. Eliot, *Dante* (London: Faber and Faber, 1965), 15-16.

This original twist that Dante gave to allegory (and how he arrived at it nobody quite understands) enabled him to produce within the reader a strong conviction of narrative truth. The symbols are not only visible — they seem tangible — but they are living persons who communicate emotion and converse in unforgettable dialogue. Such "natural symbolism," Dorothy Sayers points out, "exhibits a universal pattern [which] can be interpreted at many levels, and remains a true figure at every level."[8]

It is not only the meaning of such symbols that remains permanent. It is also the artistry with which they are handled. Dorothy Sayers was enthralled by Dante's skill in structure, by his placing of images so that they gain in significance from relations of balance and perspective, by his tact in refraining from commenting on his symbols, preferring, as she says, to set them squarely in the reader's eye, allowing them to do their own work. These are artistic qualities that can be appreciated at any period, as are the pictorial images which delight with their vivid immediacy.

Her enumeration of these qualities points to one of the Permanent Things: the human power to rejoice, to exult in creative skill, the admiration for deliberate, conscious artistry, which she communicates in such a way that the reader's heart leaps up, like Wordsworth's when he beheld a rainbow in the sky. Take, for instance, her pleasure in Dante's similes — a pleasure heightened by the fact that they are always functional, never *applique*:

> Dante's imagery . . . is always strictly functional, even when it is at its most pictorial. And pictorial it is. Dante, who was the friend of painters, and who (as we know) sometimes did a little painting himself, had the painter's eye. He had a lightning facility for fixing a scene, a look, a movement, in the fewest possible words, but unforgettably. The pictures from the *Comedy* crowd so upon us that of the mere enumeration of them there would be no end. . . .[9]

And, indeed, even to quote all the examples she gives of them would take too long, but the following passage is one of *my* rainbows in the sky. Describing the opening of *Purgatorio* and the first of the ten Heavens, she writes:

8. Sayers, *Introductory Papers on Dante*, 10.
9. Ibid., 27.

The colour is present everywhere, cool and transparent along the reedy shore, shimmering blue-violet across the limitless sea, silvery-green on the dew-soaked grass, pouring in arrowy brightness from the cloudless Northern sky. . . . All the strange geometrical pattern of the ten heavens is drawn with a pencil dipped in pure light; and in the Heaven of the Moon there is that lovely harmony of pale colour and reluctant motion whose strange lunar sheen is more moon-like than anything in all literature — except, perhaps, Coleridge's

> The moving moon went up the sky
> And nowhere did abide;
> Softly she was going up
> And a star or two beside.

In the same key, and equally evocative, is Dante's apparition of the spirits in the Moon's sphere:

> Like as from polished and transparent glass,
> Or as from water clear and luminous,
> Whose shallows leave the bottom shadowless,
> The image of a face comes back to us
> So faint, a pearl on a white forehead stirs
> The seeing sense no slowlier than this does,
> So I saw faces, many and diverse . . . (Par. III, 10-16).

So they appear, and Dante . . . looks back over his shoulder to see what forms these are, thus glassed in the lucid white moonstuff.[10]

Another aspect of Dante's structural skill which Sayers emphasizes is his ability to keep the literal story and the allegorical meanings separate, each consistent on its own level. In this he is unlike Spenser, who now and then fuses the literal and the allegorical to somewhat disconcerting effect, as when Sir Guyon and the Palmer meet the Hag, who has to be restrained before Furor can be conquered. Sir Guyon thereupon produces "an yron lock" to bind her tongue, and "yron racke" to bind Furor's hands and feet and a "hundred yron chaines." "Here," says Dorothy Sayers, "imagination boggles . . . a hundred iron chains are very heavy luggage for a knight-errant and an elderly palmer. Either there was an ironmonger's shop conveniently near (though nothing is said of it) or else we have discovered the original of Lewis

10. Ibid., 29.

Carroll's White Knight. . . ." (I have a very clear memory of hearing her reading this passage and of the joyful amusement with which it was received by the audience.) "We need not blame Spenser for this," she went on, "unless we are very literal-minded people, or lecturers in search of something to carp at."[11] The point is that this is not Dante's way of doing things. He keeps story and allegory separate, each complete and consistent in itself. The result is — and this is one of her most characteristic observations — that we have a curiously strong and convincing sense of being personally present with him throughout the journey. This sense she manages to convey, more than any other translator.

Another of Sayers's perceptions is her sense of the link between poets of all ages. There are two wonderful passages in which she communicates this. The first occurs in the lecture "Dante's Imagery: Symbolic." She refers to the picture in canto 29 of *Inferno* of the Falsifiers, who are shown afflicted with disease:

> . . . the spirits strewn through the dark valley,
> Heaped here, heaped there, enduring their distress;
> This on the back, and that upon the belly
> One of another lay, while some crawled round
> The dismal road all-fours, lethargically.
>
> (65-69)

She compares this with a description of the aftermath of battle by Sacheverell Sitwell in *Splendours and Miseries*:

> It is part of the degradation that they lie in heaps as though tipped out of a cart. There is a fatality that forces them to crawl on one another, like puppies in a new-born litter. . . .[12]

And she comments:

> Across six centuries, two poets touch hands, looking together upon the same scene. . . .[13]

11. Ibid., 35-36.
12. Sacheverell Sitwell, *Splendours and Miseries* (London: Faber and Faber, 1943), 121.
13. Sayers, *Introductory Papers on Dante*, 32.

The second instance comes from her preface to *Further Papers on Dante*. She writes:

> Here and there [in these lectures], an attempt has been made to rescue Dante from the exalted isolation in which reverential awe has placed him, and to compare him with other poets writing on similar themes. It seems to me that, in the vast and intensively-cultivated field of Dante studies, too little has as yet been done along these lines — as though, when immediate "sources" and "influences" had been discussed, the poet's achievement could be left enthroned in a vacuum. But it is· not so. Every poet that ever wore the bays is a perpetual competitor in the Olympian games, on an equal footing with his heirs and his ancestors. Poets do not merely pass on the torch in a relay race; they toss the ball to one another, to and fro across the centuries.[14]

Here indeed is a "golden thread!" This is permanence, not simply in the sense of continuous extension but of recurrence, of a circuit flowing unceasingly from past to present and from present to past. To understand the full significance of this passage we have to look at Sayers's lecture "The Poetry of the Image in Dante and Charles Williams." She says:

> A great poem like Dante's *Divine Comedy* comes to us now enriched not only with all those events and associations of the past out of which the poet fashioned his image, but also with the accreted events and associations of the six hundred years of his future and our past which lie between us and him. To him all the poets who have ever drawn sustenance from him return, bearing their sheaves with them, because he is in a manner the creator of their work as well as of his own.[15]

This is a dizzying concept, like that of eternity, which, as Keats said, "doth tease us out of thought." We find it also in Charles Williams, whom Dorothy Sayers quotes at the end of her lecture "Dante's Virgil," where she contemplates the admission of Virgil's soul to Heaven:

> Love, gratitude, prayer can operate backwards in time as well as forward. Charles Williams, in his poem, *Taliessin on the Death of Virgil,*

14. Dorothy L. Sayers, *Further Papers on Dante* (London: Methuen, 1957), v.
15. Ibid., 184.

imagines the devoted love of the Christian followers for whom Virgil had held the lantern as rushing in from the future ages to support him with the gift of their own faith in the moment of passing:

> In that hour they came; more and faster, they sped
> To their dead master; they sought him to save
> From the spectral grave and the endless falling,
> Who had heard, for their own instruction, the sound
>   of his calling.
> There was intervention, suspension, the net
>   of their loves. . . .
> Virgil was fathered of his friends.
> He lived in their ends.
> He was set on the marble of exchange.[16]

This seems like an extension of the concept of the early Church, whereby proselytes were baptized for the dead as proxies, a practice mentioned by St. Paul in 1 Corinthians 15:29. To Charles Williams it is an aspect of his doctrine of exchange, which operates from present to past and from past to present.

In her two lectures "The Meaning of Heaven and Hell" and "The Meaning of Purgatory," Dorothy Sayers examines the concept of timelessness. Whereas Purgatory, both in the story and in doctrine, is a temporal process, Hell and Heaven, though described in the story as existing in time and space, are eternal states. Both, Dorothy Sayers believed, can be experienced in this life, but only in moods and moments which give a foretaste of the quality of damnation or beatitude. "Mystics intensely," she wrote, "and many other people less intensely, know these moments of vision. . . ."[17]

She herself had no such gift — she said so categorically — and yet she was fascinated by the possibility. She planned to write a book examining its manifestation in Dante and other poets. She *did* write a novel (unfinished), about Dante and his daughter, in which she attributes to the daughter the "double vision" that the father possessed. Dorothy Sayers believed, intellectually at least, in the sacramental nature of reality and joyfully embraced Charles Williams's concept of the

---

16. Ibid., 77. (Quotation from Charles Williams, *Taliessin through Logres* [Oxford University Press, 1950.])

17. Sayers, *Introductory Papers on Dante*, 73.

Affirmation of Images. This way of meditation, followed by artists and poets, proceeds by the recognition of the infinite in the finite, the eternal in the temporal, the heavenly in the terrestrial. The Negation of Images, on the other hand, followed by many great mystics, proceeds through darkness and solitude as one by one, the finite images are rejected.

I have attempted in my book to show the extent of Sayers's experience of the Affirmative Way. I think it can only have been through her religious belief and through her creativity. There are two manifestations of this, namely *The Just Vengeance* and *The Emperor Constantine*.

Both these dramas were written during Sayers's Dante period. The first, *The Just Vengeance,* was directly inspired by her first reading of the *Paradiso.*[18] In canto 7 of *Paradiso* she found a statement of the paradox of the Atonement: if the Crucifixion was a just atonement, how could it justly be avenged by the destruction of Jerusalem? This struck her immediately, at her very first reading. She said at once in a letter to Charles Williams: these lines are "extraordinarily interesting . . . they seem to get down to something absolutely central." The words "just vengeance" ("giusta vendetta") refer to the Crucifixion, which Beatrice tells Dante was later "justly avenged" by Titus, who destroyed Jerusalem in A.D. 70. Dante cannot understand how atonement for the sins of mankind, if it was just in the first instance, could justly be avenged. Beatrice replies that if the nature assumed by God in the Incarnation is considered, no penalty was ever so just as the Cross; but if the Person who suffered it is so considered, no penalty was ever so unjust. The doctrine of the Fall and the Redemption became the subject of the drama she wrote for Lichfield Cathedral. She took Dante's words as her title, "The Just Vengeance." Three years later, in 1949, when she lectured to the Society for Italian Studies at Oxford, she referred to this passage again, in one of the most profound of her papers on Dante, "The Paradoxes of the *Comedy*":

> It is a matter for profound astonishment that this magnificent statement of Atonement theology should have been accused of Nestorianism — of the heresy, that is, which separates the two natures in the one Christ. On the contrary, it asserts . . . that the two Natures are so inextricably united in a single indivisible Person as to make the sentence of the law at the same time wholly just and wholly unjust.

18. In my book I have described in some detail what occurred.

161

> In so far as it represents God's judgment of Man it is absolute justice; in so far as it represents Man's judgment of God it is absolute injustice; and it is not possible to qualify either of those pronouncements in any way whatever.[19]

In *The Emperor Constantine,* written for the Festival of Colchester in 1951, the most dramatically powerful scene is the Council of Nicaea, in which the Nicene Creed is formulated and the Arian heresy is denounced. But the deepest and most moving scene of all — the scene between Constantine and his mother Helena — comes toward the end. Constantine is grieved and bewildered by certain sinful consequences of his attempts to do justice. Helena brings him to accept that evil can never be undone but only purged and redeemed. The price is always paid but not always by the guilty. "By whom, then?" asks Constantine. Helena replies, "By the innocent . . . And innocence alone can pardon without injustice, because it has paid the price." And Constantine asks again: "Mother, tell me, whose blood is on my hands?" She answers, "The blood of God" (act 3, scene 2).

In his very kind review of *The Passionate Intellect* in *Books and Religion,* Gregory Wolfe makes what I think is a central and fundamental statement about Sayers's approach to Dante:

> For Sayers, as for other great defenders of Christian orthodoxy of her day — G. K. Chesterton, C. S. Lewis, T. S. Eliot, and Charles Williams — Dante's balance of reason and imagination, flesh and spirit, particular and universal, became the perfect example of a wholeness of vision that could heal the tragic dichotomies of the modern world. It is this understanding of Dante that I would suggest is Sayers's greatest achievement, not her translation of *The Divine Comedy* itself. Her notes and introductions in the Penguin edition . . . demonstrate that Dante's theology, far from being some grandly conceived abstract system, was firmly grounded in an acute observation of human experience.[20]

I think this goes to the heart of the matter, or, if you like, to those

---

19. Ibid., 183.
20. Gregory Wolfe, in *Books and Religion* 17, no. 1 (Spring 1990): 11.

Permanent Things which Dorothy Sayers perceived in Dante, transmitting him to our heritage with these words:

> A great poem is not the prerequisite of scholars and critics and historians: it is yours and mine — our freehold and our possession; and what it truly means to us is a real part of its true and eternal meaning.[21]

21. Sayers, *Introductory Papers on Dante*, 19-20.

Perplexity in the Edgeware Road:
Four Quartets Revisited Yet Again

Thomas T. Howard

My title "Perplexity in the Edgeware Road" is drawn from "The Dry Salvages," the third section of T. S. Eliot's *Four Quartets*. The phrase is an apt description of the perplexity, "Whether on the shores of Asia, or in the Edgeware Road," that stands bleakly over against the Permanent Things.

What I propose is the notion that Eliot's literary and a fortiori moral testament, as it were, may be understood as pointing to these Permanent Things with a serenity, and an authority finally, that gains its force and credibility precisely via its excruciating awareness of the ambiguities of our condition — the perplexity in the Edgeware Road, if you will.

You will recall that one of the great burdens in *Four Quartets* is the question of the flux of time — present, past, and future — and how one is to come upon "the point of intersection of the timeless with time." No doubt the most familiar words from the whole poem are in the phrase, "the still point of the turning world." The question is embedded in the themes of memory, and of redemption, and of fugitive impressions from our mortal life here — what Eliot calls "hints and guesses" in the same passage from "The Dry Salvages" — and of death and vacuity, as in the lines, "O dark dark dark. They all go into the dark, / The vacant interstellar spaces, the vacant into the vacant."

The Captains, merchant bankers, eminent men of letters,
The generous patrons of art, the statesmen and the rulers,
Distinguished civil servants. chairmen of many committees,

> Industrial lords and petty contractors, all go into the dark,
> And dark the Sun and Moon, and the Almanach de Gotha
> And the Stock Exchange Gazette, the Directory of Directors,
> And cold the sense and lost the motive of action.[1]

These themes throw any notion of permanence into starker — and, it would seem, ever more unattainable — remoteness. How can we possibly speak of any Permanent Things, we who are caught in this shifting and eddying vortex of ephemera? Recall that in "Burnt Norton" we are told, speaking of that still point of the turning world which we might like to seize hold of: "And do not call it fixity, / where past and future are gathered. Neither movement from nor towards, / Neither ascent nor decline. Except for the point, the still point, / There would be no dance, and there is only the dance."[2] It is, as I say, at least partly from the excruciating awareness of flux — of the *im*permanent — that the vision of the Permanent Things in *Four Quartets* gains serenity and authority.

One of the most restless and even febrile sections in the entire work comes in the lines, in section 5 of "The Dry Salvages," which lead to the phrase which has supplied me with my title here:

> To communicate with Mars, converse with spirits,
> To report the behavior of the sea monster,
> Describe the horoscope, haruspicate or scry
> Observe disease in signatures, evoke
> Biography from the wrinkles of the palm
> And tragedy from fingers; release omens
> By sortilege, or tea leaves, riddle the inevitable
> With playing cards, fiddle with pentagrams
> Or barbituric acids, or dissect
> The recurrent image into pre-conscious terrors —
> To explore the womb, or tomb, or dreams; all these are usual
> Pastimes and drugs, and features of the press:
> And always will be, some of them especially
> When there is distress of nations and perplexity
> Whether on the Shores of Asia, or in the Edgeware Road.[3]

1. *East Coker*, III, 101-9.
2. *Burnt Norton*, I, 64-67.
3. *Dry Salvages*, V, 184-98.

The lines that follow seem to exclude the hope of doing anything about the perplexity: "But to apprehend / The point of intersection of the timeless / With time, is an occupation for the saint — / No occupation either, but something given / And taken, in a lifetime's death in love, / Ardour and selflessness and self-surrender."[4] But an allowance follows, which would seem to glance at the rest of us who will scarcely lay claim to be numbered, with Teresa, and with John of the Cross, among those saints. The poetry speaks of "hints and guesses, / Hints followed by guesses; and the rest / Is prayer, observance, discipline, thought and action."[5] I have often taken some comfort from that line. The vision, ardor, and endurance of the saint are completely foreign to my experience. But there would seem to be a prescription for me in that daunting sequence, "Prayer, observance, discipline, thought and action." How do we, who are neither Teresa nor John, propose to speak about the Permanent Things when flux would seem to be not only the condition of our existence itself, but, with what looks like increasing centrifugal speed, the special condition of our own twentieth-century *fin de siècle*?

We can pray, God help us. And we can observe — not only the liturgical calendar and the rigors of asceticism, but also *life*. To speak of observing life, of course, is to open at once the immense topic of art — of poetry, drama, narrative, painting, music, and all the rest, the work of human beings who observe life.

In *Four Quartets*, we have not a treatise like *The Ascent of Mount Carmel* on the spiritual life, nor the *Cloud of Unknowing*. Rather, we have a poem, a piece of art — like the *Divine Comedy*, the B-minor Mass, or the Sistine Chapel ceiling. The place of art in any civilization is always the same. It is to articulate, that is, give shape to what is otherwise formless or shapeless. The thing that would be otherwise formless, in the case of art, is human experience.

Primitive men, men of antiquity, medieval men, modern and post-modern men all exhibit a proclivity that is unique to our species among all the species of life that inhabit this globe, namely, the desire to *utter* experience and not simply to *undergo* experience. We share all kinds of experience with the other species of animal life: we get hungry and so do our dogs; we run out of energy and become fatigued, and so do our dogs; we suffer disappointment, and so do our dogs. Witness the dog's

4. *Dry Salvages*, III, 200-205.
5. *Dry Salvages*, V, 212-14.

tail ceasing to wag, and then drooping, as it becomes clear that he is to stay in the house when the rest of us set out for a walk. Dogs seem to have a capacity for embarrassment, and even for shame upon being discovered curled up on some forbidden sofa. But the point here is that dogs never *do* anything about these experiences, and *we do*. We not only suffer the experience: we must say something about it afterwards.

All art — all sculpture, drama, dance, painting, poetry, and story-telling — bespeaks this proclivity in us to articulate our experience. (Music presents a riddle here: no very apparent connection can be established, it seems to me, between, say, a Brandenburg concerto and any identifiable human experience: the solution to the riddle must lie somewhere in the neighborhood of talk about *pure* form, and also of our consciousness of *time*; but I suspect that to pursue this very far here would be to lead us away from our immediate concerns.)

All art, I say, bespeaks this proclivity in us to articulate our experience. This is obvious enough in the case of drama, where we all know, before we get to the theater, much too much about the pain of jealousy. Nonetheless, we have paid good money, and we wish to see this unhappy component of our experience played out yet again for us in *Othello*. Not, of course, that the play *Othello* exists solely as the dramatic projecting of the single experience, jealousy. It is a complex and manifold entity, this play; but we can at least say that every nuance in that drama is altogether recognizable to us, the audience, as being, alas, too true of our own experience of life. Nothing is false. We do not have to be wife-killers to recognize our own vulnerability to what overthrew Othello.

Similarly with painting. Why should Monet bother about all those water lilies, or Renoir about that man in the rowboat in the park with his sweetheart, or Frans Hals about all those apple-cheeked burghers, or Hieronymous Bosch about all those damned souls, when these things already exist in the real world? Aren't these artists merely gilding the lily?

No, we say: they are plucking us by the sleeve. They are laying a hand on our arm and saying, Look! Look well!

I myself am endlessly fascinated by the phenomenon of dance, whether by this we mean ballet, or folk-dancing, or ballroom dancing. It is a very peculiar phenomenon, when you think about it. Why should we get up on our toes and caper about this way? Surely it is, at the very least, somewhat beneath our dignity.

But the rejoinder to this line of questioning arises from the profoundest depths of the human spirit. We must dance. We will dance. Nay — one has only to look at the shape of Slavonic dance, Siamese dance, flamenco, Morris dancing, the highland fling, Watusi dance, and Navajo dance, to see that here we witness the exquisite articulation, by many tribes, of the whole range and scope of human experience: joy, grief, pride, yearning, rage, desolation, anticipation, delight, love. Dance gives shape, under the conditions of the human body itself, and its movements, to our experience of mortal existence.

And so it would go with all art, even with architecture. Surely, the shape of our buildings, whether we are referring to the Temple at Karnak, the palace at Versailles, the cathedral at Chartres, or the World Trade Center, speaks volumes about our own self-image, and about our notions about what constitutes appropriate space, and appropriate material, for our life and our work.

The artist, we might say, is the one who is able both to *see* the possibilities of form in our experience, and to achieve that form in some specific modality, in oil and canvas, in words, in movement, in granite or marble.

T. S. Eliot's material was words. Long before Eliot appeared on the scene, the whole human race had experienced disenchantment and ennui: but somehow he gave a particular verbal shape to that experience in such utterances as, "I should have been a pair of ragged claws / Scuttling across the floors of silent seas," or the business about "muttering retreats / Of restless nights in one-night cheap hotels / And sawdust restaurants with oyster shells: / Streets that follow like a tedious argument," not to mention wanting "to spit out all the butt-ends of my days"[6] — somehow these ways of saying it not only *express* what more than a few of us have felt, but also *bring into being* some capacity to experience the experience.

What, exactly, did *Eliot* adopt by way of "tactics"? The question is piquant, and opens, of course, onto the infinitely bigger topic of artistic strategies.

The specific mode and approach which a given artist adopts is a curious affair. It springs from the epoch in which the artist finds himself, but it must also be admitted that the artist brings something utterly

---

6. T. S. Eliot, *The Complete Poems and Plays, 1909-1950* (New York: Harcourt Brace, 1962), 3, 5.

fresh and unique to his work. To illustrate this, we need only to look at *The Iliad* to find an artifact, so to speak, that reveals a very great deal about Greece in the ninth century before Christ. The epic mode, the moral assumption, the heroic figures of Achilles, Hector, and Agamemnon, the taking for granted of battle, and of sacrifice, and of what life was like insofar as it was carried forward under the scrutiny of the gods who were themselves very far from being paragons of goodness — all of this may be said to be characteristic of that century in that country, as well as of Homer. But we must hurry to assert that the whole point of Homer is that he was Homer, or that he wrote his two epics, and not another poet. No one else could have seen things with quite his vision, and no one else would have — or indeed could have — pressed diction and meter and syntax and imagery and sensibility and vision into exactly this form.

Thus it is with all artists: the cave drawings at Lascaux; the enameled bracelets and little boxes we get from the Anglo-Saxons; the Bayeux tapestry; the poetry of Firdausi from tenth-century Persia; Samoan figurines; the music of Wagner; the choreography of Diaghilev — all of these entities present themselves to us as both characteristic of an era and as the fruit of a workman whose work cannot be duplicated.

Eliot's place in the experience of the twentieth-century West is enormous. He very quickly became the darling of the generation which was achieving self-consciousness just after World War I, with all that that implies of innocence lost, ideals decimated, world-weariness, and the refusal to be ever again "taken in." The condition implies corollaries of, on the one hand, resentment, of all that had gone into making a world in which such a war could occur, and, on the other hand, of eating and drinking and making merry inasmuch as tomorrow we would, in fact, die.

If Eliot had never written a syllable after his pre-1925 poems, which include the diseased "Prufrock," the Sweeney poems with their squalor, *The Waste Land* with its restless lassitude amongst the shards of a decaying civilization, and *The Hollow Men* with its impotence and blindness in the face of death, he would, I myself guess, still be considered a major artist whose words we all find to be painfully apt, even after the passage of seventy years.

His tactics in those days seem to have entailed the finding of a *voice* which could speak words of ennui, impotence, restlessness, and

169

demurral — words that spoke with that voice, but which would at the same time have sufficient energy and vibrancy to flag us down, engage us, hold us, and vouchsafe to us that odd catharsis, even "healing" which is the fruit of all poetry worthy of the name poetry. These tactics are not easy. How does one speak in a somnolent, attenuated, febrile murmur without lulling your readers into the very lassitude that your work as an artist fears most of all? Music that puts us to sleep loses its raison d'être at the point when we succumb. Drama that succeeds well enough to send us tottering out of the theater in pure horror or heart-break in the middle of the first act unable to sustain anymore, fails when the last theater-goer has left his seat in chagrin for the fresh air and lights of Leicester Square or the West Forties.

Somehow Eliot kept us reading, and rereading, his chronicles of dereliction. Part, if not the whole, of the reason, of course, is that these chronicles are *true*, in the sense that they accurately articulate what they set out to express. A whole generation and more hailed Eliot as poet and even prophet. He spoke the true word to the English-speaking West. Indeed, we say, this is it! Oh dear, how mordant, how pitilessly true is the word we hear from this poetry. Let us lionize the man whose poetry articulates with such implacable finality the truth of our experience.

But then, of course, a joker showed up in the pack. Eliot converted. He stepped forth in 1927 and announced that he had converted to Christian belief.

How nettlesome. How tiresome for us, his votaries. It is as though the high priest of the court of Pharaoh Amenhotep had turned to the crowds one fine morning and announced, "I believe in one God, and will no longer offer sacrifices on these altars of Osiris, Phtha, Set, or Ra." The consternation, then fury, which would have greeted this per-fidiousness would have known no bounds, surely.

Eliot experienced something like this consternation and fury from his clientele. He was betraying his sacred trust as the oracle, almost, for the English-speaking West.

But from his point of view, of course, his conversion to Christian belief did not at all change his office as poet, nor did it make lighter the burden which he, as poet, carried, if by "burden" we refer to the immense weight laid upon the shoulders of any serious artist to speak the truth. It is hard enough work to carry on with your craft if what you are producing wins accolades from your generation. But the task becomes onerous, indeed, if what you are saying (with your chisel, your brush, or your pen) is greeted with hostility, or worse, a yawn. Then the artist knows what figures like Elijah or Jeremiah faced and sustained: not only the burden of being a spokesman for the truth, but also the burden of hostility and indifference.

Most artists are all too unhappily familiar with this lot. Hostility, incomprehension, and boredom, with respect to one's work, do not spur one on to redoubled energy in applying oneself to one's task.

What did Eliot do? He produced no major poetic work for more than a decade after his conversion to Christian belief. Some essays appeared during the 1930s; his plays came later.

The major work upon which our judgment of Eliot's achievement as a Christian poet rests is *Four Quartets,* which appeared in 1943. It is this work which is a monument in the annals of the art of our century, and it is profoundly and incontrovertibly Christian. How did he do it?

At the immense risk of oversimplification, I propose an idea which makes no claim to explain, much less exhaust, Eliot's tactics or his achievement in writing *Four Quartets.* My idea here may at the least suggest one clue to Eliot's success in *Four Quartets.* It is simply this: among other things, Eliot's tactics entailed his taking what all reflective persons would be obliged to recognize as true, and then to press his inquiry about the truth in such a way that we are obliged to ask with him, "What then?" He will not allow us to stop and pitch camp on these truths: rather, the very way in which his poetry points to them reveals them as, themselves, pointers. Pointers to Something Else. Twenty-five years before he wrote *Four Quartets,* he had had his Prufrock afraid to press such questions. "Oh do not ask What is it?" We find in that poem the awful fear that if we do ask what it is we might blunder upon the answer that will destroy our pitiable attempts to garrison ourselves against the Truth. So long as we can dodge, and dodge, and dodge, we might escape the dreaded confrontation. In *Four Quartets,* our cover is blown, so to speak.

For example, in "Burnt Norton," we hear this: "What might have been and what has been / Point to one end, which is always present."[7] Anyone with the experience of the mystery of *time* is bothered by the claim the present moment has on me when it somehow arrives, implacably, at the hither end of what *has* been and what might have been.

7. *Burnt Norton,* I, 9-10.

In other words, I find myself under an imperative that ignores the distinction that I myself might like to put forward: if things had been different, I would have done better, and so on, and so forth — all the miserable protestations that I would like to regale the jury with.

In the same passage, Eliot speaks of "Disturbing the dust on a bowl of rose-leaves."[8] What bowl of rose leaves? We do not need footnotes to help us conjure the picture of that bowl, that potpourri, on the library table of some lonely soul whose life now consists in the sad and dry effort to relive past loves, with the nosegays and corsages now all dusty and desiccated. But the voice in "Burnt Norton" asks, "But to what purpose/Disturbing the dust on the bowl of rose-leaves"?[9] We find out before we have finished the poem that *memory* has a purpose much, much more serious than merely swamping us with nostalgia: it is meant to regale us with the remorseless fact of time's passing, and to "make present" to us all that has happened. At this point a Christian recognizes the true shape of things, namely, that memory, rightly used, brings us to confession; that is, fruitful confession, which is necessary to salvation, obliges me to take the past, and not merely to bewail it, but to place it *here,* and to say, in effect, "Have mercy upon me, O God, according to thy loving kindness." Furthermore, a Christian will recognize in this shape of things the Eucharist itself, since the Christian liturgy is *anamnesis,* a "remembering" which is also a "making present." We do not indulge in nostalgia at the Lord's Table, nor in mere regret for a ghastly misfortune that occurred at Golgotha two thousand years ago. No, in the divine liturgy, that whole drama is made present (the words are Christ's own — "This do for an anamnesis of me"), and thus salvific.

We have moved a very long way from the bowl of rose leaves. Or have we? It is not as though *Four Quartets* needs copious theological footnotes. We find, upon reading and rereading this poem, that, with a jewel-like lucidity, Eliot's images present stark actuality to us in such a way as to crowd us along towards the place where we are obliged to go beyond mere sterile remorse and nostalgia.

In the next section of "Burnt Norton," we find ourselves amid the circulation of the blood, and then our lymphatic system, and then the orbits of the stars, and then a boar hunt. What sort of rummage-sale of ideas have we here? The poetry quietly obliges us to admit that in each

8. *Burnt Norton,* I, 16-17.
9. *Burnt Norton,* I, 15-17.

of these phenomena we have a *pattern* of movement; even the chase involving the boarhounds and the boar is almost a dance. But you can't always descry the pattern if you are down in the middle of it. So the poetry lifts us above the trees of the forest, where we may "hear upon the sodden floor / Below, the boarhound and the boar / Pursue their pattern as before / But reconciled among the stars."[10]

"Reconciled among the stars" hints at what any reflective person hopes for: that there is — there must be — *somewhere*, some center from which the chaotic choreography takes its impulse. Anyone wishes for some such center. And Eliot's poetry quietly pursues its progress by going on to say, "At the still point of the turning world. Neither flesh nor fleshless; / Neither from nor towards; at the still point, there the dance is, / But neither arrest nor movement. And do not call it fixity, / Where past and future are gathered. Neither movement from nor towards, / Neither ascent or decline. Except for the point, the still point, / There would be no dance and there is only the dance."[11]

Who needs footnotes here? The sheer lucidity of it overwhelms us. "The still point of the turning world," not "fixity," which suggests something mechanical and bolted down; but the still point is not mere movement either, with its suggestion of mutability. Rather, that still point is in its very stillness more vibrant and energetic than all the thrashings and strugglings that mark our experience of time. The words of the poetry supply us with a way of imagining eternity — even the Godhead.

Or again, what tactics we observe here, when the poetry speaks of something we have all seen — say, on the faces of the people in the subway: "Only a flicker / Over the strained time-ridden faces / Distracted from distraction by distraction / Filled with fancies and empty of meaning / Tumid apathy with no concentration / Men and bits of paper, whirled by the cold wind / That blows before and after time, / Wind in and out of unwholesome lungs / Time before and time after. / Eructation of unhealthy souls / Into the faded air. . . ."[12] Such dereliction. How revolting. The very air itself poisoned with the eructation, the vomiting forth of used-up breath from the lungs of these forlorn souls.

And the poetry goes on: "Not here / Not here the darkness, in

10. *Burnt Norton*, II, 58-61.
11. *Burnt Norton*, II, 62-67.
12. *Burnt Norton*, III, 99-109.

this twittering world. / Descend lower, descend only / Into the world of perpetual solitude . . . Internal darkness, deprivation / And destitution of all property, / Desiccation of the world of sense, / Evacuation of the world of fancy, / Inoperancy of the world of spirit. . . ."[13]

One does not have to have read St. John of the Cross to recognize here the state to which the poetry bids us, namely, the darkness and solitude to which we all must press, *through* and *beyond* the dereliction that surrounds us in our mortal life, that darkness and solitude which alone, like the tomb of Christ, precedes any notion of resurrection.

The next section of *Four Quartets*, "East Coker," opens with these words: "In my beginning is my end."[14] No footnotes about Mary, Queen of Scots, are necessary. Anyone who will stop and think will know that indeed his "end" (his death) is both implied, and already at work, in his beginning (his birth). But, profounder than that, he will know that his *end* — his fruition, *telos*, the reason he was made — is implicit in his beginning, his conception, the way the oak is implicit in the acorn. This realization prods him to keep asking, "Well, then, what is it all *about?*" which is precisely what Eliot's poetry prods us to ask.

In "East Coker" we also find this: "Do not let me hear / Of the wisdom of old men, but rather of their folly, / Their fear of fear and frenzy, their fear of possession, / Of belonging to another, or to others, or to God."[15] Oh dear. There it is. Mere *age*, in the sense of birthdays accumulated, is very far from being any guarantee of wisdom: indeed, it may well be a tragi-comic aggregation of folly — of a lifetime's efforts to *avoid* facing things, and a sort of apotheosis of frivolousness. Alas. As we get older, we do indeed fear belonging to another — to the staff in the nursing home especially. But what if our eternal destiny *is* to belong to Another — *The Other?* That is the most frightening destiny of all for the man whose whole effort in life has been toward what is so bravely and foolishly called "self-determination," or "self-actualization," or "self-assertion." That man, eventually finds that he must either belong wholly to Another, or be damned.

My sore temptation here is to go on and on and on. What a travesty it is, to omit the words about the "wounded surgeon plying the steel / That questions the distempered part,"[16] or the words, so en-

---

13. *Burnt Norton*, III, 112-21.
14. *East Coker*, I, 1.
15. *East Coker*, III, 93-96.
16. *East Coker*, IV, 1-2.

couraging and so daunting, "And so each venture / Is a new beginning, a raid on the inarticulate / With shabby equipment always deteriorating / In the general mess of imprecision of feeling, / Undisciplined squads of emotion."[17]

There, of course, is the challenge that taxes poetry and, I think, any serious Christian: how shall he begin, yet again, to mount a raid with his shabby mental and emotional and spiritual equipment on the inarticulate, that is, attempt to take the *jumble* that is our mortal experience, and *shape* it, and call it into significant *form*, the way the Holy Ghost did with chaos at the creation? Most of us, most of the time, live in a general mess of imprecision of feeling. Our very syntax — and we are now back at the beginning of my speech — betrays this mess. "Words," as Eliot points out, "strain / Crack and sometimes break; under the burden, / Under the tension, slip, slide, perish, / Decay with imprecision, will not stay in place. . . ."[18] But beyond words, there is The Word — "The Word in the desert," says Eliot, The Word that was made flesh for us, suffering temptation and dereliction for us. That Word is the divine raid on the inarticulate; we might say the divine assault on the ruin and havoc wrought by evil. And every artist — every Christian — will see his vocation as in some sense participating in that raid.

17. *East Coker*, V, 178-82.
18. *Burnt Norton*, V, 149-52.

G. K. Chesterton among
the Permanent Poets

Aidan Mackey

Ideally, before we consider what we mean by a great poet we should first define poetry. However, limitations of space and the fact that no one has yet defined poetry prevent this. (Dr. Johnson's "Metrical utterance" is clearly inadequate and Wordsworth's "emotion recollected in tranquillity" is nonsense. Not only would it describe prose, but it could refer to thought which is entirely unexpressed.) Our dictionaries are of little real help on this subject.

We must, though, give some thought to the question of what constitutes, in our view, a great poet, before we approach the matter of Chesterton's relationship to our permanent poets. Would we include among the immortals anyone who has written a truly great poem? I think not. My own view is that quantity, though not, of course, a major consideration, must have some influence on the matter; that there must be a corpus, some solid body of work given us before we accept a man or woman as standing among the immortals. For instance, I regard the *Rubaiyat of Omar Khayyam,* that pagan counterpart of Hilaire Belloc's "Heroic Poem in Praise of Wine" as being great:

> With me along some strip of herbage strewn
> That just divides the desert from the sown
> Where name of slave and Sultan scarce is known
> And pity Sultan Mahmud on his throne.
> Here with a loaf of bread beneath the bough
> A flask of wine, a book of verse — and thou

Beside me singing in the wilderness —
And wilderness is paradise enow.[1]

But I would not accept Edward Fitzgerald as being one of our great poets.

I love, too, "The Golden Journey to Samarkand":

We who with songs beguile your pilgrimage
And swear that beauty lives, though lilies die,
We poets of the proud old lineage
Who sing to find your hearts (we know not why)
What shall we tell you?
Tales, marvelous tales
Of ships and stars, and isles where good men rest.
Away! for we are ready to a man
   Our camels sniff the evening and are glad.
Lead on, O Master of the caravan
   Lead on, the merchant princes of Baghdad.

  . . . .

White on a throne or guarded in a cave.
   There lives a prophet who can understand
Why men were born; But surely we are brave,
   Who take the Golden Road to Samarkand.[2]

That is great, very great, poetry. But Flecker, dying at the age of only thirty-one, has not left us enough to merit his inclusion in our small band.

What then, do we demand before we award the laurel wreath? A reasonable quantity of fine verse there must be. Chesterton himself showed an awareness of this when, in a review, he wrote of Alice Meynell that: "No poet, with the possible exception of Gray, has established so high a reputation on so slender a foundation, so far as mere quantity is concerned."[3]

1. Edward FitzGerald (1809-1883), "The Rubiyat of Omar Khayyam" (London: Quaritch, 1859). This is a very free translation from the Persian.
2. James Elroy Flecker (1884-1915), "The Golden Journey to Samarkand" was published in 1913 as a single poem by Secker & Co., then in his *Collected Poems* (London: Secker & Co., 1916).
3. *The Dublin Review*, Autumn 1923, 86-92.

Must this corpus be without flaw? Hardly. If we insist that a great poet must not have written any bad — really bad — verse, what a winnowing there would have to be!

Struck from our roll of honor would be Tennyson and Swinburne and Browning and Shelley and Longfellow. Beyond doubt, Wordsworth would have to be eliminated. In fact, I believe that our Hall of Permanent Fame would, at the end, house only one poet of the English language in addition to Shakespeare. John Keats is, I believe our only poet incapable of penning a clumsy or discordant line.

My suggestion is that we stipulate three requirements for admitting poets into the Hall of Permanent Fame. Firstly, that the poet is *primarily* a poet, and that his being finds its home and its expression chiefly in verse, not to the exclusion of all other considerations, but certainly before them. We have, for instance, a great deal of glorious and immortal poetry of religion and of earthly love, in which the worship of God or the love of a wife or sweetheart shines through in absolutely genuine emotion. But, I believe that for the great poet there is almost always a point at which the adoration of God or the praise of my mistress's eyebrow has to take second place to the vital concern of making that confounded penultimate line scan!

The poet does not ride, but is ridden by, his muse. This also explains why religion and earthly love, far more than any other subjects, have stimulated such an enormous body of verse which is quite admirable in intent and in genuine devotion, but utterly lamentable as poetry — because the construction has been secondary to the emotion.

My second requirement would be that we should be able, at least to a large extent, to separate the high utterance and the glory from the unsuccessful, the pedestrian, and the doggerel. With almost all of our greatest poets it is reasonably possible to ignore the failures and to be grateful for the heights upon which we may breathe the air of heaven. In the case of Wordsworth, indeed, we can almost draw a chronological line of demarcation, as did James Stephen:

Two voices are there: one is of the deep . . .
. . . and one is of an old, half-witted sheep.
and, Wordsworth, both are thine.[4]

---

4. James Kenneth Stephen (1859-1892), "Wordsworth: A Sonnet," in *Lapsus Calumi* (Cambridge: privately printed, 1891).

My third and final requirement would be that our poet should mainly, though not, of course, invariably, have the intention of addressing himself to a permanent audience, on permanent concepts, and in language which is as near permanent as can be.

The events celebrated or mourned are likely to be ephemeral in themselves, but the poet's call should be to those of our thoughts and emotions which are universal and permanent. The fact that the battles, loves and intrigues of ancient Greece are remote from our present concerns in no degree lessens the power of the great plays of Sophocles and Aeschylus to arouse and uplift us.

It seems to me a fatal weakness that so much of our present-day verse is written, not only on issues that are transitory, but in language that follows the irrational and ungrammatical fads of the moment, and which will, therefore, quickly become incomprehensible.

On that third count, Chesterton is almost entirely guiltless, very rarely falling into obscurity by using events which soon become remote. The only example I can call to mind is his poem "A Song of Swords," which would now require a short essay to render it comprehensible. Even here, he could defend himself by pointing out that when it was collected in *Poems*,[5] it appeared in a section titled "Rhymes for the Times."

It is upon the first and second counts that I must confess to reservations about Chesterton as nominee for our roll of poetic honor. He was *not* a dedicated and single-minded poet. There were too many other things in life of far greater importance to him than poetry, especially his own poetry.

It would be too simplistic of me to suggest that poetry was merely one more vehicle among the many — the essay, the novel, the debate, the letter, the play, the lecture — which he used as conveyances for his ideas in furtherance of the high causes for which he worked and fought.

There is too much magic in his poetry for it to be regarded thus, and time after time we find in him splendid lines and visions in what has set out to be no more than a squib to enliven and enlighten a passing moment. But it does seem to me that the weakness of Chesterton's verse, judging it by purely aesthetic standards, is that it was there to serve and not to be served. It is not true, as is sometimes

5. *Poems* (London: Burns Oates, 1915), 104.

179

said, that he never rewrote or corrected, but it was far from being his custom.

The great bulk — the staggering bulk if we include unpublished and uncollected material — was written out once, often for a particular occasion or riposte, and then regarded as being expended and not worth pursuing or polishing.

This reflects also upon my first and second demands, that we should be able to separate the permanent from the forgettable. G. K. Chesterton was, as that fine but neglected critic J. C. Squire wrote, "a poet of the market-place."[6] He had no interest at all in posthumous fame, wanting only to reach ordinary people with all possible immediacy of impact, and his verse, like all his writing, poured forth in a turbulent stream.

The haste with which he wrote, together with his preoccupation with matters other than aesthetic niceties, makes it difficult to find a body of his highest verse that is without flaw, in which to enshrine his name as a poet. We could quite easily isolate lovely poems that would satisfy the most fastidious of critics, but when we had done so, we would discover that we had discarded very much of what delighted and uplifted us most in his work.

We all know that vivid picture, from "Wine and Water":

The cataract of the cliff of heaven
Fell blinding off the brink
As if it would wash the stars away

and the reduction in the next line to;

As suds go down a sink.[7]

Then, in that delicious tilt at "Mr Mandragon, the Millionaire," he has the lines:

6. Sir John Collinge Squire (1884-1958), poet, author, satirist. Editor of *London Mercury*, 1919-34. This comment was made in a review of G. K. C.'s *Collected Poems*, in *The Observer*, 3 July 1927, and later collected in *Sunday Mornings* (London: Heinemann, 1930), 45-54.

7. "Wine and Water," a poem from G. K. C.'s novel, *The Flying Inn* (London: Methuen, 1914), 43-44, later incorporated in *Collected Poems* (London: Cecil Palmer, 1927), 180. It had first been published in *The New Witness*, 27 February 1913, 527, under the title "A Song of the Second Deluge."

He used all his motors
For canvassing voters
And twenty telephones.[8]

That lapse in syntax could have been remedied by the simple transposition of the first two lines — but G. K. C. was enjoying the fun too much to bother with so small a detail.

In *The Ballad of the White Horse* Chesterton has the opposing armies at the battle of Ethandune lined up in battle order, but he makes the two left flanks face each other. The error was pointed out more than once but, as his wife Frances wrote to one correspondent, he didn't think it of any importance to anyone.

This brings us to another complicating factor in any assessment of G. K. C.'s work: the deep and genuine personal humility of the man. I stress that word "genuine," because those of us who lurk on the outer fringes of the world of literature are quite capable of any amount of self-deprecation, but only on the strict understanding that this is only an expression of our sweet modesty. Heaven help anyone who takes us at our word! (Is there, in our language, a phrase more arrogant, more compact of smug self-esteem, than "In my humble opinion"?)

Although Chesterton took the beliefs for which he lived and fought very seriously indeed, he did actually believe that his own work had no lasting value. His father Edward (who lived until 1922, by which time G. K. C. had long been established as one of the great names in contemporary thought as well as in literature) had carefully preserved records and much original work by his son. After his death, Gilbert cheerfully set about the merry task of burning it all. Fortunately, the bonfire, like that later one of C. S. Lewis's work, was interrupted, but not before a great deal had been consumed.

The Everlasting Man, which I and many hold to be Chesterton's greatest book, is sprinkled throughout with the names of those minor contemporaries with whom G. K. C. argued throughout his working life. Most of them were of little importance even in their day, and it might seem that Chesterton need not have devoted precious time to them. But he never saw the situation in that light, nor would it occur to him

---

8. "The Good Rich Man," also from *The Flying Inn*. First appeared in *The New Witness*, 2 January 1913, 271, and in *Collected Poems* (London: Cecil Palmer, 1927), 189-90.

to omit those names from the book on the grounds that within a few years they would be meaningless to all but a handful of readers. He would take it for granted that if those people were to be forgotten, then so would he.

It seems to me that this deep and unselfconscious humility may be the reason, or a part of the reason, why G. K. C. appears at times to reach, in his verse, toward the heights, and then shy away, as though suddenly feeling that he is unworthy to tread such high ground.

There are, of course, exceptions in plenty, poems in which he did not flinch from high utterance, but these do not, I think, invalidate my contention that his humility militated against his nomination to the highest ranks of our poets. I use the word "nominee" and not "applicant," for in *The Outline of Sanity* Chesterton describes himself as being "a very minor poet,"[9] and so any claim for him must be made by others.

Chesterton's flawless poems are to be found, chiefly in the short, spontaneous religious poems, such as:

> The Christ-child lay on Mary's lap,
>   His hair was like a light.
> (O weary, weary were the world,
>   But here is all aright).
>
> . . . .
>
> The Christ-child stood at Mary's knee,
>   His hair was like a crown,
> And all the flowers looked up at Him,
> And all the stars looked down.[10]

You will find flawless poems among those addressed to Frances in which he achieved the extraordinary feat of bringing real newness and freshness to the ancient art of the love poem:

> My lady clad herself in grey,
>   That caught and clung about her throat;

---

9. *The Outline of Sanity* (London: Methuen, 1926), 71, and *Collected Works of Chesterton* (San Francisco: Ignatius Press, 1987) 5:35-209.

10. "A Christmas Carol," in *The Wild Knight*, G.K.C's second published book (London: Dent, 1900), 46-47, and in *Collected Poems* (London: Cecil Palmer, 1927), 308.

Then all the long grey winter day
　　On me a living splendour smote;
And why grey palmers holy are,
　　And why grey minsters great in story,
And grey skies ring the morning star,
　　And grey hairs are a crown of glory.

.　　.　　.　　.　　.　　.　　.　　.　　.　　.

My lady clad herself in blue,
　　Then on me, like the seer long gone,
The likeness of a sapphire grew,
　　The throne of him that sat thereon.
Then knew I why the Fashioner
　　Splashed reckless blue on sky and sea;
And ere 'twas good enough for her,
　　He tried it on Eternity.[11]

And flawless poems are found among those brief verses written in
the white heat of anger or satire.

Elegy in a Country Churchyard

The men that worked for England
They have their grave at home:
And bees and birds of England
About the cross can roam.

But they that fought for England,
Following a falling star,
Alas, alas for England
They have their graves afar.

But they that rule in England,
In stately conclave met.
Alas, alas for England
They have no graves as yet.[12]

11. "A Chord of Colour," in *The Wild Knight*, 7-9, and in *Collected Poems*, 294-95.
12. "Elegy in a Country Churchyard," in *The Ballad of St. Barbara and Other Verses* (London: Cecil Palmer, 1922), 9, and in *Collected Poems*, 55.

Another example is to be found in the fine, angry sonnet he wrote to a public man who applauded the calling off of a strike at Christmas:

Sonnet with the Compliments of the Season

I know you. You will hail the huge release,
Saying the sheathing of a thousand swords,
In silence and injustice, well accords
With Christmas bells. And you will gild with grease
The papers, the employers, the police,
And vomit up the void your windy words
To your New Christ; who bears no whip of cords
For them that traffic in the doves of peace.
The feast of friends, the candle fruited tree,
I have not failed to honour, and I say
It would be better for such men as we,
And we be nearer Bethlehem, if we lay
Shot dead on scarlet snows for liberty,
Dead in the daylight upon Christmas Day.[13]

Perhaps surest of all, this flawless quality is there in those glorious satires that deflate, with deadly accuracy, all pomposity and hypocrisy, as in "The World State," which opens:

Oh, how I love Humanity,
    With love so pure and pringlish,
And how I hate the horrid French,
    Who never will be English!

and ends:

The villas and the chapels where
    I learned with little labour
The way to love my fellow-man
    And hate my next-door neighbour.[14]

There are, however, four poems in particular which I find both important and illuminating. The first of these is *The Ballad of the White*

13. "Sonnet With the Compliments of the Season," in *Poems* (London: Burns Oates, 1915), 103, and in *Collected Poems* (London: Cecil Palmer, 1927), 147.
14. "The World State," in *Collected Poems* (London: Cecil Palmer, 1927), 13.

Horse, that great, sustained epic which, despite its many printings, has still not been granted its full due. The ballad form was one in which Chesterton, for all his humility, could feel at home because, despite all the glories and the heroism it has given to our literature, it remains a humble and unassuming art form:

> And naught was left King Alfred
>   But shameful tears of rage,
> In the island in the river
>   In the end of all his age.
>
> In the island in the river
>   He was broken to his knee;
> And he read, writ with an iron pen,
> That God had wearied of Wessex men
> And given their country, field and fen,
>   To the devils of the sea.
>
> .   .   .   .
>
> In the river island of Athelney,
>   With the river running past,
> In colours of such simple creed
> All things sprang at him, sun and weed,
> Till the grass grew to be grass indeed
>   And the tree was a tree at last.
>
> Fearfully plain the flower grew,
>   Like the child's book to read,
> Or like a friend's face seen in a glass;
> He looked; and there Our Lady was,
> She stood and stroked the tall live grass
>   As a man strokes his steed.
> Her face was like an open word
>   When brave men speak and choose,
> The very colours of her coat
>   Were better than good news.
>
> .   .   .   .
>
> "Mother of God," the wanderer said,
>   "I am but a common king,

Nor will I ask what saints may ask,
　　To see a secret thing.

"The gates of heaven are fearful gates
　　Worse than the gates of hell;
Not I would break the splendours barred
Or seek to know the thing they guard,
　　Which is too good to tell.

"But for this earth most pitiful,
　　This little land I know,
If that which is for ever is,
Or if our hearts shall break with bliss,
　　Seeing the stranger go?

"When our last bow is broken, Queen,
　　And our last javelin cast,
Under some sad, green evening sky,
Holding a ruined cross on high,
Under warm westland grass to lie,
　　Shall we come home at last?"
And a voice came human but high up,
　　Like a cottage climbed among
The clouds; or a serf of hut and croft
That sits by his hovel fire as oft,
But hears on his old bare roof aloft
　　A belfry burst in song.

"The gates of heaven are lightly locked,
　　We do not guard our gain,
The heaviest hind may easily
Come silently and suddenly
　　Upon me in a lane,

"And any little maid that walks
　　In good thoughts apart,
　　May break the guard of the Three Kings
And see the dear and dreadful things
　　I hid within my heart.

　　·　·　·　·　·　·　·　·　·　·　·

"The men of the East may spell the stars,
    And times and triumphs mark,
But the men signed of the cross of Christ
    Go gaily in the dark.

"The wise men know all evil things
    Under the twisted trees,
Where the perverse in pleasure pine
And men are weary of green wine
    And sick of crimson seas.

"But you and all the kind of Christ
    Are ignorant and brave,
And you have wars you hardly win
    And souls you hardly save.

"I tell you nought for your comfort,
    Yea, nought for your desire,
Save that the sky grows darker yet
    And the sea rises higher.

"Night shall be thrice night over you,
    And heaven an iron cope.
Do you have joy without a cause,
    Yea, Faith without a hope?"

Even as she spoke she was not,
    Nor any word said he,
He only heard, still as he stood
Under the old night's nodding hood,
The sea-folk breaking down the wood
    Like a high tide from sea.[15]

It was the nobility of Chesterton's expression here which evoked
C. S. Lewis's generous tribute to the ballad:

> Does not the central theme — the highly paradoxical message
> which Alfred receives from the Virgin — embody the feeling, and the

---

15. *The Ballad of the White Horse* (London: Methuen, 1911), and in *Collected Poems* (London: Cecil Palmer, 1927), 199-288. Note: the stanzas quoted here are not sequential.

only possible feeling, with which in any age, almost-defeated men take up such arms as are left them, and win?

. . . Hence, in those quaking days just after the fall of France, a young friend of mine (just about to enter the R.A.F.) and I found ourselves quoting to one another stanza after stanza of the Ballad. There was nothing else to say.[16]

The second of the four poems I have in mind is also to be found in the *Collected Poems:*

Translation from Du Bellay

Happy, who like Ulysses or that Lord
    Who raped the fleece, returning full and sage,
With usage and the world's wide reason stored,
    With his own kin can taste the end of age.
When shall I see, when shall I see, God knows!
    My little village smoke; or pass the door,
The old dear door of that unhappy house
    Which is to me a kingdom and much more?
Mightier to me the house my fathers made
    Than your audacious heads, O Halls of Rome!
More than your immortal marbles undecayed,
    The thin sad slates that cover up my home.
More than your Tiber is my Loire to me,
    Than Palatine my little Lyre there;
And more than all the winds of all the sea
    The quiet kindness of the Angevin air.[17]

The third is less well known, though John Sullivan included it in the second volume of his bibliography *Chesterton Continued,* and it was later reprinted in *The Chesterton Review:*

Sorrow

At last, at even, to my hearth I hark,
    Still faithful to my sorrow. And inside

---

16. C. S. Lewis, "Notes on the Way," *The Spectator,* 9 November 1946. Not collected.

17. "Translation from du Bellay," in *Poems* (London: Burns Oates, 1915), 130, and in *Collected Poems* (London: Cecil Palmer, 1927), 162.

Even I and all my old magnanimous pride
Are broken down before her in the dark.

Sorrow's bare arm about my neck doth strain,
　　Sorrow doth lift me to her living mouth
　　And whispers, fierce and loving like the South,
Saying, "Dear Pilgrim, have you come again?

"Whether you walked by wastes of upland green,
　　Whether you walked by wastes of ocean blue,
　　Have you not felt me step by step with you,
A thing that was both certain and unseen?

"Or haply is it ended? haply you,
　　Conquering and wholly cured of loving me,
　　Are but a wavering lover who would be
Off with the old love ere he take the new?"

But, seeing my head did but in silence sink
　　Before her ruthless irony and strong,
She gave me then that dreadful kiss to drink
　　That is the bitter spring of art and song.

Then with strange gentleness she said, "I choose
　　To be thine only, thine in all ways; yes,
Thy daughter and thy sister and thy muse,
　　Thy wife and thine immortal ancestress.

Feed not thy hate against my rule and rod,
　　For I am very clean, my son, and sane,
Because I bring all brave hearts back to God,
　　In my embraces being born again."

Thus spoke she low and rocked me like a child,
　　And as I stared at her, as stunned awhile,
On her stern face there fell more slow and mild
　　the splendour of a supernatural smile.[18]

18. *The Chesterton Review* 15, no. 4; and 16, no. 1 (double issue of November 1989–February 1990): 435-37.

The fourth and last poem is one that has not been published before. I found a typed and (of course!) undated copy of it among the treasures of Top Meadow before they were taken over by the British Library. It had been printed in *The Westminster Gazette*,[19] then forgotten and is as yet uncollected, but it will be included among the very many newly discovered poems in the definitive edition which I am editing for Chesterton's *Collected Works*, now being published by Ignatius Press.

When you are old, when candle and evening cloud
Decay beside you spinning in your chair,
Then sing this song and marvel and cry aloud
Great Ronsard praised me in the days when I was fair.
There shall no maiden spin with you or sing
But shall say "Ronsard" and the name shall ring
And sound your name with everlasting praise.
I shall lie buried and a boneless shade
By the pale myrtles pluck my last response;
You will be sitting where the embers fade,
Nodding and gazing as the last ash glows.
An old grey woman in grey garments furled.
You shall regret my love and your disdain.
Oh, do not linger, Oh, before all is vain,
Gather, Oh gather, the roses of the world.

Now there is a remarkable link between the last three of these marvelous poems. All are translations from the French. The first, a translation from du Bellay, and the only one of them to be widely known, received the highest praise. It was printed in a little book, *Masterpieces of Lyrical Translation*.[20] The editor, Adam Gowans, limited the selection to a mere thirty-four poems, saying that each had been chosen simply upon merit as an original poem which deserved immortality. In particular, he named seven "which bear comparison with any ever made in the past," and in these he included G. K. C.'s translation.

Much later, in 1966, it was included in the prestigious *Penguin*

19. "Sorrow," *Westminster Gazette*, 24 October 1908. Translated from the French of Charles Guerin. In John Sullivan, *Chesterton Continued: A Bibliographical Supplement* (London: University of London Press, 1968), 88-89.

20. *Masterpieces of Lyrical Translation* (London: Gowans & Gray, 1911), 27-28.

Book of Modern Verse in Translation. The tribute paid to it by the compiler, George Steiner, is astonishing, and must be quoted:

> At its best, the peculiar synthesis of conflict and complicity between a poem and its translation into another poem creates the impression of a "third language," of a medium of communicative energy which somehow reconciles both languages in a tongue deeper, more comprehensive, than either. In the no-man's-land between du Bellay's verse and Chesterton's English sonnet, so nearly exhaustive of the original, we seem to hear, "encore l'immortelle parole," Mallarmé's expression for the notion of a universal, immediate tongue from which English and French had broken off.[21]

This seems to me to be revealing, and very pertinent to our inquiry as to Chesterton's position among the permanent poets. My contention is that G. K. C. would feel free to soar to any heights of lyricism and sublimity in translating the poems of others, because he would not, consciously or unconsciously, feel that he was assuming a mantle for which he was inadequate. We cannot, at any point in any consideration of him, escape from the towering fact of his astonishing humility. It actually seems that the fullness of his power of sonorous and noble expression he reserved, in some measure, for the verse of poets.

I end with a quatrain which shows that this quality was part of his nature from early years. It is probably from his Slade School period, possibly even earlier, and is addressed to God:

> Hide Thou Thy face in clouds and mysteries
> Wield as Thou wilt Thy power that makes and mars
> But hear. That in Thy roaring wheel of stars
> One atom dares to love Thee ere it dies.[22]

The judgment to which these considerations force me is that G. K. Chesterton is not to be numbered among the greatest poets of our literary inheritance. He was something of even far greater importance.

21. *The Penguin Book of Modern Verse in Translation*, introduced and edited by George Steiner (London: Penguin Books Ltd., 1966), 82.

22. Verse of four lines, untitled. Holograph. Found by author in 1990 in a tin trunk which had been thought to contain only clothing and fabrics, among the archives at Top Meadow Cottage. It is printed here for the first time ever. The original, which I judged to have been written in the 1890s, is now in the British Library.

Dying and Rising:
Toward the Renewal
of the Permanent Things

Darkness at Noon: The Eclipse of the Permanent Things

Peter Kreeft

We all know what Christianity looks like when viewed from the standpoint of modernity. In this essay I shall try to turn the truth tables and see what modernity looks like when viewed from the standpoint of Christianity.

My point of view is what C. S. Lewis called "mere Christianity." "Mere Christianity" means not "little Christianity" but "big Christianity": full, biblical, apostolic, traditional, orthodox Christianity.

I shall be using many of Lewis's ideas in this essay: some explicitly, some implicitly. However, this is not a scholarly essay about Lewis but an amateur's essay using Lewis (and others) to think about the fate of the Permanent Things in the modern world. (I'm sure Lewis would much prefer his readers to think *with* him rather than *about* him; to look *along* with him rather that *at* him, to use his own very useful distinction from the essay "Meditation in a Toolshed.")

We know what Christianity looks like when viewed from the standpoint of modernity because we are bombarded with it. The media moguls, the opinion molders and real educators of our society, are the most aggressively anti-Christian propaganda elite since the Nazis. Can you remember a single movie in the last twenty years in which the Christian clergymen in it were not portrayed as hypocrites? Talk about a classic case of projection! (If you think that dig is too dirty, read Paul

---

Peter Kreeft's address at the conference was subsequently published in *Faith and Reason* 17, no. 1 (Spring 1991): 51-85. The article appears here by permission of the publisher.

Johnson's book *Intellectuals*. Someone sagely said that the title should have been *Hypocrites*.)

But what does modernity look like from the viewpoint of Christianity? Essentially, it looks like a gallows on which the Permanent Things are lynched without a trial; an altar, or a slaughterhouse in which the Permanent Things are sacrificed to the dark gods of Baal and Ashtaroth and Moloch: power and greed and lust.

Our world was aptly described by Arthur Koestler's paradoxical and prophetic title, "Darkness at Noon." A similar title by Martin Buber, "Eclipse of God," makes the same point by a similar astronomical image: we are now living in the real Dark Ages, as we approach the end of that century for which a famous religious journal named itself, with incredible naivete and false prophecy: *The Christian Century*! If there is any title we can be certain the history books of the future will never use for our century, it is that one. Much more likely is Franky Schaeffer's suggestion, "The Century of Genocide."

Of all twentieth century inventions, that is the one that has most drastically affected the most lives. We have so far witnessed five major holocausts in this century, and along with every "civilized" nation in the Western world, except Ireland, we are now participating in the sixth and largest one of all, which is also the only one that shows no signs of ending, as the other five did. What the Turks did to the Armenians, Hitler to the Jews, Stalin and Mao to their political enemies, and Pol Pot to one-third of all his nation's people, our present femininity haters who are incredibly misnamed "radical feminists" and their allies are still doing to the most tiny, innocent, and defenseless of all classes of human beings, unborn babies.

Mother Teresa said, with the simplicity of a peasant, "When a mother can kill her own child, what is left of the West to save?" (Incredibly, *Time* magazine printed that statement. Perhaps there is some hope after all.)

God asked a rhetorical question in Scripture: "Can a mother forsake the fruit of her womb? Even if she could, I could not forsake you, says the Lord your God." The rhetorical question was meant to put forth an unthinkable absurdity. Yet millions of mothers today perform that unthinkable absurdity, and many more millions, mostly men, think approvingly of that unthinkable work of Moloch.

Doubtless, most of the twenty million mothers who have aborted their babies since our Supreme Court of justice declared this injustice just were themselves victims of propaganda pressures and cultural conditioning, "more sinned against than sinning." That, however, makes things worse, not better: it implicates the whole culture in the double deed of destroying undeveloped bodies and undeveloped consciences.

If the soul is more precious than the body, the former death is worse than the latter. The soul of Western civilization is dying; that is the essence of our tragedy. When its body follows, as it must, we will see the civilizational pus ooze, but that pus is already there festering inside. The barbarians are already within the gates, writing the textbooks, newspapers, TV shows, movies, and music.

Is this going to be another one of those interminable essays on how to prevent the wreck of Western civilization? No. For as Whittaker Chambers wrote, "It is idle to talk about preventing the wreck of Western civilization. It is already a wreck from within."

Do I come to you then as a prophet of doom? No. I disavow both mantles, both prophet and doom. Perhaps there is still time to intercede for the secular city as Abraham interceded for Sodom. We do not know how much time we have left. But we do know this: if God spares New York, He will owe an apology to Sodom.

Avery Dulles has mapped out a useful chart of four possible contemporary Christian attitudes toward our secular society, in a kind of logical square of opposition. He calls the four options Traditionalism, Neo-conservatism, Liberalism, and Radicalism. Traditionalism believes in the church but not the state, i.e., not the present state of society. It is countercultural. Neo-conservatism (e.g. Richard John Neuhaus and Michael Novak) believes in both the church and the American state. Liberalism believes in Americanism but not in the church, i.e., not traditional Christianity. And Radicalism says, "A plague on both your houses."

I am a Traditionalist, as was C. S. Lewis. But I want to interject a word of caution to my fellow Traditionalists. It is the fear that Traditionalists run the same risk in idealizing the past as both Neo-conservatives and Liberals (what strange bedfellows!) run in looking benignly at the present and the future. Looking back is a posture that has been known to be very dangerous to one's health, especially if one is on a salt-free diet: remember Lot's wife.

So let's look to the future. Is it not time to be optimistic now that the Iron Curtain has fallen with an iron thud? To answer this question, let us ask two other questions, one about us and one about "them."

The one about us is this: were we more moved by the fear of God or the fear of Gorbachev? Were we wrestling against principalities and powers in the Kremlin or in Hell? Did we understand Solzhenitsyn's line about the border between Good and Evil running not between nations but down the middle of our own souls?

And the question about "them" is this: what kind of freedom was uppermost in the minds of most of the masses who poured through the newly opened Berlin Wall? Was it spiritual freedom, or even intellectual freedom? Did they, like the wise men from the East of old, come West seeking Christ? Or condoms? Did they pour into churches? Or porno shops? What excited them about the West? Did they buy Bibles or toilet paper? What freedom was legislated in Romania as soon as it had killed its dictator, who was guilty of enormous crimes? It was the freedom to kill those who are guilty of no crime at all except being in the way of someone who was bigger and already born.

So let's look to the real battle, not to the fake one. Now that that silly little temporary distraction called communism is dead or dying everywhere from Managua to Moscow — everywhere except Cambridge and Columbia — we can get back to the battle that should have been bothering Traditionalists all along: not against the the Eastern barbarianism without, but against the Western barbarianism within. The year 1984 has come and gone with few signs of Orwell's *1984* looming on our horizon, but Huxley's *Brave New World* looks like a more accurate prophecy every year. So let us be brave and look at our new world and at the internal slippery slope we've been sliding down, now that the external pseudo-threat of Communism has lost its power to distract our attention.

We're all familiar with the statistics on violent crime, rape, child abuse, drugs, and similar American leisure activities. We know that half of all marriages commit suicide, that is, end in divorce. We can read headlines well enough to be totally cynical about businessmen and politicians. Surveys tell us that this is the first generation in American history whose children are not better educated than their parents, but worse. They tell us that if teenagers don't have sex, they must be ugly, isolated, or fundamentalists. Half of all urban teenagers get pregnant, and half of them have abortions. A brave new world indeed.

I don't think we need to specify any more of the many symptoms of our decay. They are ubiquitous, obvious, and odious. The very word "decay" is evidence for our decay; for, as Chesterton put it, "our fathers said that a nation had sinned and suffered, like a man; we say it has decayed, like a cheese."

Consider just one more linguistic symptom of our decay. Whenever you hear a liberal theologian calling for a more "adult" Christianity, please remember what the word "adult" means in our culture. (What is an "adult" bookstore, or an "adult" movie?) What can be the relationship between such a theologian and a certain out-of-date teacher who said, "Unless you become as little children, you can not enter the Kingdom of God"?

What has happened? An eclipse. Nietzsche called it "the death of God," but Buber replied with an alternative image, the "eclipse of God." When the sun is eclipsed, it is still there, but no longer visible. But both death and eclipse produce a similar effect in our experience: darkness.

It is a "darkness at noon," as Koestler's title puts it, because noon is when eclipses happen. This is true both astronomically and historically. The noonday devil of pride arranges for the eclipse. It's the old Greek *hybris* plot that has been repeated many times, in ancient Israel, Greece, Rome, America. Today secularism, subjectivism, relativism, materialism, and hedonism are the craters on the moon that has risen up to eclipse the sun of God at the noon hour of human pride and cleverness, the triumph of "man's conquest of nature." Just as Lewis prophetically warned in *The Abolition of Man*, the culmination of "man's conquest of nature" has been his conquest of *human* nature by "liberating" it from the constraints of the natural moral law, the "Tao."

The change is not merely that we are behaving like beasts, but that we are believing like beasts. Man has never obeyed the Tao very well, but he at least believed in it, and thus experienced guilt. The new philosophy has removed guilt. It has made hypocrisy impossible, for hypocrisy is the tribute vice pays to virtue.

Nietzsche's "death of God" is a real event, but wrongly described. It is not the death of God but the death of seeing His image in the human soul. It is not the sun that is in darkness during an eclipse, as it seems, but the earth. "The death of God" is the pure psychological projection by a spiritual corpse.

Now when the symptoms of a terminal disease appear, whether in an individual or in a civilization, what is the reasonable response? Not despair but treatment. Not keeping our nose to the symptoms, sniffing at the decay and frothing at the mouth. Rather, we must approach the problem coldly, calmly, and logically, as a doctor would. We must be both practical and scientific. To be practical is to find out what to do, and then do it. To be scientific is to ask for a clear, step-by-step analysis and deduce a remedy for it.

Such an analysis should use the most practical and pervasive idea in all scientific thinking, the principle of causality. Every medical analysis follows the principle of causality by going through four steps: observation, diagnosis, prognosis, and prescription; the observation of the symptoms, the diagnosis of the disease that causes the symptoms, the prognosis of the cure, and the prescription for the treatment that causes the cure. The symptoms are the bad effects, the diagnosis tells the bad cause, the prognosis the good effect, and the prescription the good cause.

Every practical philosophy answers these four questions, because a practical philosopher is a doctor for the soul. For instance, Buddha's "Four Noble Truths" follow exactly these four steps. The "Four Noble Truths" comprise the whole of Buddhism, according to Buddha himself in the "Arrow Sermon." First: to live is to suffer; all life is suffering. Second: the cause of suffering is selfish desire. Third: there is a way to end suffering and achieve Nirvana: namely, to end desire. Take away the cause and you take away its effect. Fourth: the way to end desire is to practice the Noble Eightfold Path, the Buddhist yoga of ego-reduction.

Freudianism also contains these four steps. The symptoms are neurosis and psychosis. The diagnosis says the cause is the conflict between id and superego, between individual animal desire and social norms. The prognosis is homeostasis, or adjustment, a compromise of sorts. And the prescription is psychoanalysis.

Marxism sees the symptoms as class conflict, the diagnosis is capitalism, the prognosis is the classless communist society, and the prescription is a worldwide proletarian revolution.

Platonism sees the symptoms as vice; the diagnosis is ignorance; the prognosis is virtue; and the prescription is philosophical wisdom via the Socratic method.

Christianity also fits this pattern. The symptom is death, the diagnosis is sin, the prognosis is salvation, and the prescription is repentance and faith. "The wages of sin is death, but the gift of God is eternal life in Christ Jesus our Lord" (Rom. 6:23) — that single sentence sums up all Christian theology.

Let us now apply the generic form of this four-step analysis to the particular content of the deadly disease in contemporary Western civilization.

The first of the four steps of the analysis is the observation of the symptoms. I think we all know what the symptoms are and that the patient is critical; so I shall skip step one and spend most of my time on step two, the diagnosis. For that is what we mainly go to the doctor for. We go to the doctor only after we have already observed the symptoms; otherwise we wouldn't be there. "Those who are sick need a physician, not those who are well. I come to call not the righteous, but sinners" (Matt. 9:12). And once the doctor performs step two and diagnoses the disease, he or she can consult the textbooks to see whether it can be cured (the prognosis) and if so, how (the prescription).

I am going to diagnose our disease as an eclipse of the Permanent Things. I already defined "eclipse," but not "permanent" or "things." What "things" are permanent? And in what way are they "permanent"?

How can anything be permanent? Essentially, either subjectively or objectively, or both, or neither. First, something may be permanent both objectively, in itself, and also subjectively, in our consciousness. An example of this is the law of causality: nothing ever arises without a cause, *and* everyone knows that. Both the fact and the knowledge of it are permanent.

Second, something may be permanent objectively but not subjectively. For instance, the truth of monotheism tells us that if there is one God, He is permanent and eternal; but the world's knowledge of Him is not.

Third, something may be permanent subjectively but not objectively as is a permanent *illusion*, such as the attractiveness of sin, or the egocentric perspective which we carry around with us all the time, as if I had first dibs on the name "I AM" rather than God.

Fourth, something may be permanent neither objectively nor subjectively, such as fads and fashions. These do not concern us here because they are not in any sense Permanent Things. The other three are.

Take the crucial example of the Tao, or moral values, the natural moral law. There are four possible positions on it. The first position is that it is permanent both objectively and subjectively: there are eternal moral verities and our awareness of them can never be eradicated from the human heart. This is the position of St. Thomas Aquinas.

A second position holds that the moral law is permanent objectively but not subjectively; we can be changed into what Lewis in *The Abolition of Man* calls "men without chests," men whose chest, or heart, or conscience, or organ for apprehending the Tao, has atrophied.

A third position maintains that the moral law is not objectively permanent but that it is subjectively permanent, a structural illusion of the psyche. This is Freud's position: the superego is the unconscious reflection of society's constraints on the id's desires.

The fourth position believes that there is no objectively permanent moral law *and* no subjectively permanent moral law; human nature is malleable and conscience can be shaped, reshaped, or eradicated by social engineering. This is the position of Marxism and of behaviorism.

I make no apologies for calling Freud a fraud or for giving low marks to Marx, but I feel fear and trembling in arguing against Aquinas. But my daily experience of ordinary American life and people seems to tell me that the heart, the moral organ, has indeed atrophied. Perhaps the blood needed by the heart has migrated south to another, less subtle organ. There seems to be linguistic evidence for that, for the same people who confuse "adult" and "adulterous" also often confuse "organism" and "orgasm."

I don't want to spend my time arguing whether the moral law is subjectively permanent or not, but I want to ask instead what things are objectively permanent. What kinds of "things" are the Permanent Things, anyway? There are at least three of them.

First, there are permanent *truths*. These are not simply *ideas* in human minds, because our minds are *not* permanent. We change our minds faster than we change our clothes. If these Permanent Things are ideas, they must be in the divine mind. As Sartre says, "There can be no eternal truth if there is no eternal and perfect consciousness to think it." Aquinas says the same thing, in almost exactly the same words.

These permanent truths are not even the so-called "laws of nature," or laws of science. Heraclitus, the pre-Socratic Greek philosopher, first clearly realized the double truth that all matter is in motion and that there are permanent laws or formulas for this motion. He taught that "everything flows," like a river, but also that there was a permanent *logos* or law of change. For him this was the law of the transformations between fire and water, earth and air; for us it is such truths as the law of transformation between mass and energy ($E = mc^2$) or the equality between force and mass times acceleration.

But these laws of nature are not what I mean by the Permanent Things. For they are only descriptions of how matter does behave, not laws of how it must behave. Molecules do not bow down before a preexisting Ten Commandments of matter before they set out on their daily rounds. There is no permanent necessity to the laws of nature. It is conceivable that they may change billions of years from now if and when all the matter in the universe gets sucked into black holes. It is generally agreed today that the laws of nature were radically different than they are now during the first few seconds of the universe's existence, right after the Big Bang.

Instead, by permanent truths I mean things like the law of noncontradiction, and the law of causality, and the multiplication table: the objective and unchangeable laws of logic, metaphysics, and mathematics. Nothing can ever both be and not be in the same way at the same time. Nothing can ever begin to be without any cause at all for its beginning to be. Two times three can never begin to equal seven.

Can anyone deny these Permanent Things? Yes indeed. Even *they* are not subjectively permanent. For many of our currently fashionable philosophies reduce them to symbol systems, useful conventions, mental biases, cultural copings, projections of our fear of death or chaos, word games, or even patriarchal plots to oppress women. Permanent objective truths are not necessarily permanent subjectively. I spent eighteen dollars for a poorly written book by Allan Bloom because I got hooked on its wonderful first sentence: "If there is one thing every college professor in America can be certain of, or nearly certain of, it is that all or nearly all of the students who enter his classroom will believe, or think they believe, that truth is relative."

Why would someone want to deny objective truth? Who's afraid of the law of noncontradiction? What's behind the insane attempt to soften up the very structures of sanity? I think it is not logical, mathematical, or metaphysical truths that threaten, but *moral* truths. If there were permanent moral truths, that would mean that morality is no longer about nice, warm, fuzzy, vague, soft, negotiable things called "values" but about hard, unyielding, uncompromising, uncomfortable, non-negotiable things called "laws."

And their fear of permanent, objective moral laws is amazingly selective. It almost always comes down to just one area: sex. In my experience, students, like professors, bluff a lot, and do adroit intellectual dancing. But I'd bet a wad of money that if only the sixth commandment were made optional, half of all the hatred and fear of the church would vanish.

St. Augustine was one of the few honest enough to admit his obsession. After puffing great philosophical profundities about the intellectual problems that kept him back from the church, he finally admits, in the *Confessions,* "The plain fact was, I thought I should be impossibly miserable without the embraces of a mistress." If *that* profoundly philosophical motive was what held back one of the most honest, truth-seeking wisdom-lovers in history, do you really hope that nobler ideals motivate the spiritual children of Woodstock?

Thus, much more crucial than permanent *truths* are permanent *values,* or rather, permanent *moral laws,* laws as objective and unchangeable as the laws of mathematics.[1] The *application* of these laws may be uncertain and changeable, but *they* are not. Applied laws of mathematics are also sometimes uncertain and changeable, for example when you try to measure the exact length of a live alligator.

A third kind of Permanent Things emphasizes the word "things." Not only are there permanent *truths* and permanent *moral laws,* but there are also permanent *things.* There is a wonderful passage about this in *Till We Have Faces.* After Orual's sister Psyche tells Orual that she has seen the face of the god, her husband, and his palace, his house, Orual wonders whether it could be true even though she cannot see these things. She asks her Greek tutor and philosopher, the Fox,

> "You don't think — not possibly — not as a mere hundredth chance — there might be things that are real though we can't see them?"
>
> "Certainly I do. Such things as Justice, Equality, the Soul, or musical notes."
>
> "Oh, Grandfather, I don't mean things like that. . . . Are there no things — I mean *things* — but what we see?"[2]

---

1. I think Lewis made a tactical error in conceding to use the modern word "values" instead of the ancient word "law" in *The Abolition of Man.* For to the mind of the modern reader, the idea of "objective values" is simply an unintelligible contradiction in terms. For this modern mind is Cartesian and Kantian; and to the Cartesian dualist, "objective" means merely "physical," which values are *not,* and to the Kantian moralist "values" mean something posited by man's will, not God's: something subjective, though universal. You see, there is real confusion here. God did not give Moses "The Ten Values." And the currently fashionable way of teaching moral relativism in American high schools is not called "Law Clarification." There is a difference.

2. C. S. Lewis, *Till We Have Faces* (London: Collins, Son & Co., Ltd., 1979), 150.

The "things" Orual suspects are not physical things, yet they are not abstract ideas either. They are solid and substantial and real, like gods, or Platonic Forms. The immense difficulty modern students have in understanding Plato's famous Theory of Forms as anything other than abstract class concepts can be seen from their utter incomprehension (*yet* fascination) with Charles Williams's novel *The Place of the Lion,* in which the very real and active protagonists are Platonic Forms (!); and in students' equal incomprehension (*and* fascination) with the Great Dance at the end of *Perelandra,* especially this Platonic point in it:

> He could see (but the word "seeing" is now plainly inadequate), wherever the ribbons or serpents of light intersected, minute corpuscles of momentary brightness; and he knew somehow that these particles were the secular generalities of which history tells — peoples, institutions, climates of opinion, civilizations, arts, sciences, and the like — ephemeral coruscations that piped their short song and vanished. The ribbons or cords themselves, in which millions of corpuscles lived and died, were things of a different kind. At first he could not say what. But he knew in the end that most of them were individual entities. . . . Some of the thinner and more delicate cords were beings that we call short-lived: flowers and insects, a fruit or a storm of rain. . . . Oh there were such things as we also think lasting: crystals, rivers, mountains, or even stars. Far above these in girth and luminosity, and flashing with colours from beyond our spectrum, were the lines of the personal beings. . . . But not all the cords were individuals; some were universal truths or universal qualities. It did not surprise him then to find that these and the persons were both cords and both stood together as against the mere atoms of generality which lived and died in the clashing of their streams; but afterwards, when he came back to earth, he wondered.

These Platonic universals are not abstractions. They are *things.* They are gods, or spirits. In "The Descent of the Gods" chapter of *That Hideous Strength,* each of the planetary spirits is both a universal quality, like joviality, and a particular entity, like Jove. Jove, or Jupiter, does not merely *symbolize* joy; he *is* joy. Joy is not an abstract property, but a "permanent *thing,*" a reality, a god.

Lewis is so insistent on this point about the concreteness, not abstractness, of nonphysical realities, that in *Miracles* he goes so far as to call God himself a particular thing:

> What we know through laws and general principles is a series of connections. But in order for there to be a real universe, the connections must be given something to connect: a torrent of opaque actualities must be fed into the pattern. If God created the world, then He is precisely the source of this torrent. . . . But if God is the ultimate source of all concrete, individual things and events, then God himself must be concrete and individual in the highest degree. Unless the origin of all other things were itself concrete and individual, nothing else could be so; for there is no conceivable means whereby what is abstract or general could itself produce concrete reality. Bookkeeping continued to all eternity could never produce one farthing. Metre, of itself, could never produce a poem.
>
> . . . If by using the word "infinite" we encourage ourselves to think of God as a formless "everything" about whom nothing in particular and everything general is true, then it would be better to drop the word altogether. Let us dare to say that God is a particular Thing. Once, He was the only Thing; but He created, He made other things to be. He is not those other things. He is not "universal being." . . . He has a determinate character. Thus He is righteous, not amoral; creative, not inert. . . . And men are exhorted to "know the Lord," to discover and experience this particular character.[3]

We have defined three kinds of Permanent Things. All three are in eclipse in our civilization. Now I want to concentrate especially on the second one, the moral "things," and on the little classic *The Abolition of Man*, one of the half-dozen books I would like to make everyone in our culture read, at gunpoint if necessary, for the sake of their sanity and survival.

One of the things this book does for our culture is to show us ourselves in our radical distinctiveness from all previous cultures. The most enlightening single sentence I have ever read about our culture and how radically different it is from all previous cultures is this one from *The Abolition of Man:*

> There is something which unites magic and applied science [technology] while separating both from the "wisdom" of earlier ages. For

3. C. S. Lewis, *Miracles* (New York: Macmillan, 1947), 86, 88.

the wise men of old the cardinal problem had been how to conform the soul to reality, and the solution had been knowledge, self-discipline, and virtue. For magic and applied science alike the problem is how to subdue reality to the wishes of men: the solution is a technique.[4]

We usually misunderstand the spiritual significance of technology, for we associate it with science more than with magic. Of the four enterprises — magic, religion, science, and technology — most moderns would classify science and technology together and magic and religion together. Not Lewis. He sees deeper. The deepest unity, the unity of ultimate aim and purpose, unites magic and technology: the aim of both is the satisfaction of our desires by power and control. The opposite aim unites science and religion: conformity to objective truth. Just as the aim of the magician and the aim of the saint are opposites, so the aim of the pure scientist and the aim of the engineer are opposites. It is not the spirit of pure science, the spirit of pure curiosity and wonder, that our culture values, but the spirit of practical success and power. It was classical Greek and medieval civilization that valued the spirit of pure science, though they did not have the efficient method to do it very well. If there is one thing that is abundantly clear from a study of the lives as well as the writings of modern intellectuals, it is that only a small and uninfluential minority of them believe in and practice the pure love of objective truth, especially the moral truth.

Toynbee distinguished twenty-one great civilizations in human history, of which ours is the latest. Every one of them admitted the Tao, objective moral truths. Ours is the first civilization to deny the Tao. The most radically new feature of our civilization is not technology, its newly powerful means, but the lack of an end, a *summum bonum*. We are the first civilization that does not know why we exist.

Every past civilization has had some religious answer to that question. The essence of modernity is the abandoning of that religious foundation, and thus eventually also abandoning the moral first story of the same civilizational building. Morality has always rested on religion in practice, even if a few philosophers like Plato and Aristotle could defend it without religion in theory. Dostoevsky wrote, "If God does not exist, everything is permissible." History shows far more people, both

4. C. S. Lewis, *The Abolition of Man* (New York: Macmillan, 1947), 87-88.

atheists and theists, on Dostoevsky's side than on Plato's. For Sartre, "there can be no eternal Good since there is no infinite and perfect consciousness to think it." For Nietzsche, the consequence of the good news that "God is dead" is a "transvaluation of all values." Like Milton's Satan, he says, in effect, "Evil, be thou my good." He declares love, compassion, mercy, justice, impartiality, and democracy to be weak and therefore evil; cruelty, ruthlessness, war, competition, and selfishness are good. For from the natural struggle of selfishnesses emerges the strongest, the Superman.

Please do not be horrified, but I am often tempted to thank God for Hitler. For if one big Hitler and one big Holocaust had not scared the Hell out of us, we might be living in a worldwide Hitler-Holocaust-Hell right now. God rubbed our face in it — we have seen the pure logical consequences of "the death of God" in the fires of Auschwitz. Yet most of us in the West still have not learned the old and simple lesson (scandalous to modern intellectuals simply because it is simple and old) that "unless the Lord build the house, they labor in vain who build it." No one in our time has ever faced and answered the question, If there is no God, *why shouldn't I* do as I please if I can get away with it? Because it's not "acceptable," nice, humane, human, democratic, fair, just, community-building, helpful, survival-enhancing, practical, or approved? I have never heard any reply to that from any humanist. No one has ever answered Dostoevsky's "Underground Man." The existentialists refute humanism. You don't need an Augustine or an Aquinas to refute humanism, only a Nietzsche or a Sartre.

If Dostoevsky is right, morality without religion is impossible. For there is no morality without real moral laws, binding duties, objective obligations. A morality of mere convention, man-made and thus man-revisable rules of the social game, is not morality at all, only mores. Life under such pseudo-morality is not real moral warfare, only war *games*, and we are never on the hot seat, but in a hot tub.

So there is no morality without moral absolutes, and without God there can be no moral absolutes. That's the second step. An absolute law can come from and be enforced by only an absolute will. Finally, no civilization can stand for long without morality. That should be exceedingly obvious, both from common sense and from history. Thus, without religion, no moral absolutes; without moral absolutes, no real morality; and without real morality, no survival of civilization. Thus without religion, civilization cannot survive. And has not survived. This is not just a law of logic but also of history. Every civilization in history has had a religious base. Ours is experimenting with a deviation from history's most obvious and universal law. The prognosis thus does not look very hopeful. If you can't even fool Mother Nature, you certainly can't fool Father God.

This fact comes as a surprise only to this generation, the first to be biblically illiterate. All I have done is to translate into abstract, logical language the simple, punchy point of Old Testament history that a nation's *fate* rests on its *faith*.

There is one thing even more stupid than modernism's abandoning religion in society: theological modernism's abandoning religion even in religion. The essence of theological modernism is the denial of the supernatural (miracles, Christ's divinity and resurrection, heaven and hell, the Second Coming, and the divine inspiration of Scripture). These fundamentals of the faith are labeled "fundamentalistic." Modernism reduces religion to morality, morality to social morality, and social morality to socialism.

In fact, religion's instinctive gravitation to socialism is natural. For socialism and religion are the only two answers to a problem Lewis poses in *The Abolition of Man:* the problem of the Controllers versus the controlled, the Conditioners versus the conditioned. To see this, we must first review his argument in that book.

Lewis's argument in chapter 3 is absolutely stunning, both in the sense of intellectually *brilliant* and in the sense of emotionally *terrifying.* It is that "man's conquest of nature" without the Tao must necessarily become nature's conquest of man. For "man's conquest of nature" must always mean, in the concrete, some men's power over other men, using nature as the instrument. Lewis's examples of the wireless, the airplane, and the contraceptive show this: some men wield the newly won power over others as its patients. Now as long as both the agents and the patients of these powers over nature admit and work within a common Tao, or moral law, they have the same interests, rights, and values. Monarchy is not oppressive if the king and the people are working for a common goal under a common law and share a common dignity. But if the power elite, whether king, voting majority, or media elite, ceases to believe in an objective Tao, as is clearly the case in our society, then they become Controllers, Conditioners, Social Engineers, and the patients become the controlled. Propaganda replaces propagation. Propagation is "old birds teaching young birds to fly." Propaganda is programming parrots. Propagation is the transmission of tradition. Propaganda is the invention of innovation. Which of the two is piped into our brains daily by our media?

This new class of Innovators, the Tao-less Conditioners, will themselves be motivated in their social engineering, not by the Tao, which is supernatural and eternal, a Permanent Thing. Instead, they will be motivated by their natural impulses, which are non-Permanent Things: their heredity and environment, especially their environment, especially the fashionable opinions. This means they will be motivated by Nature, not by the Permanent Things, which are supernatural.

Thus "man's conquest of nature" must be expanded at both ends: the conquerors are themselves conquered by nature (Tao-less environment), and they in turn only use nature to conquer other men. Thus "man's conquest of nature" turns out to be nature's conquest of man. Man's triumph is thus man's abolition, for the new man is an artifact. Those who have been conditioned out of the belief in free will lose their free will.

Now there are only two ways out of this "abolition of man" by social engineering. One is, of course, the return to the Tao. This is unlikely because the one thing modernity resists the most is return. It believes in progress, not repentance. But this would be a solution to the alienation between the Conditioners and the conditioned because both would then be under the same moral law. That spiritual equality would overshadow all physical and social inequality. The authorities would then wield power only in the name of the common objective Tao.

The other way out is to achieve unity through socialism: not the spiritual unity of a Tao but mere physical unity, i.e. social unity, i.e. economic unity. A "classless society" will supposedly make it impossible for one class to conquer or condition others. From the history of secular socialist and communist experiments that we have seen so far, I think we must not only call all the experiments failures but also call most of the experimenters liars and hypocrites. The most systematic oppression and mass murders in history have been carried out in the name of social equality, and blessed by the intellectuals, both of the Left and the Right. Statistical studies have revealed that in Hitler's concentration camps, the cruelest torturers were the most educated.

Socialism's dream is naive because mere equality does not automatically destroy oppression. Equalitarianism can be as oppressive as any tyranny. De Tocqueville pointed out long ago that democratic totalitarianism is not a contradiction in terms, and that Americans are naive if they think that the sheer political structure of democracy protects them against totalitarianism. For democracy and totalitarianism are not opposite answers to the same question, but answers to two different questions, and thus can be compatible. Democracy is an answer to the question, *In whom* is the social-political power located? The answer is in the people at large. Totalitarinism is an answer to the question, How *much* power are the social-political authorities to have? The answer is total power, power to reshape human life, human thought, human nature itself.

Three examples of democratic totalitarianism, in theory, are Rousseau's "General Will" (*vox populi, vox dei*); in fiction, Huxley's *Brave New World;* and in fact, the American media establishment.

Only the Tao can ensure freedom. Only when we are bound to a higher law of permanent, unchangeable, objective moral absolutes are we free from being determined by the lower laws of animal instincts, selfishness, sin, and propaganda. Only conformity to the trans-social Tao can make nonconformity to a decadent society just, or even possible. For we do, and must, conform to something, or else we are formless. The only question is, to what? There are only two possible answers: to what is higher than ourselves or to what is lower, supernature or nature, the Bible or MTV, Jesus Christ or Norman Lear, the Crucified or the crucifiers.

Let's take stock for a moment. How far down the slide have we slid? How much of the Tao is already lost? How many of the objectively Permanent Things have become subjectively impermanent?

I count at least thirty-three: silence, solitude, detachment, self-control, contemplation, awe, humility, hierarchy, modesty, chastity, reverence, authority, obedience, tradition, honor, simplicity, holiness, loyalty, gentlemanliness, manliness, womanliness, propriety, ceremony, cosmic justice, pure passion, holy poverty, respect for old age, the positive spiritual use of suffering, gratitude, fidelity, real individuality, real community, courage, and absolute honesty (the passionate, or fanatical love of truth for its own sake). That's one lost value for each of the years in Christ's life.

We could, of course, profitably spend hours, days, perhaps lifetimes exploring each one of these thirty-three lost values; and we could probably add thirty-three more. But in this age of progress and time-saving devices we have no time for such important things anymore — things like conversation, debate, meditation, prayer, deep friendship, imagination, even family. (If the sexual revolution doesn't do the family in, it will die for lack of time.)

But, you may think, this gloomy picture I have painted of a spiritual Dark Ages is only half the picture. What of all the progress we've made?

Well, let's look at the progress we've made. It can be divided into two kinds: spiritual and material. Let's take spiritual progress first. I think there *has* been some significant spiritual progress in modernity in at least one area: kindness vs. cruelty. I think we are much kinder than our ancestors were, especially to those we used to be cruel to: criminals, heretics, foreigners, other races, and especially the handicapped. I think this is very real progress indeed. I wonder, though, whether one big step forward offsets thirty-three steps back, some of them also big, some medium sized, but none small.

In any situation, the case for progress and modernity usually rests on one of two grounds: either supposed spiritual progress that is not progress at all (e.g. freedom from superstition, authority, absolutist morality, biblical literalism, church dogma, and the like), or explicitly material progress, scientific and technological progress. It is this last area which is spectacular and indisputable, and thus the strongest case for progressivism.

Our civilization certainly has produced astounding, magnificent, utterly undreamed of successes in understanding and mastering the forces of nature. I think every intelligent human being born before the Renaissance, if transported by a time machine to today, would be stupefied with wonder, marvel, and admiration at the awesome progress in science and technology.

But now I ask a strange and unusual and very upsetting question: Is there such a thing as material progress at all? Or is this a confusion of categories, like a blue number, or a rectangular value? I am not sure of this, but I want to suggest the possibility that there is not and cannot be any such thing as purely material progress; that only spirit can progress.

The reason I think this surprising and unpopular conclusion is true has something to do with the nature of time. To see this, we must speak Greek for a minute. The Greek language is much richer and subtler than English when it comes to philosophical distinctions, and Greek has two words for time, not just one. *Kronos* means the time measured objectively, impersonally, and mathematically by the motion of unconscious matter through space. For instance, one day of *kronos* is always exactly twenty-four hours long, the time it takes for the earth to rotate. *Kairos*, on the other hand, is human time, lived time, experienced time, the time measured by human consciousness and purposive reaching out into a future that is not yet but is planned for. Only *kairos* knows anything of goals and values.

For instance, when St. Paul writes, "It is now time to rise from sleep, because your salvation is nearer than when you first believed," he does not mean by "time" something like "June 30 of the year 50 A.D." "It is now time to die" does not mean "it is 3:20 P.M." Ends, goals, and purposes measure *kairos*, and these things exist only in consciousness, in spirit, not in mere matter.

The reason why I think only spirit can progress is because only spirit lives in *kairos*. And only *kairos* touches eternity, knows eternity, aims at eternity. Progress means not merely change, but change toward a goal. The change is relative and shifting, but the goal is absolute and permanent. If not, if the goal changed along with the movement toward it, we could not speak any more of progress, only change. There is no progress if the goal line recedes in front of the runner as fast as the runner runs. You can't steal second base if the second baseman has already taken it and is running to third.

Think of a circle, such as a pie, with a segment of it, or a piece of the pie, as *kairos*, lived time, lifetime. The circumference of the pie is *kronos*. *Kronos* limits how much *kairos* there is (e.g., eighty years), but it does not determine the other dimension of *kairos*, the dimension of progress. Progress means getting closer to the goal, which in my geometrical image is symbolized by the center of the circle. That would be eternity, permanence. Only in the *kairos* dimension — the spiritual dimension — can we speak meaningfully of progress at all. The only thing *kronos* can do is endlessly circle around the center and limit the quantity of any segment of *kairos*, but the circumference is equidistant from the center. This symbolizes the fact that our lived time, our lifetime, can move toward eternity, but purely material time cannot. You get closer to God by sanctity, not by aging. The world gets closer to God by improving spiritually, not by improving materially. And God is the goal, the measure of progress.

The essence of modernity is the death of the spiritual. A modernist is someone who is more concerned about air pollution than soul pollution. A modernist is someone who wants clean air in order to breathe dirty words.

A modernist cares about big things, like whales, more than little things, like fetuses; big things like governments, more than little things like families and neighborhoods; big things like states, which last hundreds of years, more than little things like souls, which last forever.

A modernist, thus, is one who puts his or her faith and hope for progress in precisely the one thing that cannot progress: matter. A traditionalist, on the other hand, is one who "looks not to the things that are seen but to the things that are unseen, for the things that are seen are temporal, but the things that are unseen are eternal" (2 Cor. 4:18). A traditionalist believes in the Permanent Things, and the Permanent Things cannot progress because they are the things to which all real progress progresses.

Perhaps I should modify my stark statement that matter cannot progress at all. Perhaps matter can progress, but only with and in and for the spirit. If your body and your tools and your possessions serve your spirit, if they make you truly happy and good and wise, then they contribute to progress too.

But this modification does not help the progressive at all, since it is pretty obvious that modernity's technological know-how and power has not made us happier, wiser, better, or more saintly than our ancestors. When we speak of modern progress, we do not mean progress in happiness, in contentment, in peace of mind. Nor do we mean progress in holiness and moral perfection or wisdom. We speak readily of "modern knowledge" but never of "modern wisdom." Rather, we speak of "ancient wisdom." For wisdom is to knowledge what *kairos* is to *kronos*. *Kairos* includes the spiritual and purposive and teleological and moral dimension.

Incidentally, this point about *kairos* and *kronos* liberates us not only from the ignorant worship of "progress" but also from the ignorant lust to be "up to date." A date, being mere *kronos*, has no character. It is almost nothing. It is a one-dimensional line, the circumference. A line can have no color. Only *kairos*, only a two-dimensional segment of the circle can have character, and color. Since a date is only a point on the circumference, it has no character. Nothing can ever be really "up to date." What a wild goose chase is our lust to be "with it" or "contemporary"! What a waste of passion and love and energy!

It's all in the Bible, of course. All this stuff about "love not the world" and how hard it is for the rich to be saved — it's very practical. St. Teresa of Avila wrote, "Anyone who wishes to enter the second Mansion will be well advised, as far as his state of life permits, to try to put aside all unnecessary affairs and business." One thing painfully obvious about modern "progress" is that we all are much busier now than we ever used to be. All these time-saving devices have done exactly the opposite of saving time: they've enslaved us to time, to *kronos*, to the clock. Jesus is a very good psychologist when he says, in the parable of the sower, that we are choked and suffocated by the brambles of the cares and riches and pleasures of life, so the seed of life cannot grow, cannot progress. Progress retards progress! Progress is the enemy of progress! Business chokes our real business here. Riches make real riches extremely difficult. Remember Mother Teresa's simple, Christlike words at Harvard: "You did not invite me here from a poor country to speak to a rich country. America is not a rich country. America is a desperately spiritually poor country." America is a poor country. This only seems paradoxical to us. In fact, it is simplicity itself. It is we who are standing on our head; that's why Christ's simplicities appear to us as upside-down paradoxes. Once we get right side up again, we will see how simple it is. And the world will see *us* as upside down and strange, and "out of it." How wonderful to be "out of it" when "it" is the maelstrom.

You may doubt the paradoxical point that progress retards progress. You may think it too pessimistic, world-denying, anti-progressive, irrelevant — "out of it," in a word. Well, here is one more argument for my outrageous paradox of progress. Let's take modernity's supposed progress to its limit, its end, its success. I think its failure will be most clearly and spectacularly like a prosecuting attorney who simply lets the accused criminal talk on and on and hang himself.

Modernity's progress in conquering nature is incomplete because nature still holds one trump card over all her conquerors: death. Nature always has the last word. Suppose genetic engineering conquered death. That would be the supreme triumph. Or would it?

Let's backtrack to Eden. You remember the story, of course. It began with the invention of advertising. Satan invented the first advertisement: "Eat this; it will make you like God." It was a lie, of course, like most of the industry. Modern technology is Satan's new advertisement. It tempts us, as it tempted Eve, to become like God in power (but not in virtue). Artificial immortality would be the supreme sell job. We would mortgage our soul for that, the conquest of the very power of life. That would conquer even the highest of angels, the seraphim, whom God stationed at the gate of Eden with a flaming sword to prevent us from eating the fruit of the tree of eternal life. Death was God's severe

215

mercy, the tourniquet around the wound of sin, to limit sin to eighty years or so. Remove the tourniquet, and history would bleed to death. Imagine the Roman Empire forever. Imagine the Third Reich forever. Imagine America forever. Lewis speaks of our "nightmare civilizations" whirling around themselves in never-ending gyrations of selfishness and despair (in *Miracles*), and (elsewhere, in *Mere Christianity*) of eggs that never hatch (by death) and so went rotten. "You can't just be a good egg forever; you must hatch or go bad." Death lets us hatch; artificial immortality would make us go bad forever. Hell incarnate would reign on earth. That would have to be the end of the world. And most geneticists estimate we will have it in two to three hundred years (according to Osborn Seagerberg in *The Immortality Factor*). How wonderful progress is!

Let's now back up and ask the psychological question about motivation: why did our civilization suddenly develop this lust for power? What caused the great sea change that *The Abolition of Man* defines? How did we get a new *summum bonum*, "man's conquest of nature," or power?

I think Friedrich Nietzsche, of all people, provides us with the answer. The children of this world are wiser in their own generation than the children of light. Sometimes, Nietzsche, the prophet of nihilism, understands modern nihilism better than its critics. Viktor Frankl quotes a sentence from Nietzsche in *Man's Search for Meaning* to explain why some survived the Nazi death camps and others, often the strongest, did not: "A man can endure almost any *how* if only he has a *why*." In other words, you can endure bad circumstances, powerlessness, poverty, even a concentration camp, if and only if you have a meaning and purpose to your whole life, and therefore also to suffering which is part of life. The corollary is that if you do *not* have a "why," you will not be able to endure any little suffering.

This explains the origin of modern technology. It did not drop out of the sky. Nor did mankind suddenly get smart, by some genetic mutation. Rather, the old "why," or meaning and purpose of life, the old *summum bonum*, began to weaken and decay. Once the sense of life's significance was lost, we could not endure its sufferings. So, we *had* to invent ways of conquering nature to radically reduce those sufferings. A man with no "why" *must* conquer his "how."

St. Thomas says, "Man cannot live without joy. That is why one deprived of spiritual joy necessarily turns to carnal pleasures." The same is true of societies as it is of individuals. When "God is dead," idols must be worshiped, for man is innately a worshiper. When true joy dies, false joys must be believed in. We are addicts. That's the only explanation for the amazing fact that the whole human race idiotically tries the same experiment over and over again, with endless little variations, even though it has failed every single time, billions and billions of times: the experiment of idolatry, of hoping to find happiness, joy, and fulfillment, and adequate and final meaning in this world, trying to find the *summum bonum* in the creature rather than in the Creator. In light of the dismal track record of this vehicle, it is amazing that we keep gassing it up and putting it on the road again. It is more than amazing; it is insanity. The human race is spiritually insane. That is what the shocking doctrine of original sin means. It is shocking to us only because we are standing on our heads again, just as with the paradox of progress.

True joy is significance, false joy is power. True joy is finding truth and choosing goodness and creating beauty. False joy is fabricating ideologies and creating one's own values, and buying beauty. True joy is smelling the rose, false joy is plucking and possessing it.

Western civilization began to worship power when it began to doubt significance. The reason Lewis and Chesterton and Williams and Tolkien fascinate readers so much is that fundamentally they still live in the medieval world, a world chock full of built-in, God-designed significance. That's why they all think analogically, sacramentally, imagistically. For them, everything means something beyond itself. Everything is not only a thing, but a sign, full of significance. Modernity, confining itself to the scientific method as the model for knowing reality, deliberately induces in itself what Lewis calls a dog-like state of mind, full of facts and empty of significance. Point to your dog's food and he will sniff your finger. Show a baby a book and he will try to eat it rather than read it. Show a modern a lion and he will try to tame it and make money out of it in a circus, and smile superiorly at the quaint old medievals who saw it as the king of beasts and the natural symbol in the animal kingdom of the great King of Kings.

That's also why Tom Howard is so fascinating, especially in *Chance or the Dance?*

That's also why modern Scripture scholars tend to be either fundamentalist literalists or modernist demythologizers: neither side sees that an event like the resurrection can be both a literal historical fact and a sign or symbol. The words man makes are signs that point to things beyond themselves; but the things God makes are also signs. The whole world points beyond itself. But the whole modern mind has lost this sign-reading dimension of consciousness. Even Christians have to strain to see it. We have lost the very powerful and all-pervasive sense of significance; therefore we must replace it with science (i.e., factual knowledge) and technology (i.e., power).

At the far end of this loss of significance lies deconstructionism, which denies that even words have significance, intentionality, or a meaning that points beyond themselves. Archibald MacLeish says, "A poem must be palpable and mute, like globed fruit . . . a poem must not mean, but be." If this means what it seems to mean, it is proto-deconstructionism, linguistic nihilism, and the beginning of the end — the end of a human history and consciousness that begins with "In the beginning was the Word." Nietzsche wrote, sagely, "We [i.e., atheists] are not done with God until we are done with grammar." It looks like we are now beginning to be done with grammar. The next step can be clearly seen by reading the apotheosis of *That Hideous Strength*, the Babel scene, or its original in Genesis 11 and Revelation 18. The ancient Tower of Babel story in Genesis and the apocalyptic fall of Babylon prophesied in Revelation are the spiritual meaning of modernity. These two chapters are mirrors, reflecting each other and ourselves.

After taking so much time considering diagnosis, we now turn to make a very quick prognosis and prescription, the last two of our four steps in our spiritual medical analysis of Western civilization.

The diagnosis was very bad news indeed. I wish it were not. Honestly, I do not enjoy playing the part of the prophet of doom. Like most Americans, I like to be liked, and the messenger of bad news is seldom liked. Do you like your dentist when he says your roots are decayed? I fear many of you will remember only one thing from this essay years hence: Kreeft is a Puddleglum. Doom and gloom loom on his horizon.

Actually, I *am* a Puddleglum. The Boston Red Sox have taught me that Calvinistic, New England wisdom. Yet my prognosis is surprisingly optimistic. For seven reasons, I will not pronounce the patient dead yet, or even terminal.

First, ignorance. No one knows the future but God.

Second, free will. Repentence, turning back, has happened in history and can happen again. If the liberal claims to have a bright crystal ball, the traditionalist shouldn't claim to have a dark one, but none at all. The liberal believes in maximal external freedom because he does not really believe in the primary internal freedom, free will, and the moral responsibility that goes with it, a responsibility that extends even to our eternal destiny. We who believe in free will must never despair of the salvation of any soul (remember the thief on the cross) or any society (remember ancient Israel). As my favorite saint, Thomas More, put it, "The times are never so bad but that a good man can live in them."

Third, there is the "skin of our teeth" principle. Humanity always seems to survive by the skin of its teeth (to use the point and title of an old Thornton Wilder play). If any one of a thousand chances had gone just slightly the other way, none of us would be here now. If temperature of the primeval fireball had been a trillionth of a degree hotter or colder three seconds after the Big Bang, no life could ever have evolved anywhere in the universe. If the cosmic rays had not bombarded the primeval slime at just the right angle, protein molecules could never have come out of the stew. If Europe had not discovered ale before the Black Death polluted the water supply, most of our ancestors would have died. If Hitler had gotten the atom bomb, he would have destroyed the world. If your grandfather hadn't one day turned his head right instead of left and noticed your grandmother on the trolley, he would never have dated her, married her, and begat your father. If an Egyptian tailor hadn't cheated on the threads of Joseph's mantle, Potiphar's wife would never have been able to tear it, present it as evidence to Potiphar that Joseph attacked her, gotten him thrown into prison, and let him be in a position to interpret Pharaoh's dream, win his confidence, advise him to store seven years of grain, and save his family, the seventy original Jews, from whom Jesus came. We owe our salvation to a cheap Egyptian tailor.

Fourth, there is the rebound principle. After each night, a day. After each trough, a wave. Eclipses end. Communism is dying. Bad things die. American decadence will die. If necessary, America will die too. Diseases run their course. If our civilization is doomed, mankind is not — not until the end of the world, and that's the happiest event of all, the coming of our Bridegroom, Maranatha!

Fifth, the church is now the counterculture, not the culture, not the fat-cat establishment; North Vietnam, not South Vietnam; a catacomb church, not a Constantinian church. The church is thriving in every place she is persecuted — Poland, Lithuania, eastern Germany,

China. She is sick only where she is established: England, western Germany, Holland, Scandanivia. What an exciting change of battle plans our General is now overseeing: from defense to offense! We are now spies, guerillas. We are the barbarians at the gates.

Sixth, the church *will* win. That is guaranteed, by the only absolutely trustworthy guaranteer there is. If we only remember where our true country lies, and our true citizenship, we are absolutely certain of victory. All who seek Christ find Him.

Seventh, the strongest force in history is not man's sin but God's grace. "Where sin abounded, grace did much more abound" (Rom. 5:20). God can't lose. Othello can lose to Iago but Shakespeare can't lose. God is our Shakespeare. History is His story. Identify with our Author and in the end you can't lose either.

Finally, the prescription: what shall we do? How shall we fight the good fight? What are our marching orders as we prepare for Armageddon, or Marathon, or Waterloo?

Four answers come to mind, four practical principles, four prescriptions.

First, be countercultural. Like the Bible. Like the early church. Like Augustine's *City of God.* Like Jesus. "Be not conformed to this world, but be transformed by the renewing of your minds." Be a nut, a fanatic, a wierdo. Was it ever said of the early Christians that they were "cool," or "with it"? Or, to use exact adult equivalents, that they were "appropriate" or "acceptable"? No, here's what the world said: "These that have turned the world upside down have come here" (Acts 17:6). Let's turn the world upside down, for it's standing on its head, with its eyes in the mud and its feet kicking up in rebellion at the heavens. (Sorry, Chesterton, that's about the twentieth image I stole from you. Perhaps this confession will work the good penance of making more good thieves of your goods.)

Second, be ready. Be ready for battle, for we are at war. Edie Galbraith writes, in a letter to the *National Catholic Register,* "I'm getting tired of constantly praying for peace. What's wrong with praying for *victory* once in awhile? We belong to the church militant; we're engaged in a battle. The battle is with the powers of darkness. Since there is never any shortage of darkness, I think we should be allowed to pray for the grace to be victorious."

What difference does it make when you think you're at war? You get a sense of perspective. A matter of life and death appears as it is:

as a matter of life and death. Trivia appears as it is: trivia. No one complains that the beds are lumpy on a battlefield. No one even bleats about "sexual needs" when live bullets are whistling past the ears.

Third, be ready for the end. For we may well be very near the end. Passionate, anxious, expectant longing for the end, for the return of the Lord, was the high octane fuel of the early church. We have watered down the fuel today.

I do not think we need to make arrogant and foolish predictions in order to say "Maranatha" with an exclamation point. A good third baseman need not predict that the next pitch will be hit to him as a screaming line drive in order to be prepared for one. Let us be alert.

Alertness is not worry. Worry drains your energy; alertness conserves it, because it is calm, not agitated. Deadly calm, in the face of a matter of life or death, especially spiritual life or death. For the war we are all in, like it or not, is the war between heaven and hell, and at stake are human souls.

Finally, for this greatest of all wars we must use the greatest of all weapons, the strongest power that is.

Our enemies are supernatural, of course, but we also have natural, concrete, human enemies, those who are doing Satan's work, consciously or unconsciously, as we try to do Christ's, those who passionately hate us and want to kill us, i.e., destroy the church and make our souls like theirs. What is our strongest weapon against them?

There is one that is guaranteed to defeat them, and we alone have it. Their weapon is hate, ours is love. God's love. Agape. We can defeat our enemies by making them our friends, by loving them to death. It may take forever. But love never ends, never gives up. Not even when it sees Calvary. And once it has seen that, everything else is trivial, including the decadence of Western civilization.

In Defense of Permanent Truth and Value

John A. Sims

T. S. Eliot coined the term "Permanent Things" in reference to the enduring standards that in times past constituted the essence of our Western civilization. An impressive number of Anglo-Christians have mourned the loss of these standards and voiced the fear that their loss portends grave consequences for the future of our civilization. G. K. Chesterton, W. H. Auden, Charles Williams, Dorothy L. Sayers, and J. R. R. Tolkien joined Eliot and C. S. Lewis in a warning chorus during the first half of this century. Lewis's interest in the Permanent Things was conspicuously present in all of his writings, but his concern for the preservation of the permanent truths and values that had sustained Western civilization was carefully focused in the inaugural address he gave at Cambridge in 1955.

Magdalene College at Cambridge, Oxford's old rival, recognizing Lewis's important contribution to the field of English literary history and criticism, honored him in 1955 with a chair in medieval and Renaissance literature.[1] In his inaugural lecture Lewis described himself as "A Man of the Old West." He was, no doubt, thinking primarily of his work as a literary critic, but he was also addressing the broader commitment he had to the overarching standards of Western civilization that were quickly disappearing. Lewis's approach to literature was to take it on its own terms.

---

1. It is common knowledge that Lewis was passed over for a professorship at Oxford because of his Christian books. Many of his colleagues who did not share his faith were critical of his spending so much time on writings outside of his academic specialty. Even some of his friends expressed disapproval with what they considered his "evangelistic" style.

He did not believe that literature should be read from the perspective of a modern person's responses. "One thing I know," Lewis said, "I'd give a great deal to hear any ancient Athenian, even a stupid one, talking about Greek tragedy. He would know in his bones so much that we seek in vain."[2] Lewis's objective as a critic was not to be creative, or to add his interpretation, but to read a text as a native.

The "old dinosaur," as he called himself, desired nothing more than to stand before the modern world as that Athenian might stand — as a native who understood and appreciated the old realities. Lewis was very much aware that he was living in a new era, a post-Christian era that was radically different from the Christian and even the pre-Christian paganism of the past. That which separated the Christian from the post-Christian was more radical than that which separated Christians from pagans. "The gap between those who worshipped different gods is not so wide," Lewis argued, "as that between those who worship and those who don't."[3] Both pagans and Christians were at least open to supernatural forces.

The post-Christian had also discarded the assumption that he is fallen and in need of redemption. He confesses no belief in timeless values and moral absolutes. Consequently, there is nothing to worship but himself and the works of his own hands. He stands, as it were, as a lonely individual before an impersonal universe that has no purpose or meaning apart from that which he creates.

Lewis had no interest in merely idealizing the past. "Our ancestors," he admitted, "were cruel, lecherous, greedy and stupid — like ourselves . . . but was civilization often in serious danger of disappearing?"[4] No, he answered, but now it is. The risk of its moral and spiritual collapse is more imminent because the foundations that had supported our civilization had been eroded. The preservation of Western civilization was actually not Lewis's supreme interest. That was a secondary interest. For civilization to be safe, he knew that it must be subject to the permanent truths and values that undergird the Christian worldview, but to make civilization supreme is to make it vulnerable.[5] The safest thing for Western man would be to "seek first the kingdom of God and His righteousness" (Matthew 6:33).

2. C. S. Lewis, "The Great Divide," *Christian History* 4, no. 3 (1985): 32.
3. Ibid.
4. Peter Kreeft, "Western Civilization at The Crossroads," *Christian History* 4, no. 3 (1985): 26.
5. Ibid.

The changes that had altered the public mind about the Permanent Things in the past one hundred years were disturbing because they represented a move away from the truths and values of the kingdom of God. Any kingdom whose beliefs and values stand in conflict with the kingdom of God should not expect to stand. Augustine argued this point many centuries ago in *The City of God,* and in principle, Lewis fully agreed. It is indeed frightful to live in a world where the Permanent Things have been forsaken in favor of one in which everything is believed to be in a state of flux, where there is nothing more permanent to live for than what one "approves of" or "feels good about."

Do changeless, Permanent Things actually exist? Is there anything that remains constant? This age-old question preoccupied the ancient Greeks and continues to engage serious thinkers today. It is a very significant matter. What one believes about the existence of Permanent Things largely determines what one believes about the nature of truth and value. And what one believes about truth and value influences the way one chooses to live. It is much more than an abstract speculative question.

Throughout most of Western history the existence of Permanent Things was assumed; today, it is not. What was once the prevailing conviction among educated Western persons has, in modern times, become a "dead option" for most intellectuals. It has been taken over, Lewis believed, by the twin "myths" of evolutionism and historicism.[6]

Like the ancients, modern humanity lives by its myths. Lewis uses the term "myth" here to refer to a picture of reality that has resulted from the imagination and not from reason. He was convinced that evolutionism has been the great imaginative myth of the nineteenth and twentieth centuries. The idea found widespread expression in Romantic literature and music some time before Darwin's *Origin of the Species* in 1859.[7] The imagination of Western humanity had been prepared for evolutionism some time before its appearance in the field of science. When biological evolution established itself as scientific orthodoxy, the concept became even more marketable to other disciplines and soon found acceptance in the popular mind.[8]

Lewis was careful to distinguish the theory of evolution, held by

6. *Christian Reflections,* ed. Walter Hooper (Grand Rapids, Mich.: Eerdmans, 1967), 82-93, 100-113.

7. Ibid., 84, 90.

8. Ibid., 90-93.

biologists, from accepted popular notions about evolutionism or developmentalism. The biologist holds to evolution as a scientific hypothesis on the same grounds as he does any other hypothesis: it can account for more facts with fewer assumptions. Whether that hypothesis is true or not, it does not presume to be anything more than a hypothesis and it certainly cannot become a cosmic, metaphysical, or eschatological statement. On the mythical level, on the other hand, that is precisely what evolutionism becomes. As a scientific theory, evolution simply tries to explain changes within organic life on this planet. In the imaginative popular mind, however, it is assumed that changes imply improvement, that things are moving "onwards and upwards." What starts out as a tentative theory becomes a "factual" statement about progress on a cosmic scale:

> Having first turned what was a theory of change into a theory of improvement, it then makes this a cosmic theory. Not merely terrestrial organisms but everything is moving "upwards and onwards." Reason has "evolved" out of instinct, virtue out of complexes, poetry out of erotic howls and grunts, civilization out of savagery, the organic out of inorganic, the solar system out of some sidereal soup or traffic block. And conversely, reason, virtue, art and civilization as we now know them are only the crude or embryonic beginnings of far better things — perhaps Deity itself — in the remote future. For in the Myth, "Evolution" (as the Myth understands it) is the formula of all existence. . . . To those brought up on the Myth nothing seems more normal, more natural, more plausible, than that chaos should turn into order, death into life, ignorance into knowledge. And with this we reach the full-blown Myth. It is one of the most moving and satisfying world dramas which have ever been imagined.[9]

Being a romantic, Lewis found the myth enchanting. Though he spoke of the myth as something to be debunked and buried, he doubted that its popularity with the masses could be dispelled.[10] In the folk imagination, evolutionism is a convenient and plausible explanation of the movement of things on the cosmic scale. Everything is becoming something else, the later stages always being superior to the earlier ones. It is always a matter of the "developed" evolving from the "un-

9. Ibid., 86.
10. Ibid., 90-93.

developed," never a matter of conforming to some permanent truth or value. Love comes out of lust, virtue out of instinct. In this way one can "debunk" the respectable things by passing them off as improvements. On the other hand, disrespectable things never seem bad because they are developing into better things. Vice is only undeveloped virtue, egoism only undeveloped altruism. A little more time (and a little more education) will take care of it. Ultimately, things are not totally different in kind, only in degree. On the moral level, then, sin is never quite as bad as it seems, and righteousness never as good. There is no basis for a real qualitative difference between them.

Political parties have a stake in the myth because they all claim to represent what is positive and good in a changing society. Progressive politics never concentrates on conserving the good; it concentrates on changing things for the better in the future. Evolutionism is also an economic ally of those who manufacture and sell us goods and provide our services. Popular evolutionism suits them fine. Nothing is expected to last, and good workmanship can be minimized. Obsolescence is not only natural, it can be planned. The old models will always be superceded. The latest fashions are always superior. Consumerism is the order of the day. As Lewis noted sarcastically, in our time "sales resistance [had become] the modern sin against the Holy Ghost."[11]

Convinced that he has mastered Nature and become the controller of his own fate, modern man is ready to rule the galaxy. Lewis spoke disparagingly of modern man's vision for the future: "Eugenics have made certain that only demi-gods will now be born: psychoanalysis that none of them will lose or smirch his divinity: economics that they shall have to hand all that demi-gods require. Man has ascended his throne. Man has become God."[12]

Lewis admitted that he too felt the enchantment of the myth. The only part of him the myth did not appeal to, he noted, was his reason. It was on rational grounds that he challenged its validity.

The self-contradiction in the myth is its Achilles' heel. It asks one to accept the reasonableness of the myth while claiming that reason itself is the product of a mindless process. A materialistic evolutionary account of human thought cannot elevate it above a zoological fact about *Homo sapiens*. All that one can talk about from this perspective

11. Ibid., 92.
12. Ibid., 88.

is how the brain works. There is no basis in evolutionism for talking about a nonhuman universal reality that gives validity to our logic, including, ironically the logic of the "myth."

This irrationalism is fatal to the physical sciences, upon which the "myth" largely rests, because they depend upon the validity of inference. However, if logical inferences cannot be trusted, then the sciences themselves are groundless. Lewis explained:

> The real sciences cannot be accepted for a moment unless rational inferences are valid: for every science claims to be a series of inferences from observed facts. . . . Unless you start by believing that reality in the remotest space and the remotest time rigidly obeys the laws of logic, you can have no ground for believing in any astronomy, any biology, any paleontology, any archeology. To reach the positions held by the real scientists — which are then taken over by the Myth — you must — in fact, treat reason as an absolute. But at the same time the Myth asks me to believe that reason is simply the unforeseen and unintended by-product of its endless and aimless becoming. The content of the Myth thus knocks from under me the only ground on which I could possibly believe the Myth to be true.[13]

Lewis argued that we must give up talking about reason as something merely human. Reason is not something shut up in our heads, he said. It is something "out there," something permanent outside us that exists as an objective reality. We do not read rationality into an irrational universe; rather, our human knowledge is possible because God created us capable of responding to a rationality that saturates the universe.

> If a Brute and Blackguard made the world, then he also made our minds. If he made our minds, he also made the standard in them whereby we judge him to be a Brute and Blackguard. And how can we trust a standard which comes from such a brutal and blackguardly source? If we reject him, we ought to reject all his works. But one of his works is this very moral standard by which we reject him. If we accept this standard then we are really implying that he is not a Brute and Blackguard. If we reject it, then we have thrown away the only instrument by which we can condemn him. Heroic anti-theism thus has a contradiction in its center. You must trust the universe in one

13. Ibid., 89.

respect in order to condemn it in every other. What happens to our sense of values is, in fact, exactly what happens to our logic. If it is a purely human sense of values — a biological by-product in a particular species with no relevance to reality — then we cannot, having once realized this, continue to use it as the ground for what are meant to be serious criticisms of the nature of things.[14]

The point that Lewis is making, of course, is that neither our minds nor our moral standards are alien to reality. We can reason and we have moral standards because there is an objective truth and an objective standard of morality in the universe. Otherwise, all of our thoughts and all of our moral standards would be worthless. Lewis argued for standards of beauty on the same grounds. "There is no reason why our reaction to a beautiful landscape should not be the response, however humanly blurred and partial, to a something that is really there."[15]

The second aspect of the modern myth, historicism, is simply an extension of evolutionary thought into the realm of history. Again, Lewis was careful not to impugn a legitimate discipline. He distinguished the noble discipline of history from the "fatal pseudo-philosophy" he called historicism.

Lewis characterized historicism as the tendency on the part of theologians, philosophers, politicians, and others to interpret the historical process on the basis of their own learning or genius and to use evolutionism as their principle of interpretation. He was not opposed to finding a "meaning" in history, but he had no confidence in humanity's natural ability to read the meaning of the process out of the process itself. The meaning of history had to come from "beyond history."

Those who stare too long at the flux of history tend to see vague patterns, "like pictures in the fire,"[16] Lewis noted. But the well-defined plot of history cannot be known through speculative imagination. In the modern world, he believed, there is the tendency to adopt some "grand theory" of history and then religiously follow its path. The pantheistic thought of Hegel and the materialistic premises of Karl Marx are good examples of grand theories that have seemed promising and attractive to masses of people in the past one hundred years. Many have

14. Ibid., 66, 67.
15. Ibid., 71.
16. Ibid., 105.

followed these theories of history as one would follow a religion, trusting that world history was moving in the direction of improvement for humankind — trusting in them as one would some kind of eschatological hope. The fatal assumption has always been that the "good" emerges out of the flux of history instead of breaking into history.

Progressivism, or belief in change for the better, is not supported by the well-defined plot of the Christian story that pivots on Creation, the Fall, Redemption, and Judgment. The unchanging truth about man that we know from "beyond" history is that he is a sinner in need of redemption. No amount of change in man's environment or in his accidental qualities can alter that fact about his essence. "Whatever we have been," Lewis believed, "we are still."[17] The only two events that have ever changed man's essence are the Fall and Redemption.[18]

Lewis's emphasis upon objective truth and value was not intended to suggest that all subjective desires are suspect or that they are foreign to Christianity. There is, Lewis insisted, something within a person that says, "I want God," no less than hunger saying, "I want food," or thirst saying, "I want water." Our knowledge of God is more than a matter of raw truth. It is our heart's deepest yearning to know Him as one knows a person. We yearn to enjoy Him, to experience His presence.[19]

Subjective feelings and emotions are, in fact, closely connected to our beliefs about what is true. They are tandem experiences. It is altogether normal, for example, for a person to feel the emotion of gratitude when that person has been blessed by a benefactor. It would be unreasonable not to feel grateful. Similarly, one would expect to feel anger toward a gross injustice. The lack of it would indicate an insensitivity to the moral order that governs us. Virtues like love, joy, and peace have their emotional expression, but these emotions or subjective experiences are tied to an independent objective reality. When appropriate emotions are properly connected to what is true, stable virtues and experiences will result. Both are important to each other. Sound theology and proper beliefs shape our emotions, and proper emotions, in turn, help to establish our theology.

17. C. S. Lewis, *The Allegory of Love: A Study in Medieval Tradition* (New York: Oxford University Press, 1936), 1.

18. Kreeft, 26.

19. Jerry Root, "Following That Bright Blur," *Christian History* 4, no. 3 (1985): 27.

Lewis had no difficulty with this kind of subjectivity. It was, in fact, very important to him. One will remember that he regarded unfulfilled desires as indicators from experience that there is a realm of fulfillment beyond this world. The kind of subjectivity that Lewis rejected is the kind that disconnected emotions and desires from the Tao, the objective source of all meaning and value.[20] Instead of focusing on the Tao and allowing proper emotions and values to follow from the discovery of the object and its meaning, the subjectivist focuses on the emotions themselves and tries to create meaning and value out of his own subjectivity. Lewis illustrated the fallacy from his own experience:

> I myself do not enjoy the society of small children: because I speak from within the *Tao*, I recognize this as a defect in myself — just as a man may have to recognize that he is tone deaf or color blind. And because our approvals and disapprovals are thus recognitions of objective value or responses to an objective order, therefore emotional states can be in harmony with reason (when we feel liking for what ought to be approved) or out of harmony with reason (when we perceive that liking is due but cannot feel it). No emotion is, in itself, a judgment: in that sense all emotions and sentiments are alogical.
>
> But they can be reasonable or unreasonable as they conform to Reason or fail to conform. The heart never takes the place of the head: but it can, and should, obey it. . . .[21]

The proper relation between truth and subjectivity is not an insignificant matter. What is at stake in the relation is the doctrine of objective truth and value. To reject that relationship, Lewis reminded us, is to reject the only basis we have for saying that some attitudes are really true while others are false. Similarly, there is no basis for value apart from permanent standards. "The human mind," Lewis noted, "has no more power of inventing a new value than of imagining a new primary color, or indeed, of creating a new sun and a new sky for it to move in."[22] Once objective value has been given up, there is nothing to take

20. Lewis used the Chinese concept of the Tao to refer to the reality beyond all predicates, that which provides the basis for the doctrine of objective value — regardless of its form (Platonic, Aristotelian, Stoic, Oriental, or Christian). He rejected the notion of legitimate emotions unrelated to the Tao itself.

21. C. S. Lewis, *The Abolition of Man* (New York: Macmillan, 1973), 29, 30.

22. Ibid., 56, 57.

its place but one's "feelings." And they are the feelings that we have been conditioned to have.

The best that one can hope for when truth and objective reality have been abandoned is the gratification of one's own subjectivity and/or dependence upon practical results. This has been amply illustrated in virtually every artistic and scientific field of endeavor in the twentieth century. Existentialism and pragmatism, for example, are philosophical expressions of the subjectivist and utilitarian climate that permeates our culture. Its political manifestation is embodied in all attempts to disassociate political power from that which is true and right and attach it instead to successful propaganda. This attitude has, of course, not been restricted to any one political party or movement. It has been readily adopted by both wings on the political spectrum. Subjectivism finds its religious expression among those who value religion primarily for its usefulness[23] or because religion helps them "feel better." Religionists of this sort, Lewis noted, "only want to know if it will be comforting, or 'inspiring,' or socially useful."

Lewis traced the influence of subjectivity on science, education, and ethics in somewhat greater detail. These influences are traced in the sections that follow.

Modern technology was meant to represent man's ultimate triumph over nature. It would usher in a better and happier life for all. As it turns out, however, man's power over nature has really become a means of exercising power over other men by using nature as an instrument. The irony of the "magician's bargain" is nowhere better illustrated than in the field of applied science. The proverbial "magician's bargain" involves a would-be magician's willingness to give up his soul in return for magical powers. The fateful end of the bargain is the realization that the conferred power never really belongs to the magician but, in fact, enslaves him. That through which he meant to conquer, in the end, conquers him. Lewis alluded to the contraceptive as an example of this paradox: "As regards contraceptives," he noted, "there is a paradoxical, negative sense in which all possible future generations are the patients or subjects of a power wielded by those already alive. By contraception simply, they are denied existence; by contraception used as a means of selective breeding, they are, without their concurring voice, made to be

---

23. They are not interested in the question of truth or falsehood, of whether or not Christianity's affirmations are objectively true.

what one generation, for its own reasons, may choose to prefer."[24] In the same paradoxical way, he noted, man becomes the target for his own bombs and the victim of his own propaganda. The final stage comes, however, with man's surrender of himself:

> The final stage is come when Man by eugenics, by pre-natal conditioning, and by an education and propaganda based on a perfect applied psychology, has obtained full control over himself. Human nature will be the last part of Nature to surrender to Man. The battle will then be won. We shall . . . be henceforth free to make our species whatever we wish it to be. The battle will indeed be won. But, who precisely, will have won it?[25]

About the developments in the field of education Lewis was particularly concerned. These developments too represented acts of self-surrender. In the old system, he noted, there was the Tao, the overarching standard of truth and value to which both student and teacher were expected to conform. There was no liberty to depart from it:

> They [the old teachers] did not cut some men to some pattern they had chosen. They handed on what they had received: they initiated the young neophyte into the mysteries of humanity which over-arched him and them alike. It was but old birds teaching young birds to fly.[26]

When the Tao has been surrendered, however, there are no overarching truths and values. The only values are those of the conditioners. The conditioned are the victims of whatever artificial Tao the Conditioners have chosen. The Conditioners, by necessity, become the Motivators and Managers. Their role is to convince the conditioned that he ought to like what they say and that he ought to use the methods they suggest in order to achieve it. In a classic statement from *The Abolition of Man*, Lewis summarized the profound difference between the old attitude and the new:

> For the wise men of old the cardinal problem had been how to conform the soul to reality, and the solution had been knowledge, self-discipline, and virtue. For magic and applied science alike the

24. Lewis, *The Abolition of Man*, 68.
25. Ibid., 72.
26. Ibid., 74.

problem is how to subdue reality to the wishes of men: the salvation is the technique; and both, in the practice of this technology, are ready to do things hitherto regarded as disgusting and impious. . . .[27]

It is not that men cannot be happy outside the Tao. They can. It does not necessarily mean that they will be evil. They may not. The tragedy is that they cease to be human at all. They become specimens, artifacts. His attempt to conquer nature, which in the final analysis includes himself, results in his own abolition.

Ethics for those in pre-modern times did not necessarily produce virtuous people. To believe in a realm of objective truth and value does not of itself produce moral character. It is not enough to know the truth; we should live according to the truth. It is not enough to know the good; we are *to be* good. The justification of a virtue does not itself enable one to be virtuous. Virtuous living requires the kind of trained habit in which God is graciously willing to nurture us, but we must also be willing to practice. Moral character is more than a sudden impulse or a passing inclination. It is a moral disposition to choose and do what is right, and this disposition is the product of something more than a single factor in a person's life. In pre-modern times, developing moral character, Lewis believed, was somewhat analogous to becoming a good tennis player:

> Someone who is not a good tennis player may now and then make a good shot. What you mean by a good player is the man whose eye and muscles and nerves have been so trained by making innumerable good shots that they can now be relied on. They have a certain tone or quality which is there even when he is not playing. Just as a mathematician's mind has a certain habit and outlook which is there even when he is not doing mathematics. In the same way a man who perseveres in doing just actions gets in the end a certain quality of character. It is that quality rather than the particular actions which we mean when we talk of "virtue."[28]

Moral character was not so much a matter of our head winning out over our instincts or vice versa, but of both being ruled by what Lewis called the middle element, the "chest." The instincts or impulses

27. Ibid., 88.
28. C. S. Lewis, *Mere Christianity* (New York: Macmillan, 1971), 77.

that God has given us are not in themselves good or evil. They must be cultivated, through trained habit, into stable sentiments. Without his natural instincts man is mere spirit. Without his intellect he is mere animal. Man was not meant to be ruled entirely by his head, as the ancient Greeks supposed, or by his stomach — as many moderns seemingly believe. The Christian view, Lewis believed, is that both should be ruled by the middle element of moral discipline. Men without moral discipline are like men without chests.

"Strictly speaking," Lewis declared, "there are no such things as good and bad impulses. Think of . . . a piano. It has not got two kinds of notes on it, the 'right' notes and the 'wrong' ones. Every single note is right at one time and wrong at another. The Moral Law is not any one instinct or any set of instincts: it is something which makes a kind of tune (the tune we call goodness or right conduct) by directing the instincts."[29] Nature does not deal us all the same hand. Our instincts differ. Some have better raw material than others; some through heredity, others through training and environment. The point is that we must all play, as best we can, the hand that we have been dealt. God does not judge us on the basis of raw material but on the basis of the choices we make.

The choices we make are either making us into more "heavenly" or more "hellish" creatures. And the more heavenly we become the better we see our own badness and our need for grace. "You can understand the nature of drunkenness," Lewis noted, "when you are sober, not when you are drunk. Good people know about both good and evil: bad people do not know about either."[30]

Lewis's understanding of moral development was not one that disengaged nature from grace. Nor was it one that excluded human will and reason from the Divine Initiative. In *The Four Loves* Lewis compared the processes of moral growth to that of a garden:

> It is not disparagement to a garden to say that it will not fence and weed itself, nor prune its own fruit trees, nor roll and cut its own lawns. A garden is a good thing but that is not the sort of goodness it has. It will remain a garden, as distinct from a wilderness, only if someone does all these things to it. Its real glory is of quite a different

29. Ibid., 23.
30. Ibid., 87.

kind. The very fact that it needs constant weeding and pruning bears witness to that glory. It teems with life. It glows with colour and smells like heaven and puts forward at every hour of a summer day beauties which man could never have created and could not even, on his own resources, have imagined. If you want to see the difference between its contribution and the gardener's, put the commonest weed it grows side by side with his hoes, rakes, shears, and packet of weed killer; you have put beauty, energy, fecundity beside dead, sterile things. Just so, our decency and common sense show grey and deathlike beside the geniality of love. And when the garden is in its full glory the gardener's contributions to that glory will still have been in a sense paltry compared with those of nature. Without life springing from the earth, without rain, light and heat descending from the sky, he could do nothing. When he has done all, he has merely encouraged here and discouraged there, powers and beauties that have a different source. But his share, though small, is indispensable and laborious. When God planted a garden He set a man over it and set the man under Himself. When He planted the garden of our nature and caused the flowering, fruiting loves to grow there, He set our will to "dress" them. Compared with them it is dry and cold. And unless His grace comes down, like the rain and the sunshine, we shall use this tool to little purpose. But its laborious — and largely negative — services are indispensable. If they were needed when the garden was still paradisal, how much more now when the soil has gone sour and the worst weeds seem to thrive on it best? But heaven forbid we should work in the spirit of prigs and Stoics. While we hack and prune we know very well that what we are hacking and pruning is big with a splendour and vitality which our rational will could never of itself have supplied. To liberate that splendour, to let it become fully what it is trying to be, to have tall trees instead of scrubby tangles, and sweet apples instead of crabs, is part of our purpose.[31]

The problem with the modern ethical perspective is that it has capitulated to what men like rather than what they ought to like. Those who stand outside the Tao can only regard the "ought" as some kind of subjective feeling. They seek to debunk objective truth and value and then expect to continue on as usual under a full head of "drive"

---

31. C. S. Lewis, *The Four Loves* (New York: Harcourt, Brace, Jovanovich, 1960), 163-65.

and "creativity." The conditioners, or propagandists, become the man-molders, and the result is men without chests — men without moral discipline. "In a sort of ghastly simplicity," Lewis noted, "we remove the organ [objective value] and demand the function. We make men without chests and expect of them virtue and enterprise. We laugh at honour and are shocked to find traitors in our midst. We castrate and bid the geldings be fruitful."[32]

Lewis agreed with Aristotle who said that the "aim of education is to make the pupil like and dislike what he ought." The task is to train one's habits so that appropriate responses will follow, regardless of the actions of others. One must be true to his own nature as that nature is defined by the Tao. The difference between the old and the new education is that the one was interested in propagation, the other in propaganda. "Where the old initiated," Lewis said, "the new merely 'conditions.' The old dealt with its pupils as grown birds deal with young birds when they teach them to fly: the new deals with them more as the poultry-keeper deals with young birds — making them thus or thus for purpose of which the birds know nothing."[33]

The new education, with its appeal to "democratic" feelings and values, is undoubtedly more appealing to those who have been conditioned to value individuality so highly. But Lewis doubted that such feelings and values could continue to preserve democracy. He wrote:

> Beauty is not democratic; she reveals herself more to the few than to the many, more to the persistent and disciplined seekers than to the careless. Virtue is not democratic; she is achieved by those who pursue her more hotly than most men. Truth is not democratic; she demands special talents and special industry in those to whom she gives her favours. Political democracy is doomed if it tries to extend its demand for equality into these higher spheres. Ethical, intellectual, or aesthetic democracy is death.[34]

The concept of equality, Lewis believed, has no place in the world of the mind. He was not even sure that it could succeed as a social concept. An approach to education that forsakes the demands of ex-

32. Lewis, *The Abolition of Man*, 35.
33. Ibid., 33.
34. *Present Concerns: Essays by C. S. Lewis*, ed. Walter Hooper (New York: Harcourt, Brace, Jovanovich, 1986), 34.

cellence cannot continue to support true democracy. An inferiorly educated nation, he insisted, cannot survive indefinitely for "it can escape destruction only if its rivals and enemies are so obliging as to adopt the same system. A nation of dunces can be safe only in a world of dunces."[35]

Archimedes, intoxicated with the potential in the lever and the pulley, once announced that if he had a fixed fulcrum to work with he could move anything. "Give me a place to stand on," he said, "and I will move the world." Archimedes' enduring contribution to philosophy was his recognition of the fact that we must all have something permanent to stand on.

Lewis called himself a dinosaur, but his contemporaries found an uncanny relevance in his affirmation that there is something to stand on — a realm of Permanent Things that cannot be conditioned or relativized by the historical, the transitory, the individual. These were the realities that had attracted the Greek mind and sustained the overarching values of Western civilization until modern times.

Lewis never believed, however, that all truth exists in some abstract trans-historical realm. One will recall that it was the concrete demands of the Incarnate Jesus that pulled Lewis out of the comforts of abstract theism. After his conversion to Christianity and its Incarnational perspective, Lewis was never comfortable with either a Greek or a modern understanding of truth. In the one, the Greek, there was the tendency to remove truth from the concrete conditions of human experience. In the other, the modern, there is the tendency to restrict all truth and value to the relativities of history. Christianity, on the other hand, claims a standard of truth and goodness from beyond history but asserts that this truth has, in Jesus Christ, entered into history and the realm of human experience. Christian truth is not lost nor distorted by entering into the relativity of time. Christ alone is what gives permanent meaning to the flux of nature and history. This is, of course, the truth of the Incarnation.

We do not become more effective in this world by ceasing to think of the other world. On the contrary, we find both earthly and heavenly meaning when we begin with the heavenly perspective. The sense of eternity in what we do in the here-and-now is what gives perspective and value to the earthly task. We must never forget the importance of what we have been called to do now nor allow the mundaneness of

35. Ibid., 33.

everyday life to diminish the sacredness of ordinary tasks and relationships. In his well-known essay entitled, "The Weight of Glory," Lewis movingly reminds us of the future glory we anticipate, but he concludes by exhorting us to remember that

> the cross comes before the crown and tomorrow is a Monday morning. . . . It may be possible for each to think too much of his own potential glory hereafter; it is hardly possible for him to think too often or too deeply about that of his neighbor. The load, or weight, or burden of my neighbor's glory should be laid on my back. . . . It is a serious thing to remember that the dullest and most uninteresting person you can talk to may one day be a creature which you would be strongly tempted to worship, or else a horror and a corruption such as you now meet only in a nightmare. All day long we are, in some degree, helping each other to one or other of these destinations. It is in the light of these overwhelming possibilities, it is with the awe and the circumspection proper to them, that we should conduct all our dealings with one another, all friendships, all loves, all play, all politics. There are no *ordinary* people. You have never talked to a mere mortal. . . . It is immortals whom we joke with, work with, marry, snub, and exploit — immortal horrors or everlasting splendors. This does not mean that we are to be perpetually solemn. We must play. But our merriment must be of that kind (and it is, in fact, the merriest kind) which exists between people who have, from the outset, taken each other seriously — no flippancy, no superiority, no presumption. . . . Next to the Blessed Sacrament itself, your neighbor is the holiest object presented to your senses. If he is your Christian neighbor, he is holy in almost the same way, for in him also Christ *vere latitat* — the glorifier and the glorified, Glory Himself, is truly hidden.[36]

It is people, our neighbors whom we meet daily, who are permanent. Our highest calling in life is to help them reach that future glory for which they were created. Most of them will not find it in the lecture hall or even through the pulpit. Our Monday morning theology, our love, is more likely to lead them to faith than our expositions or

36. *The Weight of Glory and Other Essays*, ed. Walter Hooper (New York: Macmillan, 1965), 18, 19.

our arguments. The best service we can render to modern skeptics and the half-convinced is to help them find the company of those who care. In the company of those who care, they can more clearly see the truth for themselves.

"There Are No 'Trees' . . . Only This Elm": C. S. Lewis on the Scientific Method

Evan K. Gibson

Although C. S. Lewis was a specialist in English literature of the medieval and Renaissance periods, it is important to remember that his training in philosophy was as extensive as that in literature and that his first teaching at Oxford was in philosophy. So it is not surprising that when we look at his discussions of science, we find that his main interest is in its philosophical and religious implications.

He often shows an awareness of the progress of modern scientific thought and easily draws upon it for illustrations, even when discussing such an apparently unrelated subject as the Incarnation. Of the Incarnation he says in *The Problem of Pain*, "It has the seemingly arbitrary and idiosyncratic character which modern science is slowly teaching us to put up with in this wilful universe, where energy is made up in little parcels of a quantity no one could predict, where speed is not unlimited, where irreversible entropy gives time a real direction and the cosmos, no longer static or cyclic, moves like a drama from a real beginning to a real end. If any message from the core of reality ever were to reach us, we should expect to find in it just that unexpectedness, that willful dramatic anfractuosity which we find in the Christian faith."[1]

It is true that Lewis's critics have charged him with being opposed to science. And he recognized that his defense of the reality of objective value would be interpreted by some as an anti-scientific position. As he says in *The Abolition of Man*, "Nothing I can say will prevent some people from describing this lecture as an attack on science. I deny the charge, of

1. C. S. Lewis, *The Problem of Pain* (London: Geoffrey Bles, 1940), 13.

course: and real Natural Philosophers (there are some now alive) will perceive that in defending value I defend *inter alia* the value of knowledge, which must die like every other when its roots in the *Tao* are cut."[2]

The charge of hostility to science is justified if one includes as science all the extrapolations from scientific theories which the popular mind has generated. Lewis's attitude toward the theory of evolution is an example. For the hypothesis itself he shows an open mind. In "Modern Man and his Categories of Thought" he says: "With Darwinianism as a theorem in Biology I do not think a Christian need have any quarrel."[3] And in *The Problem of Pain* he discusses the fall of man but admits that we do not know exactly how creation occurred. Then he offers what he calls a legitimate guess. He speculates that "for long centuries God perfected the animal from which was to become the vehicle of humanity and the image of Himself. He gave it hands whose thumb could be applied to each of the fingers, and jaws and teeth and throat capable of articulation, and a brain sufficiently complex to execute all the material motions whereby rational thought is incarnated."[4] He says that this creature may have existed for long eons before it became a man. But in the fullness of time God gave it a new kind of consciousness. It could say "I" and "me" and could know God. We must remember that Lewis calls this picture a "guess." But it shows his sympathy with the idea that in the Lord's creation of man a day may have been thousands of years.

Again, in *Mere Christianity* he suggests that the new birth may be the "new step" in the evolutionary process. But, of the theory he adds this caveat, "though, of course, some educated people disbelieve it."[5] And in "The Funeral of a Great Myth," an ironic oration on the death of the popular fiction of "Life's" heroic struggle against the universe, he makes it clear that he is not attacking "the doctrine of Evolution as held by practising biologists" but the popular myth of developmentalism which implies that all things tend to improve. Of the doctrine itself, however, he does add as an aside, "It may be shown, by later biologists, to be a less satisfactory hypothesis than was hoped fifty years ago."[6]

2. C. S. Lewis, *The Abolition of Man* (London: Geoffrey Bles, 1946), 52.

3. C. S. Lewis, *Present Concerns* (New York: Harcourt Brace Jovanovich, 1986), 63.

4. *The Problem of Pain*, 65.

5. C. S. Lewis, *Mere Christianity* (London: Geoffrey Bles, 1952), 171.

6. C. S. Lewis, *Christian Reflections* (London: Geoffrey Bles, 1967), 83.

Although this tentative statement could hardly be called a prophecy, it is interesting that, according to a recent article by Stephen Gould, many biologists today are abandoning the gradualism of Lyell and Darwin for the once discredited theory of catastrophe as the best explanation of biologic change — for example, the claim of Nobel prize-winner Luis Alvarez that the dinosaurs were wiped out by a world-covering cloud of dust caused by an impacting asteroid.[7] In various references, however, Lewis does seem to suggest that something like the Darwinian hypothesis may have been the way that God created man. But whatever the process, the Creator was personally involved.

Turning from theories to principles, I would like to move to Lewis's view of basic scientific methods to show what Lewis sees as the limitations of the scientist's use of two tools — analysis and abstraction.

Concerning analysis, let us begin with the words of an eighteenth-century writer. "Last week I saw a woman flayed, and you will hardly believe how much it altered her person for the worse."[8] So wrote Jonathan Swift in *The Tale of the Tub,* where he observes that one of the eternal laws of nature is that she put her best furniture forward. The skinned cadaver is an ugly but perhaps fitting symbol of the ironic dean's conviction that analysis is not the road to reality.

Was C. S. Lewis a proponent of the skinned woman? That is, did he believe that the analytic method, which removes the surface and dissects the inner substance into its component parts, follows the best road to ultimate reality? In "The Seeing Eye" he points out that ordinary life is often regarded as a façade with a huge area out of sight behind it. And he says that if you listen to the physicists, you discover that the same is true of all things around us. "These tables and chairs, this magazine, the trees, clouds, and mountains are façades. Poke (scientifically) into them and you find the unimaginable structure of the atom. That is, in the long run you find mathematical formulas."[9]

But Lewis shows sympathy for Swift's concept that in appearances nature puts her best foot forward — that analysis is somehow a perversion of reality. In the article titled "Behind the Scenes" he observes that the backstage of a theater and the play proper might be used to contrast reality and appearance, but actually the play is the reality; the appear-

7. Stephen Gould, "An Asteroid to Die For," *Discover,* October 1989, 60-65.
8. Jonathan Swift, *The Tale of a Tub* (Oxford: Blackwell, 1957), 109.
9. *Christian Reflections,* 169.

ance is the thing. All the backstage "realities" exist for the play and are valueless without it.[10]

George MacDonald, Lewis's acknowledged mentor, discusses the appearance and analysis of nature in several places in his writings. Significantly, Lewis chooses a number of these for his collection titled *George MacDonald, an Anthology*. The Scottish writer says that the show of things, that is, appearances, is what God most cares for. As a mediator between God and man, nature through its appearances reveals deeper truths than can ever be accomplished through scientific discoveries. "It is through their show," he says, "not through their analysis, that we enter into their deepest truths." The face and form of a human body is the place where revelation dwells; its hidden secrets exist for its outside. "To know a primrose," he says, "is a higher thing than to know all the botany of it — just as to know Christ is an infinitely higher thing than to know all theology, all that is said about his person, or babbled about his work." He insists that he is not depreciating the labors of science, but pointing out that the gifts of nature are unspeakably more important. He admits the value of analysis, but says, "Analysis is well, as death is well."[11]

Elsewhere, in a delightful paragraph on water he asks, "Is oxygen-and-hydrogen the divine idea of water? . . . There is no water in oxygen and no water in hydrogen; it comes bubbling fresh from the imagination of the living God." Human science is the undoing, he says, of God's science because analysis always progresses backwards, away from the point where God's work culminates in revelation.[12]

Lewis's position on the question of the superiority of appearance or analysis is related to his conviction that nature must have a rational basis. He shows great respect for the reliability of logic in its relation to nature. He states, "When logic says a thing must be so, Nature always agrees."[13] In "The Funeral of a Great Myth" he says that all science is based on a series of inferences from observed facts. Science must believe that in the remotest space and time the laws of logic are obeyed.[14] And in "De Futilitate" he points out that inference is necessary for the

10. C. S. Lewis, *God in the Dock* (Grand Rapids, Mich.: Eerdmans, 1970), 248.

11. C. S. Lewis, *George MacDonald, an Anthology* (London: Geoffrey Bles, 1946), 69-70.

12. Ibid., 80-81.

13. *Christian Reflections*, 64.

14. Ibid., 89.

understanding of our existence: ". . . the material, or external world in general is an inferred world . . . therefore particular experiments far from taking us out of the magic circle of inference into some supposed direct contact with reality, are themselves evidential only as parts of that great inference."[15]

Lewis was convinced of the necessity of believing in the integrity of reason and insists that if human reasoning is not valid, no science can be true.[16] His main attack upon naturalism or philosophical materialism is that it destroys all hope of inference into the world of nature. If thoughts are only movements within a materialistic brain, they can have no relation to reality. An event among brain cells' thought can be neither true nor false. Such a philosophy proves that all proofs are nonsense.

Elsewhere he points out that if our standards of value are not from beyond the universe but only a product of this time-space-matter system, they are meaningless. If they (that is, our standards of value) are not "a light from beyond Nature whereby Nature can be judged, they are only the way in which anthropoids of our species feel when the atoms under our own skulls get into certain states — those states being produced by causes quite irrational, unhuman, and non-moral. . . . If our standards are derived from this meaningless universe they must be as meaningless as it."[17]

So Lewis concludes that the standards of value which give our life meaning must come from a reality beyond this material existence. Again from "De Futilitate": "We must then grant logic to the reality; we must, if we are to have any moral standards, grant it moral standards too. And there is really no reason why we should not do the same about standards of beauty. There is no reason why our reaction to a beautiful landscape should not be the response, however humanly blurred and partial, to something that is really there."[18]

Out of his insistence, then, upon the validity and otherworldiness of reason comes his doctrine of objective value — one of the main themes of *The Abolition of Man*. And so, if our reaction to beauty is a reaction to something that is really there, we have returned to the

15. Ibid., 62.
16. C. S. Lewis, *Miracles: A Preliminary Study* (New York: Macmillan, 1947), 26.
17. *Present Concerns*, 77.
18. *Christian Reflections*, 64.

question of the reliability of appearances in the affirmative answer and the conclusion that analysis is not necessarily the road to reality. Lewis does admit that it is a legitimate method, although whether the value derived is worth the cost is another matter.

In "Meditation in a Toolshed" he says that looking "at" a sunbeam (analysis) is not necessarily more true than looking "along" the sunbeam to that which it falls upon (appearance). Both the outer and inner may be true in different ways.[19] But his fear is that the analytical method is now so entrenched that it will destroy our confidence in the reality of the sense world around us. He says, almost wistfully, in *The Abolition of Man:* "Is it possible to imagine a new Natural Philosophy, continually conscious that the 'natural object' produced by analysis and abstraction is not reality but only a view, and always correcting the abstraction?" But he despairs of such a chimerical hope. "Perhaps I am asking impossibilities," he says. "Perhaps in the nature of things, analytical understanding must always be a basilisk which kills what it sees and sees only by killing."[20]

It is not surprising, then, that his discussions of literature and literary criticism emphasize the total impact rather than the significance of the parts. In *An Experiment in Criticism* he says that all art should be "received" rather than "used." One should not read great literature to "improve" oneself or to acquire culture. To value literature mainly for the reflections on life we draw from it or the morals which we see in it and approve of is an example of "using" rather than "receiving."[21]

To receive a literary work, our senses and imagination and various other abilities respond to a pattern invented by the writer. One should simply lay oneself open to the appearance — to whatever the piece has to offer. In fact, the judgment of literary quality can only be accomplished by taking the words seriously and holding oneself ready to conceive, imagine, and feel what the words intend.

"The true reader," he says, "reads every work seriously in the sense that he reads it whole-heartedly, makes himself as receptive as he can. But for that very reason he cannot possibly read every work solemnly or gravely. For he will read 'in the same spirit that the author writ'.

19. *God in the Dock*, 215.
20. Ibid., 53-54.
21. C. S. Lewis, *An Experiment in Criticism* (Cambridge: Cambridge University Press, 1961), 19.

What is meant lightly he will take lightly; what is meant gravely, gravely. He will 'laugh and shake in Rabelais' easy chair' while he reads Chaucer's *fabliaux* and respond with exquisite frivolity to *The Rape of the Lock*. He will enjoy a kickshaw as a kickshaw and a tragedy as a tragedy. He will never commit the error of trying to munch whipped cream as if it were venison."[22] So the appearance of the work created by the author, like "the show of things" which MacDonald says is God's final revelation, is, for Lewis, what we should give attention to.

He insists that the analysis of a literary work and its comparison with actual life is a distortion and a perversion of its purpose. One must first surrender to the word pattern and the situation. He says in "Hamlet: The Prince or the Poem?" "All conceptions of the characters arrived at, so to speak, in cold blood, by working out what sort of man it would have to be who in real life would act or speak as they do, are in my opinion chimerical."[23] The character of Hamlet is not to be analyzed as if he had stepped on to the stage from the streets of London. As a construct of Shakespeare he is a man haunted by the thought of being dead, of being in "that undiscovered country from whose bourne no traveller returns." Too many critics approach the play searching for motifs, machines, or similar abstractions of literary history. "Concrete imagination," Lewis says, "knows nothing of them."[24]

And we must approach a play like *The Merchant of Venice* "with our senses and imaginations." Otherwise, in thinking of Bassanio we may agree with the critics who say that he is a mercenary wooer. Such a charge, Lewis says, is a product of prosaic analysis. This is a story about a hero who marries a princess. A folk tale does not attempt to give us "a slice of life." What we get in a play, a poem, or a novel, the golden syllables, the clothes, the imagined situation, these are the substance. The characters as they would be in real life are only a shadow and sometimes a very distorted shadow.[25]

Thus we must conclude that although Lewis would admit the value of the skinned female cadaver in this age of medical progress, he would agree with MacDonald that "analysis is well as death is well." But, he

22. Ibid., 11.
23. C. S. Lewis, *Selected Literary Essays* (Cambridge: Cambridge University Press, 1969), 95.
24. Ibid., 105.
25. Ibid., 95-96.

would say, we must not allow the analytical method to invade and distort our appreciation of the reality of great art and literature or of the beauty with which the universe envelops us. The world which God presents to our senses is a reliable world.

But science must not only analyze. It must also abstract. It must observe how things are related, which is an exercise of the intellect. Inference recognizes similarities and ignores differences — that is, ignores them for the purposes of abstraction. As Lewis says of this second tool of science, "Abstraction is very like money. Neither gold nor paper is real wealth, but it is more convenient than real wealth for purposes of exchange."[26] He points out that abstractions are not real things — not things that occur in time and space. Or to fill out my title (from *The Personal Heresy*), "There are no 'trees', except beeches, elms, oaks and the rest. There is even no such thing as 'an elm.' There is only *this* elm, in such a year of its age, at such an hour of the day, thus lighted, thus moving, thus acted on by all the past and all the present, and affording such and such experiences to me and my dog and the insect on its trunk and the man a thousand miles away who is remembering it."[27]

Everything that exists in time and space, Lewis says, everything concrete, is an individual, as unique as "this elm." Certain heavenly bodies are classified as stars, others as planets, based on their components. But as Eustace, in *The Voyage of the Dawn Treader*, is told when he meets a Narnian star, to state what a star is made of is not to say what a star is.[28] Neither analysis nor classification expresses the essence of a thing. And Lewis would say that this is true of the works of man as well as the works of God. Like the items in nature, a poem or a great work of art should stand naked, uncluttered by categories of genus or species.

In fact, to generalize and classify is to do some damage to the discrete individuality of a thing. Lumping it with other things because of observed likenesses tends to blur the sharp lines of identity and give a false or diminished impression of the reality of the individual. Lewis would say that even our thinking about history is hampered by classification. In "De Descriptione Temporum" he agrees with Trevelyan that

26. C. S. Lewis with E. M. W. Tillyard, *The Personal Heresy: A Controversy* (London: Oxford University Press, 1965), 110-111.

27. Ibid., 110.

28. C. S. Lewis, *The Voyage of the Dawn Treader* (London, n.p., n.d.), 189.

the formation of periods of time is useful to the historian but is only a figment of the imagination and often leads thought astray. Lewis says, "Would that we could dispense with them altogether!"[29]

The blurring of the sharp lines of identity of a thing by classification may be the reason for William Blake's violent dislike of abstraction. He said, "To generalize is to be an idiot." Lewis would not go that far. He recognizes the value of general statements which classify common characteristics. He says that only science can tell you where you are likely to meet an elm. But only poetry can tell you what meeting an elm is like. Not only are trees and poems unique; a configuration, a flight of birds, a sunset, he says, may speak and say, "I am myself alone."[30]

Such a defense of uniqueness recalls the memory of the philosopher of the unique, Duns Scotus, and, perhaps, his poetic voice in the nineteenth century, Gerard Manley Hopkins. The insistence of Scotus that all our knowledge originates with sensation and that universals do not exist except as a construct in the intellect forced him to the conclusion that *haecceitas* or "thisness" is the ultimate reality of being. He would have agreed with Lewis that in "this elm," not in "trees," dwells unique existence. His intense Jesuit disciple also claims for all items of nature such an individuation. In perhaps his most Scotean poem Hopkins says:

> As kingfishers catch fire, dragonflies draw flame;
> As tumbled over rim in roundy wells
> Stones ring; like each tucked string tells, each hung bell's
> Bow swung finds tongue to fling out broad its name;
> Each mortal thing does one thing and the same:
> Deals out that being indoors each one dwells:
> Selves — goes itself; *myself* it speaks and spells;
> Crying *What I do is me: for that I came.*
> I say more: the just man justices;
> Keeps grace: that keeps all his goings graces;
> Acts in God's eye what in God's eye he is —
> Christ — for Christ plays in ten thousand places,
> Lovely in limbs, and lovely in eyes not his
> To the Father through the features of men's faces.[31]

29. *Selected Literary Essays*, 2.

30. *The Personal Heresy*, 110.

31. W. H. Gardner, ed., *The Poems of Gerard Manley Hopkins* (London: Oxford University Press, 1948), 95.

"What I do is me: for that I came." Individuation is expressed in one's *raison d'être*. However, in the sestet he declares that the individual not only acts his nature ("the just man justices," that is, acts justly) but he also acts out God's purpose in bringing him into existence. And so, on ten thousand unique stages Christ plays out the drama of grace in the lives of individual men and women.

We must conclude, then, that Lewis's flight of birds or sunset which says, "I am myself alone" belongs to this second golden thread, that of uniqueness, which, along with the reliability of appearances, is among the Permanent Things which this volume celebrates. They reach back in time not only to Hopkins and Scotus but into eternity. For one of the characteristics of the acts of the Creator, Lewis says, is uniqueness. He insists that there are no clones in God's universe. As the Hymn of the Great Dance in *Perelandra* declares of God, "Never did He make two things the same; never did He utter one word twice. After earths, not better earths but beasts; after beasts, not better beasts but spirits. After a falling, not recovery but a new creation. Out of the new creation, not a third but the mode of change itself is changed for ever."[32]

But if uniqueness is a fundamental characteristic of the universe, what room is left for natural laws, those repetitions of actions and conditions which scientists have noted and employed to manipulate nature for our benefit? Although Lewis often refers to natural law, he says of causation, "In the whole history of the universe the laws of Nature have never produced a single event," and he points out that natural laws are only patterns to which events conform, but not their source or cause. "The laws of Nature explain everything except the source of events." They are indispensable for manipulating the universe, but they do not exist anywhere in the continuous cataract of real events which make up the actual universe. And so he says that the mathematics of physics may be true about reality, but "it can hardly be the reality itself."[33]

As a Christian Lewis was, no doubt, influenced by the Hebrew approach to the natural world. The Old Testament contains no deistic concept of an absentee landlord and a nature run by self-operating laws. Because it was the creation of God, nature, to the Hebrew, was useful in giving insights into his character. But, though separate from God, it

32. C. S. Lewis, *Perelandra* (London: The Bodley Head, 1943), 246-47.
33. *God in the Dock*, 77-78.

did not exist apart from him. The explanation of the creation and its workings was to be found in God's decisions and actions alone. His intimate presence and the possibility of his miraculous actions effectively negated any concept of a mechanical universe.

But Lewis's interest in the philosophical implications of natural law carries him further. At least three times in his book titled *Miracles* he refers to the theory that the laws of nature are merely averages, that if we could delve deeply enough we would find that nature is lawless. The illustration often given is that although a stream of electrons may seem to obey certain patterns, each individual electron, if we could follow it, would show variations which indicates that it was not bound by the strict "law" which man thinks he has observed. If this theory is true, one could conclude that even the smallest physical particles are unique. Then we could say that the immanent God, who, we are told in Scripture, upholds all things and in whom all things hold together, has allowed man to see a divine regularity and to formulate what he calls natural laws, which give him a greater mastery over his environment.

Lewis does not build an argument upon this theory. He admits that scientific opinion often changes and brings down like a house of cards any philosophical construct erected upon it. But, he says, if there is a level at which natural law does not operate, then, in addition to the supernatural, there is also a subnatural, a second door of escape out of the straitjacket of a mechanical universe.[34]

The uniqueness of God's creation need not mean, however, the isolation of each unit, for he says in the already quoted passage from *Perelandra*, "The edge of each nature borders on that whereof it contains no shadow or similitude."[35] The fabric of creation is interrelated and interwoven. Or using a different figure in the essay titled "Miracles," he says, "Divine reality is like a fugue. All His acts are different, but they all rhyme or echo to one another."[36]

Of course, if this is so, then every item of creation is different, from snowflake to human being. And here is where the dark side of uniqueness appears. A unique being with free will may choose to turn from his Creator and go his own way. To the self-centered one his own

34. *Miracles*, 24, 68, 128.
35. *Perelandra*, 247.
36. *God in the Dock*, 37.

uniqueness repels all other beings. Lewis implies that one who turns from God will also turn from the "edge of each nature" that borders on it. As Screwtape tells Wormwood, "The whole philosophy of Hell rests on recognition of the axiom that one thing is not another thing, and, specially, that one self is not another self. My good is my good and your good is yours. What one gains another loses."[37] And so, turning inward and eventually worshiping nothing but himself, the one driven by his rebel moves farther and farther away. Like Napoleon in *The Great Divorce*, his hell will be a residence light years from his nearest neighbor, a hell of distance without and a hell of hatred within.[38]

But those who agree with Tennyson's great line that "we needs must love the highest when we see it,"[39] will each have a unique relationship with the God who never does the same thing twice. It will *be* a unique relationship, Lewis says, because the Creator has made only one of you, and alone knows you completely. None of your friends, for instance, can know the secret thread which connects the books which you really love. No one can see the world as you see it. Sharing a landscape which speaks to you of the elfin music of another world, you discover that to your friend the scene is mundane, or calls up an alien vision. The ineffable longing which Lewis calls "Joy" in his autobiography always seems to deliver a solitary melody heard by you alone. As he says in *The Problem of Pain*, "We cannot tell each other about it. It is the secret signature on each soul, the incommunicable and unappeasable want, the thing we desired before we met our wives or made our friends or chose our work, and which we shall still desire on our deathbeds, when the mind no longer knows wife or friend or work. While we are, this is. If we lose this, we lose all."[40]

It is this "signature on each soul," the "hallmark" of the Master, which is the guarantee of its uniqueness. And most important of all, Lewis would say, is that it is a guarantee that each of us will have a unique relationship with God and a unique place in heaven. As he says in the same book, "Your place in heaven will seem to be made for you and you alone, because you were made for it — made for it stitch by

---

37. C. S. Lewis, *The Screwtape Letters* (London: Geoffrey Bles, 1954), 92.
38. C. S. Lewis, *The Great Divorce* (London: Geoffrey Bles, 1946), 20-21.
39. Alfred Lord Tennyson, *Idylls of the King*, "Guinevere," l. 655.
40. *The Problem of Pain*, 134-35.

stitch as a glove is made for a hand."[41] This unique relationship, he says, is the "white stone" promised in Revelation[42] to each redeemed soul — a secret name which defines some one aspect of the divine beauty which he shall forever know and praise better than any other creature can. If each soul were the same, the church could praise God with only one note. Uniqueness allows us to produce a symphony.

41. Ibid., 135-36.
42. Rev. 2:17.

Some Ideas on a Christian Core Curriculum from the Writings of G. K. Chesterton, T. S. Eliot, and Dorothy L. Sayers

Alzina Stone Dale

These comments should be taken only as some "thoughts," or, to use Eliot's careful phrase, some "notes towards a definition" of what kind of education — or more specifically — the kind of core curriculum we need in order to preserve the beliefs, values and standards of orthodox Christianity. As you will note, my research did not lead me to a definite conclusion about the content of such a "canon," but instead suggested some of the problems we face in developing one. My choice of topic originally grew out of my own experience — not as a writer, but as an artist in residence working in Chicago's inner-city schools. For nearly a year I assiduously collected clippings and articles, jotted down notes, and marked up books, ending up with enough material for several volumes. In the process I found that the terms "curriculum," "core," and "canon" are being used in an ongoing public "dialogue" cutting across all educational institutions from pre-school to graduate school.

When I tried to organize my thoughts on paper so that I could present a platform on which to stand, I realized that I must redefine my topic. I could explain my three authors' thoughts on the issue and describe the present-day heretics who are undermining their position, but for a solution I had to look to a dialogue with others, both to help me define the Permanent Things and to suggest strategies appropriate to the current age.

On the other hand, thanks to my three mentors, Dorothy L. Sayers, G. K. Chesterton, and T. S. Eliot, whom I picked because in their works they had transmitted the Permanent Things to me, I already knew what kind of a "final solution" they would have proposed. It is not a new idea, but we still have not achieved it. These three authors would agree that the ideal way to preserve the Permanent Things is to apply one remedy mankind has never yet tried — Christianity. The remedy would require us to build Chesterton's Uncompleted Temple (or Eliot's Christian Society) instead of continuing to live in neutral or pagan cultures where in Chesterton's graphic phrase, "Christendom" is still only "a half-built villa abandoned by a bankrupt builder" in a world "more like a deserted suburb than a deserted cemetery."[1]

Knowing the ultimate cure we seek may help us to focus more clearly on ways and means. As G. K. Chesterton in his marvelous beginning to *What's Wrong with the World* observed,

> modern social enquiry has a shape that is somewhat sharply defined. It begins . . . with an analysis, with statistics, [and] . . . tables [on such things as the] growth of hysteria among policemen; . . . it ends with a chapter . . . called "The Remedy." It is almost wholly due to this careful, solid, and scientific method that "The Remedy" is never found[;] . . . sociology is always stating the disease before the cure. But it is the whole definition and dignity of man that in social matters we must actually find the cure before we find the disease.[2]

At the same time, no matter how loudly they proclaimed our spendthrift dependence on our diminishing Christian capital, Sayers and Eliot agreed that a Christian country does not exist nor should one be expected to come into being. Instead, they both believed that in a fallen world, Christianity or the Church must always stand against the state and the world, rather than be co-opted by it — or control it. In addition, no matter what kind of society may exist, all three agreed that the way to preserve Christianity's Permanent Things was through education, of which Eliot said that culture was only a by-product.

The difficulty is that my authors do not explain precisely how to get the education we want in our society today. They would not be unequivocally in favor of a nation of parochial schools, funded by vouchers, because the schools may end up another variety of state-dictated schools, since he who pays the piper calls the tune. In fact, our

1. G. K. Chesterton, *What's Wrong with the World* (Leipzig: Bernhard Tauchitz, 1910), 46-47.
2. Ibid., 9-10.

three authors were educated in circumstances that can best be described as only nominally Christian. Even Sayers, the child of the parsonage absorbed in Prayer Book culture, had little formal Christian education. But all three were taught — at home — to think about what they heard and read. As a result of that home nurturing, once their formal schooling was completed they continued their studies, and as adults, became convinced, orthodox Christians.

This pattern raises the age-old question, Can Christianity be taught or must it be caught? If it must be caught, what becomes of my search for a Christian core curriculum, my "Great Books" list meant to be a canon for us to use when debating with today's educational heretics? At the same time, how can we continue to have a culture that has any Christian capital left, if, as modern education theorists are doing, we keep pushing Christian texts off the academic lists or refuse to allow a Christian to teach them?

As I searched for clues in the works of these Christian "ancestors" of mine, I was reminded that the whole issue of curriculums and canons, however trendy, is not new. My own college education followed exactly the pattern Dorothy L. Sayers had described in *The Lost Tools of Learning*. I, too, studied history and literature under various "subject categories" like economics, psychology, sociology, and criticism. The one idea lacking was that these specific disciplines might interrelate or offer a coherent meaning for existence. Not until I studied those disciplines a second time at divinity school did I began to see how, in Charles Williams' sense, they could co-inhere, letting me make sense of the story of Western civilization. I was also fortunate to be a pupil of Jaroslav Pelikan, a brilliant Lutheran theologian deeply interested in *The Vindication of Tradition* and *Mystery of Continuity* — titles of two of his recent books. Pelikan showed me that the angle of vision with which one studies something — including any classic — determines its significance and that no one approaches a text or a topic with a blank point of view. Thus, the Permanent Things must be taught by the community of believers — the church — rather than by heretics or cultured despisers of the tradition.

But if we conclude that education within some kind of believing community is crucial, the way to accomplish that in today's world is still a mystery. Part of the answer seems to lie in the way suggested by C. S. Lewis in *Surprised by Joy* when, reading Chesterton's *The Everlasting Man*, he commented that "a young man who wishes to remain an atheist cannot be too careful of his reading."[3] Great books can "speak to our condition." But it is also clear that Lewis did not come to Christianity simply by being bombarded by Bibles and Christian texts out of the blue. Like Eliot and Sayers, Lewis was part of a community in which those books were still available to him, and he also debated them with people who either believed in them or attacked them. Chesterton, on the other hand, had reversed the process by reading and debating with the heretics.

These "ancestors of mine" all had "ancestors" or "sponsors" of their own, from whose works they "caught" Christianity. While all three are classified as "moderns," both Sayers and Eliot, like Lewis, recorded their recognition of Chesterton as an "ancestor," who had transmitted and translated Christianity to them effectively. Sayers wrote that

> To the young people of my generation, G. K. C. was a kind of Christian liberator. Like a beneficent bomb, he blew out of the Church a quantity of stained glass of a very poor period, and let in gusts of fresh air, in which the dead leaves of doctrine danced with all the energy and indecorum of Our Lady's Tumbler. . . . It was . . . stimulating to be told that Christianity was not a dull thing, but a gay thing, not an unintelligent thing but a wise thing, and indeed a shrewd thing — for while it was still frequently admitted to be harmless as the dove, it had almost ceased to be credited with the wisdom of the serpent.[4]

Similarly, Eliot in his *Times* obituary, praised G. K. C. for his "lonely moral battle" against the time, and for his bold combination of "genuine conservatism, genuine liberalism, and genuine radicalism." He declared that G. K. C. had done more than any man in his age to maintain "the existence of the important [Christian] minority in the modern world."[5] To transmit the tradition, then, takes not just a group of approved texts, but special teachers to translate it and students able to receive the message being transmitted. I might add that when I say "special" teachers, they must have the liveliness and creativity characteristic of my authors, or no one will listen.

3. C. S. Lewis, *Surprised by Joy* (New York: Harcourt Brace, 1955), 190-91.

4. D. L. Sayers, in the preface to G. K. Chesterton, *The Surprise* (London: Sheed & Ward, 1952), 5.

5. T. S. Eliot, quoted in Alzina Stone Dale, *T. S. Eliot, the Philosopher Poet* (Wheaton, Ill.: Harold Shaw Publishers), 1988, 130.

At this point, before describing the other kinds of teachers (or Chestertonian heretics) abroad today, I thought I might learn more about my teachers as well as our situation by compiling a list for use both as a canon and as a weapon. To do so, I chose specific texts of my three authors, which, following the classic Christian tradition of St. Augustine, had been written at times of personal or national crisis.

More specifically, Chesterton wrote *Orthodoxy* in 1908 to celebrate his conversion to Christianity, *What's Wrong with the World* in 1910 as Liberal England broke into pieces, and *The Everlasting Man* in 1925, after the destructive peace had left Europe, in Eliot's phrase, a "Waste Land." Eliot, whose own conversion had been celebrated in *After Strange Gods* in 1934, published *The Idea of a Christian Society* in 1939, followed in 1948 by *Notes Towards the Definition of Culture*. Sayers, the birthright Christian, had begun to speak out on public issues in the mid-thirties, but she first really examined her conscience and her beliefs in *Begin Here*. Published in 1940, it foreshadowed her classic description of the artist as subcreator in *The Mind of the Maker* in 1941, and her ideas on education in *The Lost Tools of Learning* in 1947. While thinking and writing about these matters, Sayers and Eliot also had participated in Archbishop Temple's great mid-war religious conference at Malvern. All these events in turn pointed towards Eliot's postwar comedies like *The Cocktail Party* and Sayers's translation of Dante's *Divine Comedy*.

Our whole world is not as visibly or totally at war today; but it may be that upheavals like the destruction of the Berlin Wall reflect a turning point for civilization. If so, we must always bear in mind that, whatever plan or system we create, none of my authors — nor St. Augustine himself — believed that "progress" towards the perfection of human society was inevitable or one of the Permanent Things.

As I compiled my tentative list of texts that these authors had found significant, I discovered that they had chosen many of the same books, borrowed books from one another, and read one another. (An intriguing example was my discovery of Sayers using Chesterton's argument against the historical thesis of "Northernness" or "Prussianism" as the source of modern democracy. Instead, Sayers, too, came down solidly in favor of Rome as the fountainhead of Western civilization.)

My so-called "master list" — not surprisingly — turned out to sound like many others already in existence. It includes not only ancient fathers like Aristotle, Plato, Aquinas, and Augustine, but also the Bible and the Book of Common Prayer, as well as Dante and Dostoyevsky, representing Western and Eastern orthodoxy. Then it became largely British in cultural background, including all the great English poets from Chaucer, Shakespeare, Milton, Donne, Blake, Browning, and Eliot, as well as essayists and historians like Launcelot Andrewes, Hooker, Lamb and Chesterton, Macaulay, Morris, Ruskin and Carlyle, together with all major English novelists from Jane Austen, Sir Walter Scott, the Bröntes, Charles Dickens, and George MacDonald, to Sayers, D. H. Lawrence, James Joyce, Chesterton, Lewis, and even Virginia Woolf.

As befitting artists, their combined list was both literary and humanistic. It also showed both a Western civilization and an English language bias, perhaps appropriate in a world where English has become the new universal language, but a fact sure to be attacked by my heretics. They also would not like either Chesterton and Eliot's "idea of Europe" or "Rome," or Sayers's interesting projection of both the Roman and British Empire as exporters of Christian culture, dramatized in *Man Born to be King*. The list itself raised another question: how much are Christianity and Western civilization the same thing?

These mentors of mine also saw the past itself, in Chesterton's words, as a "consensus of common human voices" that is preserved by "giving votes to the most obscure of all classes, our ancestors . . . [by preserving] the democracy of the dead," while Sayers stated bluntly that the roots of our civilization "for good or evil . . . [are] western, Mediterranean, and Christian."[6]

At this point I was reminded of categories of European thought described by Leslie Workman. His comments help describe the way in which my writers understood the Permanent Things.[7] As "classicists," they were intent upon emphasizing the forms and continuity of tradition; as "medievalists," these three had become practicing Christians in a modern Anglican Church devoted to the idea of repossessing its medieval roots. Contrariwise, my contemporary heretics, who cheerfully "dump" Christianity together with medievalism and all its works to embrace the idea of change, also still cling to Workman's "classical tradition" of a uniform standard and form, even when insisting upon believing in Toynbee's cluster of multiple and co-equal cultures. Thus, they are still a part of Western civilization, and subject to the same

6. D. L. Sayers, *Begin Here* (New York: Harcourt, Brace and Co., 1941), 25.
7. Leslie Workman, "Pagan Classicism and Christian Medievalism" (lecture given at Hope College, 1982).

classical-medieval dualism Workman saw as fundamental to the European mind.

Far from being fashionably intellectual, however, my three authors were rank individualists and democrats, more amateur readers than academic critics. Each in his or her different way personified the meaning of Sayers's delicious claim about the "importance of being vulgar."[8] They were not wedded solely to "great texts" of high seriousness. On the contrary, these three Christian authors were true cultural "democrats." Like Eliot, they were rescuers and redeemers of forgotten literary treasures; like Chesterton, they were readers of all kinds of popular fiction; and like Sayers, they were translators of ideas from one genre to another. To speak to the modern world, they found medieval knight-errants in modern detectives, made theological arguments based on Lewis Carroll, and quoted Sherlock Holmes in religious drama. They went to meet readers where they were, bringing the Christian message with them.

It was also their Christian conviction that in education, as in everything else, the individual is the important one to speak to, not cults, sects, special interest groups or nations, whether sexist, racist, Third World, or whatever. Two generations before Gertrude Himmelfarb labeled modern studies the "New History," they had encountered its fragmentation of human personality. In *Begin Here*, after Sayers had graphically described the incomplete images of economic, scientific, and psychological man, she suggested that the artists, or creative man, are the only ones able to give us back the whole man who was once the ideal of Western Mediterranean civilization. She went on to elaborate on this idea in *The Mind of the Maker*, with her still superb description of man the craftsman, made in the image of God. But despite her efforts, today we seem to have more and more post-Christian artists for whom the Christian tradition is only a shorthand way to make personal or group political statements.

Finally, I discovered that for my three authors, the most important thing was their point of view, not the texts that made up their reading. All three knew that there is a world of difference between understanding other cultures and accepting their values, and all three came down squarely and uncompromisingly in favor of a necessary connection be-

8. D. L. Sayers, "The Importance of Being Vulgar," unpub. lecture, given February 12, 1936.

tween Western civilization and orthodox Christianity. They would never have agreed with G. B. Shaw (described by Chesterton) that the Golden Rule is that there *is* no Golden Rule. My authors also roundly declared that it was irrational and unbalanced — really insane — to accept just anything as art, because there was always a danger of propaganda being disguised (and protected) as art. Each of them exemplified the comment made about Chesterton that

> the sense of the world as a moral battlefield is at the centre of [his] thought. . . . It made it possible for him to live in a world of anarchies and negations and yet preserve that moral energy that he called optimism.[9]

Because of their consciousness of being at war and their points of view, they must be our models when considering today's educational heretics who threaten the orderly transmission of the Permanent Things. They all talk of standards, but have very little authority on which to base the standards they want to teach, and, I have suggested, most of our contemporary educational theorists are like those G. K. C. described in *The Everlasting Man,* when he said that

> the next best thing to being really inside Christendom is to be really outside it. [But] . . . the popular critics of Christianity are not really outside it."[10]

Although our opponents still base many of their arguments upon the remnants of Christian capital, they talk as if they were only arguing among themselves. Christendom — even the Idea of Europe — is long gone from their educational and cultural vocabulary. This fact was demonstrated to me by a Chicago public school principal where I was teaching. She had meticulously arranged to help Muslim children observe Ramadan and allowed the girls to wear Islamic headdresses to gym, but she became visibly uneasy when I told a class that some family holidays, like Christmas, are also Christian holy days.

The idea of ethnicity as a desirable social concept ends abruptly

9. Samuel Hynes, *Edwardian Occasions,* quoted in Alzina Stone Dale, *The Outline of Sanity* (Grand Rapids, Mich.: Eerdmans, 1982), 297.

10. G. K. Chesterton, *The Everlasting Man* (New York: Dodd, Mead, 1925, reprint New York: Doubleday Image Books, 1955), 9.

when it reaches the "WASPs." As one by birth and upbringing, I even hesitated to make these remarks, not because they are untrue, but because I am well aware of the "flak" generated when Chesterton, Sayers and Eliot in turn tried to say similar things about culture.

One prototypical heretic exemplifies the ultimate in residual culture. He is intent on providing "the many" with a lowest common denominator education. The second is such an elitist he would be happiest if formal education were once again restricted to "the few" worthy of it. The third larger, more varied kind of heretic is still committed to the once abhorrent and supposedly outmoded concept of "separate but equal."

My first two examples are E. D. Hirsch, author and promoter of *Cultural Literacy*, and Allan Bloom, author of *The Closing of the American Mind*. Both have written best-sellers which are used pejoratively to address the issue of culture and its development by means of education, that is, curriculum. But they do not view one another as colleagues. Bloom, startled at finding himself "trendy" when he expected to be scolding his academic peers, regards Hirsch and people like him as part of the problem. Hirsch is outspokenly unimpressed by Bloom who is "only concerned about the spiritual condition of undergraduates at elite universities," and insists that "we aren't part of the same temper of the times."[11]

Although in both cases, people have argued that either Hirsch or Bloom *is* upholding the Permanent Things, I believe, that in many ways they are different versions of a romantic return to the certainties of a classical — and pagan — past. I have even nicknamed them "Hudge and Gudge" in memory of Chesterton's Tory and Socialist portrayed in *What's Wrong with the World*, who turned out to be equally contemptuous of the rights of the ordinary Jones to a home and education of his own.

What I think both men really want is a return to an age in which one kind of education — or the lack of it — would solve society's problems. Hirsch dislikes Bloom's antiscientism and he declares that Bloom believes in the "Decline of the West" and "loves Heidegger and Nietzsche,"[12] an unfair comment since Bloom is clearly on the side of

11. E. D. Hirsch, quoted in Christopher Hitchens, "Why We Don't Know What We Don't Know," in *The New York Times Magazine*, 13 May 1990, 32-62.
12. Ibid., 51.

any humanist who is not Germanic. Hirsch considers himself a disciple of the optimistic Enlightenment tradition, an egalitarian who preaches the re-establishment of a national education consensus on "what every American needs to know."[13] But his standards of reference, like his list of terms, is strangely eclectic, including the Bible Belt but not the Bible, Shakespeare, and songs like "We Shall Overcome." Although Hirsch's declared intention is to establish a "core curriculum" of facts that will stop chaos and decline in the classroom by giving everyone a common body of knowledge, *The Dictionary of Cultural Literacy* really is only a tool for playing "Jeopardy" or "Trivial Pursuit."

By contrast, Allan Bloom is more concerned with the unfortunate "democracy of the disciplines." For him, liberal education has lost its focus and has no content. He is contemptuous of today's students who "lack curiosity and are less cultivated than any generation he has known" but also argues that "there is a new language of good and evil that prevents us from talking about good and evil anymore. It is the language of "value relativism" which is a change in our view of things moral and political, a change as great as the one which took place when Christianity replaced Greek and Roman paganism."[14] He insists that this change is "part of the German invasion of the U.S." To counteract this antisemitic influence, Bloom wants students to read Hobbes, Locke, and Rousseau, but nowhere does he suggest that he would point out to his students how the Christian tradition molded those writers.

Despite an appeal to common standards or values, neither author is engaged in translating or transmitting the Permanent Things from our Judeo-Christian heritage, except when some references to that heritage still appear in ordinary speech and need to be "translated" for today's students. Bloom's strictures against the sloppiness of much education would be applauded by Sayers and Eliot, but he and Hirsch want their students acquainted with the major thoughts of the past because all students are entitled to have "intellectual capital" with which to develop new wealth for themselves. Still, these two "cultured despisers" would leave some texts from which their students might catch Christianity.

This is not true of the third group of heretics who brought Hirsch

13. Ibid., 62.

14. Allan Bloom, quoted in "Today's University — Where Democracy is Anarchy," in *University of Chicago Magazine*, Summer 1987, 6-12.

to my attention. Although Hirsch (rightly) insists he is not trying to forcefeed what he calls "contemporary WASP culture" on everyone, this third group is wildly insulted by the very idea of a common curriculum in our multicultural, multiracial society. They see both Hirsch and Bloom's concern with factual information and the mental tools to use it as an obstacle to progressive education. They still prefer to believe (against virtually all current educational statistics) that students learn by doing and develop skills by realizing their own potential.

These "defendants" attack all standardized tests (and fear national ones) because they are culturally biased. They insist that "culture" is the legitimation of a particular way of life, and that schools transmit a culture that is specific to class, gender, and race. While Bloom presumably is in favor of exactly that result, Hirsch responds that "All education is going to acculturate. . . . If it's social change you want, then acculturate first, so everyone can argue in the same language."[15] The difficulty is whether they will know anything substantive to argue about.

Dr. Alberta Arthurs, a 1972 graduate of Bryn Mawr and the black Director for Arts and Humanities of the Rockefeller Foundation, is typical of this third group. In the winter 1990 issue of *The Bryn Mawr Alumnae Bulletin*, under "Cultural Pluralism," Dr. Arthurs wrote that

> We are living in a diverse, multicultural society and in an interdependent world . . . undergoing unprecedented international change. These realities inform the funding priorities of the . . . Rockefeller Foundation and I believe they will also have a profound effect on American colleges and universities in the next decade . . . [together with] the shrinking of the world . . . , and perhaps in reaction to the mixing of people of different cultures, fundamentalist and ethnic heritage movements have spread and grown stronger; regional and national identities are assuming new importance. Differences are being stressed and even cherished. Over the past twenty years, scholars have been exploring the experiences of those invisible in the traditional formulations of American culture and in the "canon" of cultural artifacts usually assumed to represent it. . . . [They want] to examine the cultural blinders with which non-Western peoples have been studied. . . .
>
> In an attempt to promote this . . . intercultural dialogue . . . the

15. E. D. Hirsch, 32-62.

Foundation supports . . . research on non-Western societies and American cultural pluralism . . . [and is] only indirectly involved in the issues of curricular revision, cultural literacy, and inclusion currently being debated on college campuses and in public fora. . . . It seems to me that the arguments over the curriculum are only part of a larger struggle over the nation's culture . . . as well as over America's changing position in a complex world. As we move toward the 21st century, those of us in policy-making positions in the independent sector and in education must work to incorporate and apply the insights gained from the dialogic scholarship that depicts American and non-Western culture in newly inclusive and complex terms."[16]

From the standpoint of preserving the Permanent Things, I confess that I find Arthurs' vision of a world fractured into a thousand warring factions, each crusading for its own culture or subculture, more frightening than the minimalist approach of Hirsch or the elitist approach of Bloom. At least those heretics will leave me some chance of a few Christian texts surviving in the common culture where they may capture the attention of some future Lewis or Eliot.

In dealing with this third heresy, I am somewhat more comfortable with the approach of a former professor of Oriental Studies at Columbia University. In "Asian Classics and the Humanities," Professor de Bary said that the

challenge . . . to the so-called WASP canon . . . in the name of so-called non-Western cultures, is revealed in its negative and incoherent formulation, for "non-Western" stands for nothing in itself and is meant less to affirm these alternative traditions than to call into question the validity of any tradition at all. . . . It often amounts to nothing less than a radical, cultural-revolutionary challenge to any kind of canon — East or West.

Having stated the problem well, de Bary went on,

. . . we cannot simply mount a defense of established practice, or superimpose a preconceived definition of the canon on other cultures. Rather we must examine what other traditions have considered classic and develop criteria that may contribute to an enlarged conception

16. Alberta Arthurs, "Cultural Pluralism," *Bryn Mawr Alumnae Bulletin*, Winter 1990, 21.

both of the classics and the humanities — in short, a working, con-
testable canon for educational purposes. One need not imagine it
possible to isolate such an enterprise from all politics or ideology nor
suppose that education can be free of indoctrination. Better instead
that the premises and purposes of an educational program be made
explicit, and that faculties openly take responsibility for the values
their curriculum is meant to serve. . . . A common body of required
texts and source readings is used to encourage the individual's confrontation with challenging questions and ideas, as well as to facilitate
discussion. Through common readings and the exchange of ideas . . .
students learn to think for themselves and express themselves. . . .
"Core" then refers not just to canon but to process and method.

He adds that

. . . one's own cultural tradition should have priority in undergraduate
education anywhere. The globalization of culture may well produce
a "global village" but there are grounds for doubt whether it will retain
any . . . distinctive culture . . . of their own traditions."[17]

Instead of Arthurs' "open" point of view, which leads to confusion
of purpose, DeBary's goal is to establish a "Great Conversation for all
the world."[18] But his multiracial, multicultural approach to education
still depends ultimately on texts being taught not from within the
tradition of the Permanent Things, not from the perspective of other
cultures and traditions, like Islam, but taught by "neutral" cultured
despisers who disapprove of any culture or creed being given top billing.

So, what are we to do? Back in 1939 Eliot did not see any societies
that he would call "Christian," but he wanted to encourage ordinary
people to consider thoughtfully what such a society would be like. He
questioned the possibility of defining "culture," and he deplored the
modern tendency of equating "culture" with "education." Like my other
mentors, Eliot also felt that the spiritual foundations of Western civilization had been undermined, but he insisted that even in a Christian
state there would "always remain a dual allegiance to the State and to
the Church, . . . a tension [which is] . . . essential to the idea of a

17. William Theodore de Bary, "Asian Classics and the Humanities" in *Columbia
College Today*, Spring/Summer 1990, 19-21.
18. Ibid., 24.

Christian society."[19] His argument was repeated by Sayers in a postwar article which sounds very timely today: ". . . it is not yet clear what the New Age of the world is going to be like. But however it may turn out, the Church's duty towards it will be one and the same, namely to bear resolute and incorruptible witness against it. This is the business of the Church in every age, no matter how enlightened."[20]

All three authors tell us that our job today is to redefine — as they did — the presuppositions which underlay a Christian approach to education. They saw this process as an ongoing battle never won, but needing to be fought over and over, just as the White Horse needs to be "scoured" by every generation. They insist that we must take more care to know our enemies and read and argue, as they did, with the "heretics" than to preach to the converted. Even the unconverted Eliot in *Tradition and the Individual Talent*, published in 1919, wrote that "tradition . . . cannot be inherited, and if you want it you must obtain it by great labour." He added, in words that could have been written by Chesterton or Sayers,

> [Tradition] involves . . . the historical sense [which] compels a man to write not merely with his own generation in his bones, but with a feeling that the whole of the literature of Europe . . . and within it the whole of the literature of his own country has a simultaneous existence and composes a simultaneous order. This historical sense, which is a sense of the timeless as well as of the temporal and of the timeless and the temporal together, is what makes a writer traditional. And it is at the same time what makes a writer most acutely conscious of his place in time. . . .

He concluded in words almost identical with those used by Chesterton in *The Victorian Age in Literature*, "No poet, no artists of any art, has his complete meaning alone. His significance, his appreciation is the appreciation of his relation to the dead poets and artists."[21] The language of tradition itself helped to convert Eliot. As each generation

19. T. S. Eliot, "The Idea of a Christian Society" in *Christianity and Culture* (New York: Harcourt Brace Jovanovich, 1940, 1968), 44.

20. Dorothy L. Sayers, "The Church in the New Age," in *World Review*, March 1941, 11-15.

21. T. S. Eliot, "Tradition and the Individual Talent," in Frank Kermode, *Selected Prose of T. S. Eliot* (New York: Harcourt Brace Jovanovich, 1975), 38.

works to repossess its cultural tradition, the very act of doing so may have the effect of converting the unconverted.

But in today's eclectic intellectual climate, to care about the Permanent Things by definition means to be dull as ditchwater because eternal truths are neither intriguing nor contemporary. We need to reestablish the validity of Chesterton's comment that his scientist friends had told him that ditchwater was teaming with quiet fun. Even though we need to appeal to the man in the street, we simply cannot ignore the fact that for my mentors, the tradition or Permanent Things were "embedded in" what Chesterton called either "Rome" or "Christendom," what Eliot called "the idea of Europe," and Sayers, "Western — Mediterranean — Christianity." Like them we have to stand up for that transmission in the face of great pressure to deny it.

Finally, however, all three insisted that education in the end comes down not to the state but the family. The Permanent Things themselves may have to be passed along through the family, however weak a reed it seems for such a task today. But, taking their lives as models, our three authors offer some hope that even dysfunctional families — to use modern jargon — may be an important resource.

In *What's Wrong with the World* where he defends the right of families to inculcate their own beliefs and value systems in their young, Chesterton wrote that

> education is a word like . . . "inheritance." . . . [I]t is not an object, but a method. . . . It is giving something — perhaps poison. Education is tradition, and tradition (as its name implies) can be treason. . . . Dogma is actually the only thing that cannot be separated from education. It IS education. A teacher who is not dogmatic is simply a teacher who is not teaching.[22]

Then he added that "there are no uneducated people . . . ; only most people are educated wrong" and "the true task of culture today is not a task of expansion, but . . . of selection — and rejection. The educationist must find a creed and teach it. Even if it be not a theological creed, it must still be as fastidious and as firm as theology. In short, it must be orthodox. . . ."[23]

In discussing the "idea" of a Christian society, Eliot repeated his

22. G. K. Chesterton, *What's Wrong with the World*, 188-90.
23. Ibid., 203.

argument from *After Strange Gods* that such a society must be developed within a culture that is organic and homogeneous. The family, even today, exemplifies these traits more than any other social unit and provides a nurturing ground whose lessons, for good or ill, are rarely forgotten. Thus, in the end, the way one learns is crucial.

All three of these artists were nurtured at home by their mothers, "those solemn and star-appointed priestesses . . . of democracy and tradition,"[24] whom Chesterton called the only true universalists. All three subsequently found school — and later, the world — less exciting, and finding few teachers, they became largely self-taught.

Of the three, Sayers is probably the most explicit about what is wrong with the way we teach today. In her little pamphlet *The Lost Tools of Learning* she begins by explaining that

> I, whose experience of teaching is extremely limited, and whose life . . . has been almost wholly out of touch with eductional circles, should presume to discuss education is a matter . . . that calls for no apology. Bishops air their opinions about economics; biologists, about metaphysics, celibates . . . about matrimony . . . and plain, blunt men write to the papers to say that Einstein and Picasso do not know how to draw. Up to a certain point . . . these activities are commendable. Too much specialization is not a good thing. There is also one excellent reason why the veriest amateur may feel entitled to have an opinion about education . . . we have all, at some time or other, been taught.[25]

Then she explains her basic idea, which is to use the medieval academic discipline as a model to teach students how to think for themselves:

> . . . amid all the multitudinous subjects which figure in the syllabuses, we are really teaching the right things in the right way . . . [if] by teaching fewer things, differently, we might not . . . produc[e] a better result . . . a society of educated people, fitted to preserve their intellectual freedom amid the complex pressures of our modern society. . . . Today when the proportion of literacy throughout Western Europe

---

24. G. K. Chesterton, *Orthodoxy* in *Collected Works* (Ignatius Press: San Francisco, 1986), 252.

25. Dorothy L. Sayers, *The Lost Tools of Learning* (London: Methuen & Co. Ltd.), 1.

is higher than it has ever been . . . people . . . have become susceptible to the influence of advertisement and mass-propaganda to an extent hitherto unheard-of and unimagined . . . in a day when armour was never so necessary. . . . They are a prey to words in their emotions instead of being the masters of them in their intellects. . . . The truth is that for the last 300 years or so we have been living upon our educational capital. . . . Right down to the 19th century, our public affairs were mostly managed, and our books and journals were for the most part written, by people brought up in homes, and trained in places, where that tradition was still alive in the memory and almost in the blood. Just so, many people today who are atheist or agnostic in religion, are governed in their conduct by a code of Christian ethics which is so rooted in their unconscious assumptions that it never occurs to them to question it. But one cannot live on capital forever. A tradition, however firmly rooted, if it is never watered, though it dies hard, yet in the end it dies. . . .[26]

My three mentors offered no formula for transmitting the Permanent Things to the twenty-first century. Although they share the ideal of a Christian society, they also concluded that the "New Jerusalem" cannot be built here any more than it was in England's green and pleasant land. They saw education and the transmission of values and standards as beginning with the family, without telling us exactly how we are to keep that family functional and Christian. Instead of a Christian canon of "great books," they suggest that we look at every book from a Christian standpoint and criticize all contemporary culture in its light. Finally, by their example, they urge us all to work at the task of translating the tradition into popular, contemporary forms accessible and acceptable to today's societies.

26. Ibid., 30.

C. S. Lewis and the
Conversion of the West

William J. Abraham

C. S. Lewis was one of the two internationally famous theologians which Ireland has produced in its long embrace of the Christian tradition. The other was John Scotus Erigena. I find Lewis an intriguing figure as I seek to come to terms with what it means to engage in evangelism in our contemporary Western culture. Even a cursory reading of Lewis reveals a network of proposals which deserve the closest attention. In fact, it is a great pity that those interested in the conversion or evangelization[1] of the West have paid next to no attention to Lewis and what he has to say to us. I can think of at least two reasons why this is the case. First, those interested in evangelism have tended to restrict evangelism either to proclamation or to numerical church growth. In both cases the help that Lewis can tender has been totally shut out as irrelevant. Lewis is seen either as a useful pre-evangelist in his role of apologist, or he is construed as a kind of valuable intellectual nursemaid who can help retain converts once they have accepted the good news, committed themselves to Christ, and joined the church.

Secondly, those interested in Lewis have tended to be so consumed with the Lewis phenomena — its origins, its associates, its intrinsic content and value — that they have rarely explored the great potential Lewis represents in the field of evangelism. Lewis has in fact both formally and materially much to say to it and I hope that someday someone will take up this subject and give it the extended treatment it deserves.

1. In the title of this essay I am using conversion as a synonym for evangelism.

I think there are two hands in evangelism, one where we reach out to share, the other where we reach out to receive. With the one hand we reach out to declare with a passion and flair the good news of the arrival of God's kingdom in Jesus Christ. With the other hand we reach out with intelligence and love to receive those who respond to the gospel, seeking as best we can to ground them in the fullness of God's rule on earth. Elsewhere I have spelled out the grammar and practical content of this vision of evangelism.[2]

Here I intend to consider how we should construe the West that we are seeking to convert. I perceive the modern world as thoroughly fragmented and chaotic. In fact, to speak of a single modern world is an oxymoron. Our Western world is a world of ghettos bound together by airline traffic, democratic capitalism, T-shirts, and the ideology of pluralism. Whatever it is we hold in common, what strikes me are the differences that confront us in the particularities of our subcultures. Even to speak of our culture as "postmodern," whatever its value for certain purposes, is a risk, for such talk posits a monolithic generalization which is deeply distorting in the field of evangelism. If we look at our culture as a whole, we are confronted by a *discord* of voices, of worldviews, of moral traditions, of lifestyles, and of inner informal logics which cannot be flattened out into a comprehensive theoretic analysis — whether intellectual, economic, or sociological.

Interestingly, this situation leads automatically to the first lesson Lewis has to teach us about evangelism. Our first task is to acknowledge the vagaries and diversity of our culture. To be sure, Lewis was well aware of the global trends in highbrow culture. He had no hesitation in making generalizations about the cultural elites he knew. Yet, this was tempered by a refreshing realism about our culture. Nowhere is this more aptly stated than in his essay, "Revival or Decay."[3] Lewis there pokes fun at a headmaster who reveled in optimistic generalizations about religion in the West. Lewis aptly ruminates on the "approaches" to "religion" he has *actually* met.

An anonymous postcard tells me that I ought to be flogged at the cart's tail for professing to believe in the Virgin Birth. A distinguished

2. *The Logic of Evangelism* (Grand Rapids, Mich.: Eerdmans, 1989).
3. In C. S. Lewis, *Undeceptions: Essays on Theology and Ethics* (London: Geoffrey Bles, 1970), 207-10.

literary atheist to whom I am introduced mutters, looks away, and swiftly walks to the far end of the room. An unknown American writes to ask me whether Elijah's fiery chariot was really a Flying Saucer. I encounter theosophists, British Israelites, spiritualists, pantheists. Why do people like the Headmaster always talk about "religion"? Why not religions? We seethe with religions. Christianity, I am pleased to note, is one of them.

Is there a monogeneous "West"? I doubt it. Everything that can go on is going on all round us. Religions buzz about us like bees. A serious sex worship — quite different from the cheery lechery endemic in our species — is one of them. Traces of embryonic religions occur in science-fiction. Meanwhile, as always, the Christian way too is followed. But nowadays, when it is not followed, it need not be feigned. That fact covers a great deal of what may be called the decay of religion. Apart from that, is the present so very different from other ages or "the West" from anywhere else?[4]

We can capture the main point here by simply suggesting that we are back in the position of the church of the first three centuries. Christians live in a world that is radically pluralistic and fragmented. For the most part the age of Christendom is gone, and we must now happily acknowledge our marginal, minority, and even sectarian status in the conflict of ideas and ideologies.

The second lesson Lewis has to teach us lies openly in the neighborhood of the first. It is this: in seeking to convert the West we must take our bearings concerning the *content* of the gospel not from our culture but from the great eternal verities of the gospel itself. To take the negative side of this, we might say that to take our bearings from our culture as presently constituted is to commit suicide. It would mean allowing the gospel to become the mirror of a set of contradictory alternatives which would willy-nilly entail its fragmentation and dissolution. This does *not* mean that we be insensitive to the particularities of our subcultures; much less does it mean that we become uninformed or ahistorical in our thinking about our culture. It simply requires us to be ruthlessly honest about the consequences of modernity. Its fragmentation may provide an opportunity for evangelization which may surprise us, but it would not have surprised Lewis. This has already happened in Anglo-American philosophy. Witness the extraordinary spectacle of a minority of significant, contemporary philosophers

4. Ibid., 209.

who got enough distance from Christianity in their training to treat it as an amazing surprise in the welter of alternatives available. Likewise, in certain circles it is possible for distinguished scholars in various fields to give apologetic lectures on behalf of Christianity precisely because it is allowed equal time alongside, say Marxism, radical feminism, deconstructionism, Dianic witchcraft, and the like.

We do not, however, take our bearings from such considerations. Our second task is to relearn the language of faith, to steep ourselves in the creeds, to dig deep in the commonalities of the Christian tradition, and to learn again the gospel of the kingdom embedded in the scriptural record. This is the place to start as evangelists; and to these fountains we must return again and again with open hearts, self-critical minds, and bended knees. Lewis grasped and lived out this admonition with characteristic thoroughness and flair.

Our third task is to express the faith boldly in ways accessible to the common people. Lewis expresses this with an interesting practical suggestion in a letter addressed publicly to W. Norman Pittenger:

> In both countries [Britain and the U.S.A.] an essential part of the ordination exam ought to be a passage from some recognised theological work set for translation into vulgar English — just like doing Latin prose. Failure on this paper should mean failure in the whole exam. It is absolutely disgraceful that we expect missionaries to the Bantu to learn Bantu but never ask whether our missionaries to the Americas or England can speak American or English. Any fool can write *learned* language. The vernacular is the real test. If you can't turn your faith into it, then either you don't understand it or you don't believe in it.[5]

Typically, Lewis exaggerates a little here, but is it asking too much to expect the evangelist to translate everything the gospel says into vulgar English? For over two centuries revivalists of one sort or another have used this technique, with results thoroughly mixed in character. Nevertheless, Lewis's approach to Christian apologetics should not be limited to his literary or homiletical works. Today, the Western world needs another Charles Wesley to help us sing the gospel with enthusiasm. I am currently experimenting in this domain by working with two Dutch country and western singers who have set Wesley's poetry and hymns to the rhythms

5. Ibid., 283.

suitable for autoharp, banjo, and guitar. What a surprise it would be if Wesley's genius could be recovered in this thoroughly unlikely fashion! Lewis might not approve of the music, but I think he would respect the intention, and even the results. From the interview with Dr. Stephen Olford in the Wade collection at Wheaton, we know that Lewis was sufficiently in tune with revival meetings to share his own testimony. Christians must find a way to enter the popular culture with the gospel without capitulating to the culture's narrowness or its norms. In Wesley's terms, we must consent to be more vile; in Lewis's terms, more vulgar. In doing so we shall be emulating the kenosis of our Lord and Savior.

Thus far I have highlighted three principles which should inform our evangelistic strategies. We need to acknowledge the radical discontinuities in our culture, we need to be faithful to the gospel, and we need to risk translating the faith into the vernacular. I would now like to turn to another question which involves two issues that are likely to be sharply disputed. The general question is, How far can Lewis help us in the field of pre-evangelism? The two ancillary issues are how far Lewis can really help us in the field of apologetics, and what help can be garnered from Lewis's notion of "mere Christianity."

For many, apologetics has been Lewis's strongest suit, but in more recent times this assumption has been subject to stringent analysis. For example, John Beversluis has argued that after the stunning defeat by Anscombe in the famous Oxford debate at the Socratic club, Lewis in fact abandoned serious apologetic work, turning to fiction as a better way to open up the faith to unbelievers.[6] And, A. N. Wilson in his biography of Lewis suggests that even if Lewis did not abandon apologetics, he really should have done so. Wilson sees Lewis as an intellectual bully whose arguments are shallow and insensitive. In contrast, Wilson is very laudatory in his appreciation for Lewis's literary-critical work, and he is far from unkind in his analysis of Lewis's own literary creations.

A second case against Lewis as an apologist has been made because of recent developments in epistemology. In the last twenty years philosophers like Alvin Plantinga and Nicholas Wolterstorff have made compelling cases against any evidentalist defense of the rationality of religious belief. It would be fair to say that with the crumbling of most forms of Enlightenment foundationalism, Christian theists find themselves in

---

6. John Beversluis, *C. S. Lewis and the Search for Rational Religion* (Grand Rapids, Mich.: Eerdmans, 1985).

a radically different position from that prevalent a century ago. In our situation the use of narrative, allegory, drama, fantasy, poetry and the like may prove extremely important in the articulation of the Christian faith and in opening up the heart and mind to the depth and simplicity of the gospel. Hence Lewis's heart may prove more lasting than his head at this point.

But I am reluctant to limit Lewis's role in the field of apologetics to his heart. There is nothing inherent in Reformed epistemology that would prevent Lewis from performing a useful service as an intellectual apologist. Indeed, Plantinga and his many friends are happy that arguments be deployed to defend Christianity. Their objection is not directed to the use of argument but to the status of argument in the cognitive scheme of things. They are keen to insist that argument is not essential to the rationality of Christian faith. Moreover, good sense and diplomatic strategy surely suggest that Christians not play off the one side of Lewis against the other. There is surely a place in evangelism both for narrative and for argument. Each has its proper place.

The crux, here, is whether Lewis has any good arguments at all. If he does not, then that game is over, and we should turn to his narratives. In my judgment the game is far from over. The matter can best be expressed by noting that the deep logic of Lewis's account of the rationality of the Christian belief has a distinguished pedigree both before and after him. Before him stand figures like John Wesley, Joseph Butler, John Henry Newman, and William Tennant; after him follow a whole crew of figures, most notably, Austin Farrer, Basil Mitchell, John Lucas, and Richard Swinburne. Lewis's epistemological thought exists in a tradition in which rational adjudication depends on the assembling of cumulative case arguments rather than on strictly inductive or deductive arguments. Consequently, Lewis cannot be dismissed by the kind of psychological and reductionistic accounts deployed by Beversluis and Wilson.

Lewis presented at a popular and vulgar level what can, in fact, be argued at a thoroughly sophisticated level. At a popular level this is bound to appear as bullying, precisely because ancillary arguments or deeper presuppositions have to be set aside in order to get an opponent to see the force of a piece of evidence. In short, then, I think there is more intellectual horsepower in Lewis than he is currently allowed, and it would be a grave mistake to set aside his usefulness and his challenge as passé.

Evangelists today will discover that their apologetics will not be adequate if they simply repeat Lewis or study what Lewis has achieved. As the founders of the C. S. Lewis Centre have recognized, we need to do now what Lewis did for his day and generation. Evangelists need to develop their own account of the various opponents faced today, and should develop their own arguments to articulate and defend the Christian faith. They must find their own voices and take into account the changed contexts and circumstances in which they are called to operate. Naturally, this applies both to the creation of appropriate fiction, fantasy, allegory, poetry, and to the development of apologetic literature. For the evangelist there is still considerable intellectual horsepower in Lewis's work in apologetics.

The other question I want to take up has a very different focus and it cuts much more deeply into the Lewis agenda. You will recall that central to that agenda was a certain way of construing the heart and defining the essence of the Christian tradition. Lewis isolated a common core of Christian teaching which, following Baxter, he dubbed "mere Christianity." This allowed Lewis to set aside what he considered to be peripheral or secondary matter, and it enabled him to concentrate on the big themes of the Christian tradition. It also, incidentally, gives us a way to distinguish what is peripheral and central about Christianity in Lewis's thought. Hence, we should not confuse Lewis' opinions about gender or his allegiance to Idealism or his particular political judgments with the heart of the Christian message. The questions we must face here are very radical. Is Lewis's apologetic strategy satisfactory? Is there such an animal as "mere Christianity"? Is it a convenient invention on the part of Lewis? Is the notion even coherent?

These issues have been raised of late by a scholar thoroughly sympathetic to Lewis, James Patrick. In his full-scale study of Lewis at Oxford, he puts the issue succinctly:

> His theology is always migrant; the mere Christianity he defended consists of those doctrines he shared with most of the men who met in the Eagle and the Child on Tuesdays. It had no home; it was in its way as idealistic as the philosophy of Bradley, but the vagabond has been a welcomed and comfortable guest almost everywhere.[7]

---

7. James Patrick, *The Magdalen Metaphysicals* (Mercer, Ga.: Mercer University Press, 1985), 132.

The matter is also forthrightly raised by Father John Randolph Willis. In the introduction to *Pleasures Forevermore: The Theology of C. S. Lewis*, Willis

> attempts to show that the basis for *Mere Christianity*, the via media of the Anglican church, does not from the Roman Catholic vantage point exist at all. Hence, from the logical point of view, Lewis' foundations for *Mere Christianity* must collapse, because the very topics he attempted to avoid — pope, magisterium, sacraments — are essential ingredients to the theological whole.[8]

Not surprisingly we already have a rejoinder to charges like these from Walter Hooper, who takes a conciliatory line in his response and concedes that Anglicanism is inadequate in that it does not possess a seat of doctrinal authority. Yet, Hooper is keen to insist on the generally Catholic character of Lewis's piety, as well as Lewis's potential openness to the "the spectacle of a Pope actually functioning as head of Christendom." However, he thinks that Lewis is entirely within his rights to articulate and defend "mere Christianity." According to Hooper, Willis has made two mistakes, one of interpretation, the other of strategy. Regarding the interpretation of Lewis, Hooper believes that Willis has failed to interpret correctly the extremely limited purpose of Lewis's move. Lewis merely wants to lay out what Christians hold in common and thus get folks interested and started on their journey. Regarding strategy, Hooper believes that Willis has failed to see the importance of a place from which to begin when dealing with the seeker or outsider. The place to begin is not with infallibility but with the common verities of the Christian tradition. This is precisely the strategy Lewis commends and uses.

My sympathies are entirely with Hooper in these matters. It seems to me that both Patrick and Willis are deeply mistaken both in matters of fact and logic. "Mere Christianity" is neither merely the doctrines held by the group who met in the Eagle and Child on Tuesdays, nor is it a vagabond without a home, nor is it the failed via media of the Anglican tradition, nor does it form a logical point of view collapse without foundations if it is not systematically integrated with pope, magisterium, and sacraments.

8. John Randolph Willis, *Pleasures Forevermore, the Theology of C. S. Lewis* (Chicago: Loyola University Press, 1983), xx.

Moreover, besides the issue of intent and strategy identified by Hooper, there are two other considerations which support these contentions. The first is Lewis's own clear account of the concept of mere Christianity, an idea important enough to be quoted at length. It occurs in a striking passage in "On the Reading of Old Books."

I myself was first led into reading the Christian classics, almost accidentally, as a result of my English studies. Some, such as Hooker, Herbert, Traherne, Taylor, and Bunyan, I read because they are themselves great English writers; others, such as Boethius, St. Augustine, Thomas Aquinas and Dante, because they were "influences." George MacDonald I had found for myself at the age of sixteen and never wavered in my allegiance, though I had tried for a long time to ignore his Christianity. They are, you will note, a mixed bag, representative of many Churches, climates and ages. And that brings me to yet another reason for reading them. The divisions of Christendom are undeniable and are by some of these writers most fiercely expressed. But if any man is tempted to think — as one might be tempted who read only contemporaries — that "Christianity" is a word of so many meanings that it means nothing at all, he can learn beyond all doubt, by stepping out of his own century, that this is not so. Measured against the ages, "mere Christianity" turns out to be no insipid interdenominational transparency, but something positive and self-consistent, and inexhaustible. I know it, indeed, to my cost. In the days when I still hated Christianity, I learned to recognize, like some all too familiar smell, that almost unvarying *something* which met me, now in Puritan Bunyan, now in Anglican Hooker, now in Thomist Dante. It was there (honeyed and floral) in François de Sales; it was there (grave and homely) in Spenser and Walton; it was there (grim but manful) in Pascal and Johnson; there again, with a mild, frightening, Paradisial flavour, in Vaughan and Boehme and Traherne. In the urban sobriety of the eighteenth century one was not safe — Law and Butler were two lions in the path. The supposed "Paganism" of the Elizabethans could not keep it out; it lay in wait where a man might have supposed himself safest, in the very centre of *The Faerie Queen* and the *Arcadia*. It was, of course, varied; and yet — after all — so unimistakably the same; recognizable, not to be evaded, the odour which is death to us until we allow it to become life: "an air that kills/From yon far country blows."

We are all rightly distressed, and ashamed, also, at the divisions of Christendom. But those who have always lived within the Christian fold may be too easily dispirited by them. They are bad, but such people do not know what it looks like from without. Seen from there, what is left intact despite all the divisions, still appears (as it truly is) an immensely formidable unity. I know, for I saw it; and well our enemies know it. That unity any of us can find by going out of his own age. It is not enough, but it is more than you had thought till then. Once you are well soaked in it, if you then venture to speak, you will have an amusing experience. You will be thought a Papist when you are actually reproducing Bunyan, a Pantheist when you are quoting Aquinas, and so forth. For you have now got on to the great level viaduct which crosses the ages and which looks so high from the valleys, so low from the mountains, so narrow compared with the swamps, and so broad compared with the sheep-tracks.[9]

In this passage Lewis refutes the claim that "mere Christianity" is merely the historically relative opinions of Anglicans or the men in the Eagle and Child. Lewis was drawn to this notion precisely because it was none of these. On the contrary, it was to be found in the old books, in the classics of the faith. Furthermore, it is not a homeless or vagabond body of material. Its strength is that it can fit into several homes without fuss and tension. It is not a vagabond but a movable feast which Christians of varying and even conflicting traditions can share with delight and integrity. In this role it should not be asked to achieve more than it intended, for its purposes and usefulness are modestly circumscribed. Finally, it does not collapse, as Willis believes it must, because it does not belong *essentially* to some doctrine of infallibility, whether Roman Catholic or Evangelical in content. Indeed, the quest to base "mere Christianity" or the eternal verities of the faith upon some doctrine of infallibility is deeply misguided. It betrays a lack of understanding of the scope and nature of "mere Christianity." It assumes that "mere Christianity" needs to be based on some deeper religious dogma of infallibility, say of scripture (the Protestant move) or Church (the Roman Catholic move). It implies that "mere Christianity" needs a deeper religious foundation. However, the critical point to note about "mere Christianity" is that its content is the foundation and basis of the Christian faith. To look for something more basic or more foundational is to play

9. *Undeceptions,* 163-64.

a Cartesian game which is certainly not obligatory and may well be strategically misguided. Of course, this does not in itself prevent anyone from believing in some doctrine of infallibility. All sorts of doctrines can be added, and they can even be added as equally foundational. However, there is nothing *in logic* which makes these other additional doctrines essential to the deployment or coherence of the idea of "mere Christianity." Moreover, there is nothing in Lewis which would preclude one from attempting to ground the content of "mere Christianity" in something else. If we are to ground it in something else — a task long embraced by the tradition of natural theology, we will be required to engage in work of the highest order in the field of epistemology. The question of the usefulness of Lewis's "mere Christianity" will not be resolved by some kind of doctrine of infallibility. As I suggested above, Lewis himself was no mean intellect in this domain, even though he did not continue his work as a philosopher after switching to the field of literature. Lewis's concept of "mere Christianity" should have a place in the ministry of evangelism.

However we work through the significance of Lewis for evangelism, we must always remember that conversion involves some kind of consent which is not under our control. Conversion always involves the secret action of the Holy Spirit in our culture and in our hearts. Lewis was well aware of this. What he may not have sufficiently stressed, however, at least in his formal essays, was the necessity and concurrence of the action of grace. Grace is vital to conversion, because it means that prayer and fasting are as critical in evangelism as some grand scheme of preaching or apologetics. An understanding of grace also means that we need to relax and release all our work into the hands of God.

Another serious problem we face in evangelism lies not in our culture or the decay of Western civilization or the supposed loss of the Permanent Things. It lies in ourselves and in our churches. We simply do not possess the theological base and heritage out of which evangelism can emerge naturally and joyfully. In our culture is the flotsam and jetsam of the classical Christian heritage dismantled and scattered like leaves off a tree. The good news is that while our churches only fitfully own and possess Christianity, it lies there at hand to be embraced and celebrated. We do not need a new Kant to make it intellectually feasible. We do not need a new Schleiermacher or Bultmann to repair and reconstruct it. Christianity lies there awaiting to be repossessed in our old books, hymns, and liturgies. In them is all the basic ontology and metaphysics we need.[10] Here is all the cleansing water we require. Here is all the bread and wine we can swallow. Here are enough spiritual exercises to equip us for war. Here is enough mystery to baffle and absorb us. Here are adequate spiritual gifts to keep us at work in the service of our God. It was part of the genius of Lewis to see this legacy and to make it live again when so many had given up hope or gone after soft and deceptive alternatives. Lewis laid hold of the Permanent Things, the enduring ingredients of the faith, without which we die and by which we live.

Where does "mere Christianity" or its functional equivalent belong in the ministry of evangelism today? It does not quite belong in the forefront of the gospel. It is not the gospel. The gospel is Jesus Christ crucified and risen. The gospel is the story of the breaking in to the world of God in Christ through the Holy Spirit. The gospel is the dawning of God's new age in power and weakness, in mercy and judgment, in death and resurrection. The gospel is Jesus, and Him we proclaim in the power of the spirit. "Mere Christianity" is what we pass on when people respond initially to Christ and His gospel. In doing so we will be moving to reinstate the catechumenate of the early second-century church or its functional equivalents, we will be handing over the intellectual basics of our faith, and we will be engaging in the kind of Christian initiation which will present a serious alternative to the voices commonly heard in our culture.[11]

Let me illustrate. Recently, I drove from Maynooth outside Dublin to Belfast to visit my favorite uncle. He lives and breathes the Permanent Things naturally, even casually. We talked about his early Christian initiation. There was no talk of any dramatic religious experience; Irish Presbyterians can be shy on these matters. What was amazing was how he spent his Sundays while growing up in Northern Ireland. He got up, went to Sunday school, went home for tea, went back to church, and then went to an open-air meeting. Today, we look back in astonishment at such a schedule; we may even slightly despise it as cruel and impossible. However, the one thing this process did was to ground my

10. This statement should *not* be taken to mean that there is no room in the Christian tradition for extended technical work in ontology and metaphysics.

11. I have argued this case in *The Logic of Evangelism* (Grand Rapids, Mich.: Eerdmans, 1989).

uncle in the faith. It gave him time and space to lay hold of the Permanent Things. In my own case, I am eternally grateful for the hymns of Charles Wesley. When I came to Christ I was immersed in the hymns of the faith. In what many would regard as a cultural desert and a liturgical backwater, I was baptised in a sea of song and faith which Lewis brilliantly identifies and summarizes.

I do not know the full story of our culture and civilization, although I am profoundly skeptical of the varied analyses of diagnosis and prescription that preoccupy us. They often look too much like exercises in dialectical philosophy which are liable to impress only the uninformed. I do not know if a third great awakening is in the making; I do not know if we are destined to destruction and decay; I do not know if Islam will be the religion of the twenty-first century. Yet this I do know: if we fail to teach the basics of the faith, we will never withstand the ravages of the world, the flesh, and the devil. I cannot outline how this should be done,[12] but I will insist that if we do not teach the faith in our churches as an essential element in our evangelism, we will languish, and we will deserve to.

We have churches and buildings all over the land. We have hosts of viable universities and educational institutions. We have publishing houses, and radio and T.V. stations. We have think-tanks, and conferences, and institutes, and agencies galore. We have a magnificent intellectual heritage behind us. We have historians and sociologists; we have scientists, poets, playwrights, prophets, English professors, philosophers, and even a few theologians. We have saints, martyrs, priests, deacons, and evangelists in our midst. We have great novelists and fantasy writers and literary critics. And in and through these, we have the presence of the Almighty Father, the Only-Begotten Son, and the All-holy and good and life-giving Holy Spirit. What more can we ask? What more do we need?

---

12. I have sought in conjunction with a local church in Uvalde, Texas, to develop a modern course for catechumens.

The Recovery of the Permanent Things: Eliot circa 1930

Marion Montgomery

One can . . . be a relative idealist or a relative realist. What it seems to me to lend itself to most naturally, is a relative materialism — or at least this is the way in which my sympathies incline.

Eliot to Norbert Wiener, January 6, 1915

I am still a relativist, a cracker of small theories like nuts, essentially an egoist perhaps. . . .

Eliot to Aiken, August 21, 1916

The point of view I am struggling to attack is perhaps related to the metaphysical theory of the substantial unity of the soul: for my meaning is, that the poet has, not a "personality" to express, but a particular medium.

"Tradition and the Individual Talent," 1920

The use of criticism as Eliot sees it in his Harvard lectures in 1932-33 is to discover the degree of a proper accommodation of the poet

---

This essay is part of a book-length work, "Memory and the Recovery of the Permanent Things: A Reading of T. S. Eliot."

as a person to his work, in a just judgment of both poet and poem.[1] The judgment is not so limited as it had seemed in 1920 when Eliot published *The Sacred Wood*. Then, what was required of the poet as poet was a complete escape of *person*, though person was very superficially understood by that younger Eliot. (He was thirty-two years old then.) The poet was required to act from a gnostic position of depersonalization. As he put it in "Tradition and the Individual Talent," "The progress of the artist is a continual self-sacrifice, a continual extinction of personality."[2] Again, poetry "is not the expression of personality, but an escape from personality." And, most tellingly of the gnostic view in the Eliot before *The Waste Land*, "the more perfect the artist, the more completely separate in him will be the man who suffers and the mind which creates."

By the time of his Harvard lectures, Eliot's position is fundamentally changed. Not that he believes any final judgment is possible to the critic concerning the "person" of the poet in relation to the poem. As he says in approaching the concern in *The Use of Poetry and the Use of Criticism*, the lectures as published in 1933, "Criticism . . . never does find out what poetry is, in the sense of arriving at an adequate definition. . . . Nor can criticism ever arrive at a final appraisal of poetry. [The] critic who remains worth reading has asked, if he has only imperfectly answered" two questions: "What is poetry?" and "Is this a good poem?" But the questions are deceptive in their seemingly simple straightforwardness. In the critic's attempt to answer them, he at once encounters the complication of the poet's presence, despite his attempt as critic to remove the poet from consideration. What are we to say of Shelley, having attempted these questions in reading him?

One may not, Eliot now holds in the 1930s, set aside from a critical reading of a poem the philosophical element permeating the poem, however subtly managed by the poet's artistry. No longer will he say, as he had in a letter to Norbert Wiener, in the year *Prufrock and Other*

---

1. The Charles Eliot Norton Lectures at Harvard were given beginning on November 4, 1932, and concluding on March 31, 1933. They were published by Faber and Faber that year under the title, *The Use of Poetry and the Use of Criticism: Studies in the Relation of Criticism to Poetry in England*.

2. This essay, first published in 1919 and then collected in *The Sacred Wood* (1920), has been a staple of modern critical texts since the rise of the New Criticism. The citations are to the text in Eliot's *Selected Essays*, the Harcourt, Brace & World edition of 1960.

Observations was published, that "all philosophising is a perversion of reality," leaving him inclined through "a relative materialism" to "the mechanistic world" generally accepted by the intelligentsia out of the new science.[3] By 1930, the "personal" is no longer to be denied a relevance to art. The critic, in justice to the poetry, must attempt to see the truth of two aspects of the poem: the thing itself and the presence in it, to some degree, of the maker of that thing. For there is a symbiotic existence not to be disjoined, lest one be left with only, in Eliot's words, "the debris of poetry, rather than the poetry itself," as he will be prepared to say at Harvard in 1932-33.

In raising this critical problem in relation to Shelley as poet, Eliot feels obliged to account for his own early enthusiasm for Shelley, as it contrasts to his present (1933) inability to read that poetry except for such purposes as the present lectures. His early enthusiasm he now believes to be explained by youthful circumstances as reader more than by Shelley's abiding accomplishments. With age, Eliot's circumstances have changed, but more importantly, he himself has changed. He is not the same person he was. Or more accurately, he is now more fully the person it was possible for him to become than he was when only fifteen. At fifteen, he recalls being fascinated "because the question of belief or disbelief did not arise." Shelley's "cloudy Platonism" did not intrude into the encounter of his poetry by a cloudy fifteen-year-old. Or, put another way, the mutual cloudiness proved compatible. And so at fifteen, he had been "in a much better position to enjoy the poetry," an enjoyment limited because it was directed by his own adolescent mind more than by the insufficiency of Shelley's vision. He was thus able to read Shelley with enthusiasm. He is prepared, in 1933, now a venerable forty-year-old critic and poet, to conclude that "the question of belief or disbelief, in the intellectual sense, never arises when we are reading well," that is, reading in accordance with present capacities.

Still, one must make certain clarifications about this assertion. For, if one is to read well, there must be some coincidence of intellectual limits of both poet and reader, circumscribed by the poem as a thing in itself. The reader's degree of intellectual maturity and that of the poet's

3. Valerie Eliot, ed., *The Letters of T. S. Eliot*, vol. 1: 1898-1922 (New York: Harcourt Brace Jovanovich, 1988). The irony here, which would have been apparent to Eliot after *The Waste Land*, is in the date of his letter to Wiener, January 6th of 1915 — that is, Epiphany. (See note 14 below.)

encounter each other through the poem, the made thing. Thus it is that one says, as Eliot does, that the poem exists "somewhere between the writer and the reader." And in the poems that lie between Eliot and Shelley in the 1930s the question of belief at last intrudes itself inescapably for Eliot. After reflecting upon that intrusion, Eliot concludes that, judging both his and Shelley's relative maturities of mind, a shortfall of maturity lies in Shelley. In some degree Shelley is, in Eliot's judgment, a failed poet. However, it will not follow from such a judgment that Eliot would cast Shelley into outer darkness, as we shall see. But he is nevertheless required to conclude a failure in the poetry, in relation to the poet himself.

The maturity at issue for Eliot has to do with what Keats, in a letter Eliot quotes, has called the "proper self."[4] The concern is with the degree of fulfillment of the gifts of personhood, if we may translate Keats's phrase to its scholastic implications.[5] It is not simply a matter of intellectual facility, for one does not deny Shelley's remarkable intellect. It is rather that in the end even so remarkable a gift as Shelley's results in an insufficient resonance of person caught up by vision in the poem itself. Thus the waking of such resonances in the reader himself is limited by the poem, since it has been limited in its making. We are dealing with a sort of relativism here, but it is not the relativist Eliot of 1920. This new relativism means that some poems are better than others, not because of the poet's "depersonalization," but because some

4. Eliot quotes Keats's letter to Bailey (1817): "I must say one thing that has pressed upon me lately, and increased my Humility and capability of submission — and that is this truth — Men of Genius are great as certain ethereal chemicals operating on the Mass of neutral intellect — but they have not any individuality, any determined character — I would call the top and head of those who have a proper self Men of Power." No doubt Eliot would have been reminded by Keats's "ethereal chemicals" figure of his own earlier characterization of the poet's mind as a "shred of platinum," the "catalyst" to the making of sulphurous acid. But Eliot's figure intends a separation in the poetic process of "the man who suffers and the mind which creates." Keats's distinction is between just such a reductionism of the self, the "man," to "individuality," as opposed to a desirable wholesomeness in the poet, a "proper self."

5. Scholastic concepts are a part of Eliot's thought and become important to his poetry at last. Note for instance the concluding lines of "The Hollow Men." There the shadow falls upon intellect (a shadow which will prove in the event a light whereby intellect discovers flowers in an abandoned garden as having "the look of roses that are looked at"). Intellect arrested finds itself in suspense between *conception* and *creation*, between *potency* and *existence*.

poets not only possess gifts differing from one another in respect to their ability to make a poem, but they also possess relative vision of the truth of things independent of particular gift or artistry. This is to say that such "relativism" is prescribed by an absolute, most immediately manifest by the reality of existence itself. In consequence, one may value Dante as a greater poet than Shelley, but not be required by that judgment to cast Shelley into an outer darkness from the critical mind.

There is that other possibility, of course: a lack of maturity in the reader, whatever his age. But Eliot speaks with a confidence in his own growth. Because of that confidence he suggests that the adolescent is wrongly belabored if his teachers require of him a full response to the resonance of such great poets as Shakespeare or Dante. He recalls his own experience as a child: "The only pleasure I got from Shakespeare [was] the pleasure of being commended for reading him; had I been a child of more independent mind I should have refused to read him at all." Fitzgerald's *Rubaiyat* was a different matter. At fourteen, the poem struck him "like a conversion," whereupon he took "the usual adolescent course with Byron, Shelley, Keats, Rossetti, Swinbourne."[6]

We are thus led by Eliot to what seems an inevitable conclusion, remembering that intellectual snobbery is very far removed from what Eliot is saying, though intellectual snobbery is an attitude often attributed to him. That conclusion is that a poet, insofar as he has made a significant work, requires of us a maturity of response, a response to which the work itself serves as medium. Through a proper intellectual encounter with a good poem, one puts the question of belief or disbelief in its proper perspective in relation to the limits of art as art. Those limits at some point in our intellectual response touch upon legitimate questions of belief or disbelief. Lest such a term as "intellectual" be misunderstood here, let us be reminded that it is a term more inclusive than its synonym "rational," for intellect is complex, involving the "intuitive" as well as the "rational." Most anciently the poet has engaged the tensional poles of his own intellect, metaphorically described as the tension between heart and head.

In a proper, mature, intellectual encounter with the poem, one

6. Eliot recalls in a letter to his mother (July 10, 1919) that when his father rewarded him with twenty-five dollars for having won the Latin prize in his St. Louis youth, "I stole two dollars out of it to buy a copy of Shelley's poems, and no one ever knew." In Valerie Eliot, ed., *The Letters of T. S. Eliot*.

encounters a mystery not to be denied, lest poetry itself be denied: the poet, given his gift and a devoted practice of craft, is also given a passion for the truth of things, without which his made thing is still-born or born retarded. The poem, by its aspect of being a made thing, bears an inescapable presence of the more or less passionate maker. For by the very act of his pressing art to its limits as art, he not only effects a thing, the poem; he also affects that made thing in its created nature, as a continuing presence in it. Thus to isolate the poet from his poem — by setting aside the particular maker who is always actively present in the made thing — distorts our perspective of the poem. The attempt, says Eliot, speaking directly to us, leads us into the error "of seeking from poetry some illusory *pure* enjoyment, of separating poetry from everything else in the world, and cheating yourself out of a great deal that poetry has to give to your development."[7]

Poetry rightly taken, then, contributes to the development of person. That is the position Eliot has come to, and it is a considerable distance from what he held at the time he published *The Sacred Wood*. He now holds that the reader, coming into a fullness of his potential as an intellectual creature, is enabled to embrace more and more of "everything else in the world," insofar as that everything else is truly seen as existence — as *thing else*. That is the enlarged view upon existence that Eliot has celebrated so tellingly in his poem "Ash-Wednesday," in which a flowering of the desert is recognized as never before by the poet. Such growth not only leads to his witness in that poem; we discover through the poem a possibility of that growth in ourselves.

It will not follow from this argument, as Eliot is quick to insist, that the "good" reader as here characterized — that is, as intellect in the act of maturing — must embrace the poet's particular vision as his

---

7. Eliot's words here ought to make one cautious about treating him as simply a "New Critic," if one means by that term to describe a critic who holds the text as independent of the poet himself and of all else — as is now commonly meant by the term. For instance, Gerald Graff, in a generally healthy argument against critical walls built between literature *per se* and the fullness of intellectual being, faults Eliot as a chief instigator. Eliot regrets in several places a general neglect of his position after *The Sacred Wood* (1920), remarking about the popularity of such pieces as "Tradition and the Individual Talent" and "The Perfect Critic" to the neglect of his later critical position. In his preface to the 1964 edition of *The Use of Poetry* he speaks of "Tradition and the Individual Talent" as "perhaps the most juvenile" of his essays, but that essay continues to be the anthologized piece in texts to represent Eliot as critic.

own belief. One discovers that Shelley, for example, is unsupportable even at his best, being limited by his own intellectual immaturity. Eliot will demur from Coleridge's dictum that we must suspend disbelief to read a poem, not only because it is impossible to do so. One cannot do so because the very act of openness to a poem involves some degree of judgment. But the attempt is dangerous as well because the very attempt tends to erode our capacity to believe what is worthy of belief if and when we encounter the worthy. This is to say that the openness of mind as popularly urged is most dangerous in its tendency to a reductionism whereby all *things* are reduced to a parity that denies the particular nature of the particular thing.

It is of course difficult to speak of such intellectual concerns, as we have hinted, without appearing to be an "elitist," to use a currently popular term thrown against the moral necessity of making intellectual discriminations. Those discriminations are to be measured by the truth of things themselves, as opposed to our measuring things by our feelings or impulses enslaved by passing ideology — by that false love of the self which is our day's dominant creed. That false creed was held at least tacitly by Eliot before *The Waste Land* out of a disposition partly inherited from the intellectual milieu of Puritanism focused at Harvard at the turn of the century.[8] A Cartesian ideology in him took to the Symbolist movement instinctively, since the Symbolist address of the art of poetry seemed the most viable means of imposing intellect's desire for order upon an existence no longer admitted as bearing any order in itself. Indeed, even the existence of a world separate from intellect no longer enjoyed easy acceptance by the intelligentsia, a climate of thought haunting Eliot's early poetry.

Now to have recovered oneself from such dislocation, as Eliot had done in the 1930s, might tempt one to turn his gift of making poems or of making criticism into something quite other — into the making of theology, perhaps. For intellectual action presupposes judgment, which involves belief, which may all too easily tempt one to advocate the belief itself, as if advocacy were proof of art. Eliot had at hand an instance of that sort of error: while he was lecturing at Harvard, Ezra

---

8. I have explored at length the transformation of Puritanism to gnosticism in three volumes, *The Prophetic Poet and the Spirit of the Age,* calling particular attention in volume 3, *Why Hawthorne Was Melancholy* (1984), to Charles W. Eliot's role through his educational program established at Harvard after 1867.

Pound was in Italy extolling the virtues of the latest savior of the body social, Mussolini, with the fervor of a disciple of a new spiritual revelation. Pound mistook his authority as disciple to be justified fundamentally by his gifts as poet. What Eliot wished to keep in mind was that the poet's and the critic's discrimination is an intellectual one, first of all, though rooted in his spiritual being. And so he practices a species of philosophy, not of theology, as was Pound's inclination. The difference lies in Eliot's attempt to bear witness, in contrast to Pound's fervor to convert mankind.[9]

As critic, even if one rejects the muddled Platonism of a Shelley or a Pound, one may nevertheless recognize that an inadequate vision may serve intellectual as well as, ultimately, spiritual ends. That is, an illusion embraced by a poet as reality or embraced as a pragmatic convenience to his writing is reflected in his art.[10] But illusion may serve to alert intellect and thus contribute to intellectual maturity. That is, intellect may, in recognizing the alternate claim of illusion and vision, conclude that such alternation speaks necessarily of a reality. The problem then remaining is to determine which is illusion, which vision. That is the theme of Keats's best poetry, made explicit for instance in his "Ode to a Nightingale." As for a possible virtue in art sprung from the poet's illusion, one may especially value the poet's passion, his intention to the truth of things, however much he may fail that truth. It is this passion in Keats that Eliot has come to value highly by the time of his Harvard lectures. The disparity between illusion, recognized as illusion, and intimations of truth (reflected as necessary by the very attempt that

9. In speaking of Pound as "theologian," I recall Eric Voegelin's examination of Plato's introduction of this "neologism of world-historic consequences." In the *Republic,* Plato declares that both negative and positive propositions are types of theology, both types measured by an absolute and so either negative or positive in that light. Propositions believed justify destructive or constructive actions of mind, in which actions that mind deports itself with "theological" conviction.

10. Eliot says that Shelley "borrowed" a philosophy for his poetic purposes. One might compare Wallace Stevens, a very strict Cartesian idealist in his poetry, to which he brings a Symbolist deportment to imagery not unlike Eliot's early deportment. Stevens makes a remarkable poetry in which there is seldom to be detected the sort of unrest with the implicit philosophical position one finds in the early Eliot. That Stevens' role as poet is so deliberately set aside from his more inclusive life underlines his use of the "philosophy" as a convenience, as opposed to a principle to which he is committed with some passion, as is Shelley.

leads only to illusion) proves movingly effective, not simply as the dramatic energy in the poem itself, but as evidence of a necessary growth in us as persons which Eliot has come to witness, a growth that is spiritual as well as intellectual. In Keats's "Ode to a Nightingale" one encounters an arrest of, but not the absolute death of, a desire for the truth of things. For where there is an absolute death of desire, all poetry ceases, since the intellect itself is suspended. Keats makes a most poignant acknowledgment of arrest:

> Was it a vision, or a waking dream?
> Fled is that music: — Do I wake or sleep?

The poignancy for us lies in our tacit realization, however deeply buried in intellect, that though Keats in these lines thinks himself a victim of the final rebuke to intellect, the death of desire, the very raising of the question speaks to the contrary. It is not high dramatic irony as in *Oedipus Rex*, but it is dramatic irony of the same species, dependent on the disparity between the speaker's belief and our tacit knowledge of an envelopment of that belief by a larger reality.

Eliot has himself caught most poignantly that same suspension between illusion and reality in "The Love Song of J. Alfred Prufrock," Prufrock being an extreme intellectual idealist drowning in the caves of his own consciousness, unable to break free to the risks of the larger ocean of being by which he is contained as but one of many things. We find the state of mind reflected in this poem also reflected in other of Eliot's poems contemporary to it, in "Preludes" and "Rhapsody on a Windy Night" for instance. And so we come to realize, as Eliot did himself, that the poem's maker at the time of writing was very much caught in an ambiguous suspension of intellect, with the promise of rescue left obscure in the very ambiguity of that suspension. Intellect's dream world as justified by Cartesian philosophy bears its self-contradiction, bears the implications of a world into which it may suddenly wake, as Eliot finds himself to have done by the time of "Ash-Wednesday."

One matures, then, through an ordered consent to the passion stirred in us by desire for some worthy object. And it is intellect's office to make consent orderly and proportionate to worthiness. But it is more usual to us, because we have lost the virtues of intellect, to be left lamenting the death of passionate desire, confused as to whether any object is worthy. It is this failure of intellect, exacerbated by the collapse of philosophy and theology from their proper support of ordinate consent to passion, that has supplied the most typical themes of modern literature, a literature in which we have come to call the protagonist the "antihero." Such is the theme in Eliot's early poetry, as his skillful deployment of epigraph and allusion underlines. Dante shows us Guido in Hell proper, but we are hard pressed to justify J. Alfred Prufrock worthy even of Hell. And Agamemnon's cry of woe is beyond Sweeney's hearing in "Sweeney among the Nightingales."

What Eliot's later poetry reveals is an emergence of the soul as potentially heroic beyond its worldly entrapments, a heroism possible even in its day-to-day endurance of the mundane. But the circumstances of the ordinary lack the spectacle one finds in Greek or Renaissance tragedy. It is nevertheless possible to rise from the subheroic condition of a Prufrock through a surrender which, as Eliot will phrase it in his last important poem, *Little Gidding,* "costs us no less than everything" by that action. In the "waste land" halfway through Eliot's personal journey, as bracketed by "Preludes" and *Little Gidding,* Eliot speaks of an overwhelming action at a level removed from the spectacle of our world as *spectacle* is ordinarily taken in that world. That hidden, heroic action is the "awful daring of a moment's surrender," which will "not be found in our obituaries," for it is a surrender of the person to the reality of existence, a surrender to which spectacle is at best but an uncertain sign. We must especially notice in this portion of *The Waste Land* that intellect speaks to "heart," toward a reassociation of sensibilities significant to spiritual recovery. The "dissociation of sensibilities" is no longer for Eliot a matter of English literary history. Meanwhile, Ezra Pound's spectacular position in Italy grows as a reminder to Eliot that his own attempt to make passion ordinate toward a worthy object is not the only possible issue of passion to the soul.

It is not too large a generalization to say that, since Eliot's "Hollow Men," our world has been largely given over to conflicts effecting awesome and cataclysmic destructions. The poem itself is to some degree an effect of one such destruction, World War II, which left the West spiritually debilitated. Few columns remain unbroken, few heaps of broken images restored by a patient labor signifying visions of recovery. Nor is it too large a generalization to observe that in our century's descent into chaos, encounter between the subhero and the antihero provide only the spectacle of chaos. What we have lost, in regard to drama's spectacle, is the steadying assurance of the abiding. Oedipus's crown and robes speak an order to be held, an order to which a general consent is granted, even though he falls from that order. But the turmoil of World War I, of World War II, of the general dislocations of common consent in the 1960s — to touch significant low points of community disintegration — serve only to underline in our experience that in our day any spectacle reflects disorder as our common ground. Where is the order common and worthy by which we may measure actions in art or in life itself?

What we must not mistake here is the role passion has played in establishing chaos as the measure of our human predicament, lest despair consume us. Neither passion lost, as to the hollow men, nor passion perverted, as by Conrad's Kurtz, is sufficient justification for rejecting passion, however, as if passion were now or ever and always falsely spent in the world's and humanity's destruction simply because it is passion. That is the restoring lesson of the Cross, toward which Eliot tends in his poetry as he sees his world increasingly given to chaos. It is also the lesson gradually and gropingly and even grudgingly sought in this last quarter of our century, though such struggling pilgrims, as we encounter them, appear often as confused or more confused intellectually than Shelley in his murky Platonism.

And so Eliot's arresting epigraph to "The Hollow Men": "Mr. Kurtz — he dead." It sets action, or rather inaction, in relation to Kurtz's violently misspent passion, making the loss of ordinate passion more poignant and stirring. The arrest of spirit lamented in the poem becomes intolerable as we read it. But insofar as one experiences through the poem a growing recognition that such an arrest is intolerable, the reader is less likely to escape into a merely violent action of his own, namely, a rejection of the hollow man because he is judged as existing where all the indicators read absolute zero. A response of despair is insufficient to the poem, though its voice reflects deep despair. The reader's surrender here would but be an attempt to escape his own dilemma of frustrated desire. The solution does not lie in such a great refusal as this. For it would be a great refusal in that the reader is himself deeply at risk. The solution is rather a recovery of intellect to its proper office through a reflection that comes to understand just what is always at risk in passion: the person — the specific, discrete existence named John or Mary, Paul or Magdalene. In that recovery lies a recovery of the implication of reality itself, whether in the reader or in the poet. And it is a recovery made possible in some degree through the poem itself, through this imitation of possible actions by persons relative to their becoming out of sheer being.

It is this possibility in poetry that Eliot has come to recognize, witnessed by "Ash-Wednesday" and remarked in his Harvard lectures thereafter. For poetry may have the virtue of returning us to reality itself. And so long as the maturing which is reflected in that turning is an openness to existences, that openness makes the person less vulnerable to despair, even as it will dictate restraint in the tendency to absolute judgment of rejection out of despair. One holds a Shelley with intellectual caution, lest one's own finite intellect judge unjustly out of illusion rather than through a maturing vision of the truth of the thing judged. In a truth-full judgment not only the limits of the judging intellect are honored, but the limits of being in the thing judged are therefore more clearly perceived.

It will not follow, of course, that such openness to things means an abandonment of judgment out of our fear of unjustness to things. Judgment is discrimination, measured by the reality of the things judged. After all, poems are not paintings; art is not life. And more insistently demanding upon intellect, whether one is critic or poet, all poems are not great poems any more than all poets are equal in their particularizing gifts. The desirable openness to things as existences independent of intellect makes it not only possible but obligatory for that intellect to discover and credit by intellectual judgment likeness in unlike things, unlikeness in like things. It is through such judgment of thing among things that one comes to recognize and accept the hierarchy, the order, in existing things. In the growing capacity for distinction among existent things out of an intellectual openness to being, intellect will neither confuse stones with trees, nor trees with their resident owls, nor whales with persons. Nor will one confuse a particular person with another particular person.[11] One need not demonstrate how far removed we are

11. The order here meant, I believe, to be recovered to the poet's good health through the Thomistic "principle of the proper proportionality," which does not mean that that principle dictates. It is a principle discovered rather than applied, through a realism grown out of common sense. Etienne Gilson expounds the point in *Methodical Realism*, essays published in the 1930s but only recently (1990) collected under the title. Gilson sets Realism against Cartesian Idealism, arguing that there can be no middle ground between the two. Through the Thomistic principle, one recognizes the distance between things in their specific and particular natures, as opposed to the nature of their Cause, God. Discrimination allows the exploration of relative distance of thing from

today from making such discriminating judgments required of intellect by piety toward the complexity of creation itself. From evening news to learned academic argument, sentimentality replaces the proper offices of judgment so that proper discrimination may be avoided. The warm glow of feelings in place of thought casts a twilight spell on the chaos steadily encroaching upon consciousness. Not, of course, that the openness of intellect to the orders of being, governed by the necessities of discrimination among beings, may deny to any particular thing the virtues peculiar to it and it alone as the thing it is. The destruction by intellectual indiscrimination lies precisely here: in a judgment absolving particular things of their limits, resulting in what is in truth sacrilege against the holiness of particular things. It is such violation that we practice, for instance, when we announce as a principle of political order that anyone can be whatever he wants to be. This is the confusing message permeating social and political thought in our time, a message leading to the despairing confusions among our young persons. For the maturing of the powers of discrimination is the process of life itself to rational spirit, to person becoming person out of discrete gifts. And it leads to a truth not to be denied except at great cost to the person each is: things, by the very fact of their existing at all, are not equal in their actualities, however much we pretend otherwise.

It is an immature capacity for discrimination in Eliot at fifteen that led to his excessive infatuation with Shelley, which in retrospect he sees as suitable enough to the conditions of his early encounter. It

---

thing within creation, without violation of any thing, discovering unlikeness anchored commonly in a fundamental likeness, namely being as the ground out of which specific beings exist. The distinction between *ens* and *esse* is intrinsic in creation, not a conceptual creation by intellect itself, so that one recognizes ordered hierarchy in existing things as independent of intellectual *conceptions* born in the intellect out of the reality of existences. The poet might well approach existence through this experience of proper proportionality in order to recover a viability in metaphor out of analogy of proper proportionality, as Thomas distinguishes that analogy from the analogy of inequality or the analogy of attribution. Ezra Pound and William Carlos Williams were deeply suspicious of metaphor, without making such distinctions. For the analogy of attribution is so facilely handy to lesser poets: this corrosive inclination in Imagism led Pound to reject it for Vorticism and Williams to reject it for Objectivism. Wallace Stevens, on the other hand, took exceptional pleasure in the freedom of analogy by attribution, keeping a playful detachment from the game he thus played, not committed consequentially to his intellectual actions as poet. On this important point, see St. Thomas's *On Being and Essence* and Gerald B. Phelan's exploration in *St. Thomas and Analogy* (1941).

is that same limiting circumstance that made him as a child not respond fully to Shakespeare. For, as he says, the "perception of *why* Shakespeare, or Dante, or Sophokles holds the place he has [in our literary tradition] is something which comes only very slowly in the course of living." And, we add, it is a growth in a tradition of the blood more or less sustaining one toward a capacity to perceive and understand the *why*.[12] In the course of living, one grows toward a belief or disbelief which is therefore neither precipitately arbitrary nor absolute. Again, in a scholastic perspective, one comes more and more into the actualities of one's personhood, within the limits of the potential given to one: one's *specific* being as person, that complex particularity where one *is* and *becomes*.

Having come to this realization through "Ash-Wednesday," Eliot does not condemn himself for that earlier infatuation, any more than he repudiates some of that earlier criticism with which he has come to disagree very radically. For that criticism has been in part the means whereby he has come to his personhood. Even so, he would likely rebuke us were we not at least to caution any forty-year-old poet or critic who clings to the infatuations of his intellectual youth. If there is such a creature as the popular "dirty old man" of sexual forwardness, then the forward intellectual is also a creature warranting caricature: atrophied through neglect of mature discriminations and pretending to an intellectual virility through empty enthusiasms collected from youth. It is he who will prove the bane of humanistic recovery in the academy for this decade.

12. We should remember that in the same year in which he gave the Charles Eliot Norton Lectures at Harvard, Eliot also gave the Page-Barbour Lectures at the University of Virginia, also published in 1933 as *After Strange Gods*. In these lectures, Eliot makes a distinction between *tradition* and *orthodoxy* that is central to his new position as critic and poet, so that these lectures complement his *Use of Poetry*. *After Strange Gods* has been unjustly abused and neglected, out of a critical timidity uncertain of its own authority, its own ordinate judgment, in minnowing wheat from chaff in the essays. In an age lacking heroes, we tend to despair angrily as well as timidly when a hero proves imperfect, we having long neglected the difference between hero and god, a discrimination necessary to both a tragic and comic vision of man. Eliot, of course, was very much aware that ours is a world capable for the most part only of a pathetic, as opposed to tragic or comic, vision. That is what his own poetry is largely "about." Anyway, a discomforting suspicion of Eliot as too much under the influence of Charles Maurras in the late 1920s and early 1930s does not justify a neglect of the viable; it only requires a separation of the true from the false in a journey toward the good. *After Strange Gods* requires our recovering the valid in it.

We would seem, by this point of our consideration of Eliot, to have reached a dilemma in his position. That is, we would seem to have merely substituted one sort of arrest for another. Prufrock, in terror that any act will limit his potential, will not act at all. He argues, with a wily spiritual cowardice, that any act would inevitably be taken by the always hostile world of the tea party as the true revelation of his full being. Thus he projects his own intellectual deception upon all intellects. All those others are Prufrocks also, and his only recourse is to out-Prufrock them. Note his reason for not moving overtly to engage the particular woman among the women who come and go talking of Michelangelo. There is a hint of sensual attraction to her. What, he postulates, if I were to say to her, in words bearing witty sexual innuendo, "I am Lazarus come from the dead"? Unlikely that she knows John Donne, but even so the words would be discomforting, given their coming from Prufrock. Even if he should act so daringly, however, she would merely say, turning from him to escape with her eyes out the window into the empty, vacuous night, "That is not what I meant at all." In short, Prufrock can be comfortable with her only so long as he can assume her to be a female Prufrock, thus justifying his inaction with her.

So Prufrock is contented by a supposition obviating any action. To act is for him not to judge — that most fundamental ground in any action — but to be judged, to be "formulated." Here Prufrock the wily logician avoids action by attributing its primary ground of judgment to others, refusing its presence as the ground of inaction in himself. He does so through the subtle confusion of the passive voice. His justification is that the "formulated phrase," with which he would be "fixed" as specimen in consequence of overt action, is never a sufficient representation of the essence of the thing formulated, least of all his own person. He takes refuge behind a scholastic principle: that the sign is always insufficient to the thing itself. Prufrock proves adept at manipulating the scholastic concept to justify his arrested spirit, the consequence of which manipulation is that he is a hollow man. Eliot very deliberately plays out this consequence in "The Hollow Men," as we have noted, in the play of the shadow that falls between contingent terms voiced in the concluding lines of that rather desperate poem; for instance "Between the *potency* / And the *existence*" (emphasis mine).

Such manipulation is an advantage to the intellect if it is to delay, by denial, its own existence in a present moment at a particular place, the only point of one's being where any action is ever possible. Prufrock's denial of present circumstances that impinge upon his actual existence, those pre-conditions to any action, *has been managed* insidiously by his intellect's shifting of formulations at the grammatical level. It is the procedure whereby his intellect separates "the man who suffers and the mind which creates," to quote Eliot's argument from "Tradition and the Individual Talent." By the illusion of a separation in the self, he establishes the illusion that thereby he is "the more perfect [as] artist" of his argument. An aspect of a more inclusive person reduced to formulaic name, J. Alfred Prufrock if nothing else is skilled rhetorician. Or perhaps we might better say, a skilled sophist whose extreme skepticism is necessarily extreme, if intellect is to maintain the emptiness of person as the principle of any escape from the risks of action. Here it is well to recall that Eliot, in a letter to his Harvard mentor J. H. Woods (January 28, 1915) speaks fearfully of his own "fatal disposition to scepticism."

Through manipulation of verb tenses, Prufrock maintains his dislocation from a present and a place, speaking authoritatively of a spent past and prophetically of a failed future: "Would it be worthwhile, if one, turning toward the window. . . ." Thus managed by insidious intellect, the insistent present is denied implicitly, though it still impinges upon the denial despite the conditional mood of the verb. For even as one formulates such phrases, the very action of formulation is made possible only by a present existence of the formulator. Thus is Prufrock caught up in a perpetual contradiction, a denial of the present which alone makes any denial possible: it is only *now* that I may think of *past* or *future*. Such is the inescapable present that in whatever signs we use, whatever poem or argument, the action of those words is always out of a present, an immediacy of circumstances without which words could not even exist. To use words is to establish *my* existence *here* and *now*, even though the words are inadequate to circumscribe the here and now.

As a reader who is in some degree a Prufrock, as we all are, I am stirred from Prufrock's reductionisms of himself. For it is Prufrock who is reduced by his words. In that stirring of a response within me, there may rise at least a shadow of humility, somewhat displacing the Prufrockean assumption of intellectual autonomy to which I am susceptible. And I may suspect such a shadow to be cast by a light not that of my own intellect, as if the shadow were caused by a memory of some light other than my intellect's presumption of itself as ultimate. That response has the look, no less than have roses, of something looked at, to borrow and adapt a phrase from *Burnt Norton* signaling this recognition in Eliot himself. I may be stirred to recognize that every such assumption of autonomy by renegade intellect is focused away from a present moment in one way or another, away from this present of my own being in relation to the particulars of place. That is the aspect of gnostic autonomy which accounts on the one hand for futile nostalgia and on the other for projected utopias: the one disregards the present for the past; the other the present for an illusion of the future. Both require speculative denials of the existential actuality of the person who is doing the speculating. Marvelous dreams may be spun out of such things, of course, an illusional alchemy blinding intellect to its present being in a substantial person and within an inclusive complex reality.

But the shadows in me, stirred by my encounter with Eliot's poem, include a knowledge of substantial being, a once known but forgotten thing whose recovery makes possible a new light *to* intellectual light.[13] That knowledge of substantial being, as St. Teresa might put it, is in intellect "like feeling someone near one in a dark place." Such is her description of intellectual vision, that interior illumination whereby being is recognized as actual and not a shadow, though always contingent in its actuality to Being Itself; that is, to the Cause of being we call God. It is this intellectual vision we acknowledge when we say that anything — a rose or birdsong, the laughter of children, stones in a garden — has the look of a thing that is "looked at," a phrase Eliot uses to rescue Prufrock's wiley misappropriation of the passive.

With the stirring in me of known but forgotten things, initiated by my own surrender of autonomy through faint stirrings of humility, I may refrain from casting Prufrock into outer darkness, however irritating his false intellectualizing. And in so refraining, I may also begin a rescue of my own Prufrockean self. If one puts the point as St. Thomas might put it, I will have begun to remove obstacles to grace. Even so, though I avoid absolute condemnation of Prufrock on the urging of my recovering humility, I may not refuse all judgment on the authority of that humility, for that is false humility — one which does not value things

13. This rather cryptic remark on substantial being as encountered in experiencing things, including those things called poems, is helpfully expanded by Gilson in *Methodical Realism*, and developed by me earlier in the book from which the present essay is taken.

as they are. Judgment arrested by a pretense of humility denies the most salient aspect of intellect in its true nature: any act of intellect, even a refusal to act, advances a judgment. What is at issue is just judgment under the limits of finitude, the finitude of myself in particular circumstances out of a particular history.[14]

One must, then, assert at last the adequacy or inadequacy of "The Love Song of J. Alfred Prufrock" to satisfy belief or to escape our disbelief. That is what Eliot, in his own retrospective reflections upon his poems and criticism, his more mature reading of his past work, comes to see. The subtleties of a buried spiritual dimension in this psychological portrait of intellect, as Eliot caught it very early in his writing (1909-10), are rather certainly there in the poem all along, though he need not nor could not at the time have intended those subleties. What we must say to that paradox is that the poet, insofar as he is true to the necessities of his art — true to a vision he holds of the nature of what his art imitates — will have written more largely than he may know in and by the writing, by his present action of making. Such an explanation of his deepening understanding of his own earlier poems Eliot might well have

14. We are saying, then, that Eliot has come to accept the responsibility of judgment as critic with a humility one hardly finds in him in his early criticism. There he is dismissive of philosophy and history as advanced by philosophers and historians, neither discipline being sufficient to his critical requirements. In "The Perfect Critic" (1920), for instance, it is the poet who is the proper judge, not philosopher or historian, and there is more than a hint that he means the poet such as himself to be capable as critic. This is a position out of that early relativism which only his own mind can justify. Our remark seems severe, but it is no more severe than Eliot's own subsequent judgment of his earlier intellectual deportment as characterized by "a stiffness and an assumption of pontifical solemnity" — as he describes his presence in *The Sacred Wood* in his preface to the 1928 reissue of the work. Here let us also recall some of his words to Norbert Wiener, in a letter written January 6, 1915, the year of *Prufrock and Other Observations*. Anticipating a final revision of his doctoral thesis on F. H. Bradley, he says: "I shall attack first 'Reality' second 'Idea' or ideal content, and then try to show sufficient reason for attempting to get along without any theory of judgment whatsoever. . . . [N]o definition of judgment, that is, is formally either right or wrong: and it simply is a waste of time to define judgment at all." Given our advantage of perspective upon the whole of his life, we remark an irony: the letter is written on Epiphany, which coincidence seems to have escaped Eliot. That realization calls our attention to the general attitude toward Holy Days and Saints Days, let alone Saints themselves, as reflected in Eliot's letters up to 1922, the year of *The Waste Land*: Holy Days are welcomed, in that they allow him an escape from his bank job, usually to the country, for the purpose of writing essays or reviews.

encountered in Maritain's *Art and Scholasticism*, to which he pays tribute in his Harvard lectures. But he could as well have come to it on his own in revisiting the stages of his own growing, as reflected in the body of his poems from "Preludes" to "Ash-Wednesday." Those reflections are part of his manner as poet, the revisiting of his past through a developing insight, with an increasing discovery of his own maturing toward the fullness of personhood. That he does judge that maturing in art is abundantly evident in "Ash-Wednesday," which is a poem to be juxtaposed to "Gerontion" to discover how changed the poet has become.

At the outset of "Ash-Wednesday" there is a paradoxical prayer: "Teach us to care and not to care." We may adapt that prayer in relation to our present point: "Teach us to judge and not to judge." For there is no escape from an abiding tensional necessity in us to judge. As intellectual creatures, we are required to judge, but further required that judgment be ordinate — that is, to judge in relation to our finite encounter of the truth of things. It is a necessity impinging from our will upon all aspects of our life, made tentative as judgment by a proper humility. By acknowledging our intellectual insufficiency to absolute judgment, we are not thereby excused from the consequent agonizing intellectual action of judging truth perceived. And in judging ordinately we seek a balance in that tensional dynamism which characterizes us, intellect bodily alive. That is what Eliot is about when he says in *The Use of Poetry*, "We must write our poetry as we can." In turn, we must read his poetry as we can, just as we must live as fully as we can within our gifts as intellectual creatures. To insist upon the point, we must act within our recognitions of our finitudes of body, mind, spirit, toward the true, the good, the beautiful. There is an insurmountable discomfort in us always, consequent upon such recognitions of our limits, which may tempt to an arrest that is the death of spirit. Yet, that discomfort, the uneasiness in our recognition of our finitude, is and must be always with us.

Still, given that discomfort and the necessity of an accommodation to it which requires that we care and not care, we are more Prufrockean than we may admit. Eliot recognizes this common likeness in us when he says in concluding his Harvard lectures, "our lives are mostly a constant evasion of ourselves, an evasion of the visible and sensible world." That is a rather precise characterization of Prufrock, who so conspicuously attempts to reject "the visible and sensible world," which is always screaming to us "Here! Now!" Eliot will dramatize a Prufrock more deeply seen than in his 1909 poem, putting himself in that role directly but speaking for that which is common to us all. In *East Coker* (1940) he says that we are always

> In the middle, not only in the middle of the way
> But all the way, in a dark wood, in a bramble,
> On the edge of a grimpen, where is no secure foothold.
> And menaced by monsters, fancy lights,
> Risking enchantment.

These are words most pregnant of the mystery of intellect in its tension between illusion as an ideal projected by desire and a reality feared in its very actualities, of intellect whose surrender to reality costs "no less than everything" in its surrender of autonomy.

At the beginning of World War II, Jacques Maritain gave a lecture at Oxford, "The Human Person and Society." As the war was coming to an end, he gave another at Rome, "The Person and the Individual." We shall likely discover that Eliot knew these lectures. In the 1920s, he had become acquainted with Maritain and his work, which he translated and published (for instance Maritain's "Poetry and Religion" in the May 1927 issue of *Criterion*). But whether or not he knew these particular pieces, what is certain is that both Maritain and Eliot, in the midst of wartime horrors, sought to recover that center to the meaning of existence which is our personhood.[15] One finds that concern in

15. Maritain's lectures are brought together in *The Person and the Common Good* (1946). The crucial distinction he makes is between *person* and *individual*. "Thomistic personalism stresses the metaphysical distinction" between the terms. In the distinction lies the center of that mystery Eliot speaks of as our deportment of caring and not caring. "As an individual," Maritain says, "each of us is a fragment of a species, a part of the universe, a unique point in the immense web of cosmic, ethical, historical forces and influences. . . . Nonetheless, each of us is also a person and, as such, is not controlled by the stars. Our whole being subsists in virtue of the subsistence of the spiritual soul. It is as person that we love. . . . For love is not concerned with qualities or natures or essences but with *persons*." Again, "Personality is the subsistence of the spiritual soul communicated to the human composite." And once more, "it is the human *person* who enters society; as an individual, it enters society as a part whose proper good is inferior to the good of the whole [of that whole constituted temporally of persons]. . . . [B]ecause of the highest requirements of personality as such, the human person, as a spiritual totality referred to the transcendent whole, *surpasses* and is superior to all temporal societies. . . . With respect to the eternal destiny of the soul, society exists for each

Eliots's *Little Gidding*, in which the London fires seem almost to call God's providence into question. "The dove descending breaks the air" over London, "With flame of incandescent terror" under Nazi bombardments, leaving as the only hope "the choice of pyre or pyre — To be redeemed from fire by fire." So terrifying that necessity that one might well demand to know, as does the speaker in *Little Gidding*, "Who then devised the torment?"

What the poem gradually reveals is that beyond the inescapable horror of mass destruction that war brought upon Western civilization, there is an inescapable Love more destroying in its rescue than words may say. In the shock of that moment, when death is to be reckoned by a mathematics of individuals, an accounting of horror that deadens horror by the very calculation, the reality of Love is forced upon Eliot's awareness as he walks the burning London streets as air-raid warden. Who then devised such destruction? Who let it happen? Man alone? That is the old question which Eliot found Dame Julian of Norwich asking long before modern efficiencies in the destruction of material existences, including those counted as individuals rather than persons. Before her initial vision, Dame Julian had also questioned God's providence. "Why by the great foreseeing wisdom of God the beginning of sin was not letted: for then methought, all should have been well."[16]

That is the ancient standing question, to which a rational explanation is always inadequate. It is then that Dame Julian receives her vision of Christ crucified, speaking to her. "Jesus . . . answered by this word and said: 'It behoved that there should be sin; but all shall be well, and all shall be well, and all manner of thing shall be well." Sin, "the utter naughting that he bare for us in this life," one must accept as "behovable," though it will not follow therefrom that one may cease enduring the journey because of the necessity otherwise to wrestle intellectually with evil's nature and causes. To accept sin as allowed by God's providence does not grant intellect perpetual holiday. And so Dame Julian, contemplating her vision for fifteen years, comes to an understanding of its meaning, by an

---

person and is subordinate to it." Teach us, as individual, to care, as person, not to care for the temporal world in which we journey.

16. *Revelations of Divine Love, Shewed to A Devout Ankress by Dame Julian of Norwich*. Edited from the MSS. by Dom Roger Hudleston (London: Burnes Oates, 1927). This edition would probably have come to hand for Eliot at about the time of "Ash-Wednesday."

intellectual vision, an interior illumination. Such a vision differs from supernatural manifestations or sensible revelations through image, such as had been her first vision. It is of this intellectual vision that St. Teresa speaks when she says that it is "like feeling someone near one in a dark place." Darkness is the literal circumstances to Eliot's encounter by intellectual vision of the "voice of that Calling" as he walks the darkened London streets under blitz, remembered in *Little Gidding*.

He may have been aware of a coincidence: we learn in Dame Julian's *Revelation of Divine Love* that only after a fifteen-year interval of meditation upon that supernatural vision in which Christ visited her so palpably that she came to understand its meaning through her "ghostly understanding," through intellectual vision. Eliot, walking the blackened London rubble, would recall his own earlier encounter with the Word in the desert, which he memorialized in "Ash-Wednesday." He, too, walked in a newly lighted darkness thereafter, and then at almost the same interval of fifteen years he is forced to deal with immediate evidence of a radical evil in London rubble.

What came to Dame Julian as intellectual vision, after long meditation, is movingly echoed in Eliot's song in *Little Gidding*, and in that poem's final lines:

"Wouldst thou witten the Lord's meaning in this thing?
"Wit it well, Love was his Meaning.
"Who showed it to thee? Love.
"What showed he thee? Love.
"Wherefore showed it he? For Love."

It is Love's relation to undeniable evil, one fire to another, that Eliot now understands and embraces, after which we note he no longer writes poetry:

Who then devised the torment? Love.
Love is the unfamiliar Name
Behind the hands that wove
The intolerable shirt of flame
Which human power cannot remove.

The human power of intellect cannot remove, dissolve, the agonizing paradox of flame contending with flame within the person, within the soul, any more than within the general world, despite intellect's strongest attempts to declare the meaninglessness of existence as its only defense. For the first mystery to intellect it cannot deny: its very attempt to do so establishes a mystery it cannot resolve unaided by grace: *existence is*.

Long before all our agitations over Descartes' *Cogito*, St. Augustine had made the same point about existence. What, he asks himself, if I am deluded about my own existence? Ah, but I must exist, else I cannot be deluded.[17] That is the secret, at first undetected by Eliot, underlying the sardonic desperation in "Preludes," where the speaker, unable to find any meaning in consciousness itself and so suspicious of consciousness as an illusion, can only conclude:

> Wipe your hand across your mouth and laugh;
> The worlds revolve like ancient women
> Gathering fuel in vacant lots.

Long after, the hidden mystery in that point of departure upon both his poetic and spiritual journey brings him to sing with a joy recovered:

> We only live, only suspire
> Consumed by either fire or fire.

Such are the conditions to our finite but free existence as intellectual creature. When one is consumed by the fire of that heaven which holds the earth, as Dante imagines it for us, one must conclude, as Eliot does in the final lines of his final poem,

> All manner of thing shall be well
> When the tongues of flame are in-folded
> Into the crowned knot of fire
> And the fire and the rose are one.

What we learn from Eliot, then, in reading his poetry as one long poem, is that short of a beatific vision toward which we properly tend, we may be held in the way despite the way's seeming darkness and our own inclination to waywardness. We are held, insofar as we learn at each present moment and in each particular place of our being both to care and not to care through intellectual judgment of all manner of things contingent to our present place.

17. *City of God*, XI, 26.

Contributors

From 1985 to 1995 **William J. Abraham** was McCreless Professor of Evangelism and Professor of Philosophy of Religion at Perkins School of Theology, Southern Methodist University. In the fall of 1995 he was appointed Albert Cook Outler Professor of Wesley Studies at Perkins. In 1991 he wrote the article "The State of Christian Theology in North America" for the *Encyclopaedia Britannica's Great Ideas Today*. His books include *The Divine Inspiration of Holy Scripture, Divine Revelation and the Limits of Historical Criticism,* and *The Logic of Evangelism.* He currently serves on the editorial board of *Interpretation.*

William F. Campbell, professor of economics at Louisiana State University, is president of the Association of Christian Economists and past president of the Philadelphia Society. He has also served on the national Graduate Fellowship Board, later known as the Jacob Javits Fellowship Board. Among the journals in which his articles have appeared are *American Economic Review, Journal of Economic Issues, History of Political Economy, Modern Age,* and *Intercollegiate Review.*

Ian Crowther, a writer and broadcaster, is literary editor of *The Salisbury Review.* His book *Chesterton* was published in 1991 by The Claridge Press.

Alzina Stone Dale is the author of ten books, including biographies of Dorothy L. Sayers (*Maker & Craftsman*), G. K. Chesterton (*The Outline of Sanity*), and T. S. Eliot (*The Philosopher Poet*). In addition, she has edited a collection of essays, *Dorothy L. Sayers: The Centenary Book,* as well as *Chesterton on Dickens,* volume 15 of Ignatius Press's collected works of Chesterton.

David Dooley is an Emeritus Professor of English, St. Michael's College, University of Toronto. His publications include books on Sinclair Lewis, Compton Mackensie, the moral vision in the Canadian novel, and, with Margaret Morriss, *Evelyn Waugh: A Reference Guide.* He has also edited the first volume in the collected works of G. K. Chesterton, which included *Heretics* and *Orthodoxy.*

Evan K. Gibson, Ph.D., recently deceased, held teaching positions in English at the University of Washington, Oregon State University, and Seattle Pacific University. In addition to numerous contributions in the fields of religion and literature, he authored *C. S. Lewis, Spinner of Tales* and the article "The Centrality of *Perelandra* to Lewis's Theology," which was published in *The Riddle of Joy.*

Kent R. Hill, president of Eastern Nazarene College and former president of the Institute on Religion and Democracy (Washington, D.C.), taught Christian apologetics at Moscow State University in 1991. He is the author of numerous articles; his most recent book is *The Soviet Union on the Brink.*

Thomas T. Howard, professor of English at St. John's Seminary College, has written nine books, including *The Novels of Charles Williams* and *The Achievement of C. S. Lewis.* His many articles have appeared in such journals as *The New York Times Book Review, The New Oxford Review, Studies in the Literary Imagination,* and *Modern Age.*

Between 1951 and 1991, **Russell Kirk** published thirty books in diverse disciplines; among the better known of them are *The Conservative Mind, Eliot and His Age, The Roots of American Order, The Wise Men Know What Wicked Things Are Written on the Sky,* and *John Randolph of Roanoke.* He also wrote five volumes of fiction. Until his death in 1994 he was the president of the Marguerite Eyer Wilbur Foundation, president of The Educational Reviewer, Inc., and editor of *The University Bookman,* the quarterly publication of the latter foundation.

Peter Kreeft, professor of philosophy at Boston College, has authored over two dozen books, including *C. S. Lewis: A Critical Essay, Summa of the Summa,* and *Making Sense of Suffering.*

Aidan Mackey is founder and administrator of the G. K. Chesterton Study Centre, Bedford, England. For ten years, he was chairman of the Chesterton Society in England. He is the author of *Mr. Chesterton Comes to Tea, Hilaire Belloc and His Critics, The Wisdom of G. K. Chesterton,* and numerous articles and reviews.

Michael Macdonald is professor of European Studies and Philosophy, and Director of the C. S. Lewis Institute at Seattle Pacific University. He has written numerous articles and reviews, as well as *Europe: A Tantalizing Romance, Philosophical Questions: An Introductory Anthology* (with Richard Purtill and Peter Kreeft), and he co-edited *The Riddle of Joy* (with Andrew Tadie).

Marion Montgomery is a poet, fiction writer, and critic who lives in Crawford, Georgia. He has recently published *Liberal Arts and Community: The Feeding of the Larger Body* and *The Men I Have Chosen for Fathers: Literary and Philosophical Passages.*

Professor of English **George Musacchio** holds the Frank W. Mayborn Chair of Arts and Sciences at the University of Mary Hardin-Baylor in central Texas. He has published many articles on C. S. Lewis, including "Fiction in *A Grief Observed,*" and he is the author of *Milton's Adam and Eve.*

John Peterson has published and edited the monthly *Midwest Chesterton News* since its inception in 1988. His extensive Father Brown bibliography accompanied *The Mask of Midas,* Chesterton's final Father Brown story, published in 1991, and his new selection of Father Brown stories will be published by Ignatius Press.

Barbara Reynolds, former lecturer in Italian at Cambridge University, is the author of *Dorothy L. Sayers: Her Life and Soul; The Passionate Intellect: Dorothy L. Sayers's Encounter with Dante;* and the translation of the Penguin editions of Ariosto's *Orlando Furioso,* Dante's *La Vita Nuova,* and Dante's *Paradiso,* with Dorothy L. Sayers. She is the general editor of the *Concise Cambridge Italian Dictionary*, and holds honorary doctorates from Wheaton College and Hope College.

Professor **John A. Sims** teaches in the theology department at Lee College and is the author of *Edward John Carnell: Defender of the Faith* and *Power with Purpose: The Holy Spirit in Historical and Contemporary Perspective.*

Andrew Tadie is English professor and director of the Faith and Great Ideas program at Seattle University. He prepared the introduction to a new edition of Mark Twain's *Personal Recollections of Joan of Arc* and co-edited with Michael Macdonald *The Riddle of Joy.*

John G. West, Jr., assistant professor of political science at Seattle Pacific University, is a senior fellow at the Seattle-based Discovery Institute where he directs the program on religion, liberty, and civic life.

David Whalen, English professor at Hillsdale College, is the author of *The Consolation of Rhetoric,* "John Henry Newman: The Rhetoric of the Real," and "On a Summer-Stricken Stream."

Gregory Wolfe is publisher and editor of *Image: A Journal of the Arts and Religion* and the author of *Malcolm Muggeridge: A Biography.* With his wife, Suzanne M. Wolfe, and William Kilpatrick, he wrote *Books That Build Character,* a guide to children's books.

Appendix

Participants at the 1990 Conference on the Permanent Things

William Abraham
Judy Arnold
Kelley Arnold
Sarah Beattie
Ian T. Benson
Janet Blumberg-
  Knedlik
Cornelius Burns
John Burton
Leo Bustad
William Campbell
Roger Campbell
Dick Caster
Richard Caulkins
Rev. Gerald T. Cobb, S.J.
Martha Cotten
Alzina Stone Dale
David Dooley

Margaret Dornay
Deb Easter
Steven Faulkner
Rev. Joseph Fessio, S.J.
Karen Finch
Miles Finch
Kathryn Flower
Mary Flynn
Robert Flynn
Ridgway Foley
Steve Garber
Kathleen Geraghty
Kim Gilnett
Margaret Goodman
Nadine Gray
Raymond Gray
Tom Gray
Kelly Griffin

Scott Heaton
Kent Hill
Diane Hood
Walter Hooper
Thomas Howard
Rev. Ronald Hoyum
MeLinda Hughes
David Huisman
Eric Jacobsen
Deborah Jacobson
George Kendall
Nellie Kester
Ralph Kester
Julie Kim
Pastor Roger Kinkead
Russell Kirk
Peter Kreeft
James Kushiner

Dolane Larson
Rev. David Leigh, S.J.
Winifred Leighton
Mrs. Bill Lewis
Linda Lusk
Michael Macdonald
Aidan Mackey
Carol Martin
Curtis Martin
Regis Martin
Spencer Masloff
J. Stanley Matson
Ronald McComb
Sara McLaughlin
Marion Montgomery
Rebecca Moxley
George Musacchio
John Peterson
Eugene Petrich
Lysle Pickard
Helen Puccetti

Victor Puccetti
Richard Purtill
Barbara Reynolds
Barry Rigney
David Ringer
Virginia Rober
Carol Russell
Roger Schmeckly
Ben Schuller
Joseph Schwartz
Luci Shaw
John Sims
Patricia Sims
Thomas Slate
Henrich Stammler
Pamela Stromberg
Eugene Sullivan
Donna Sullivan
Margaret Sundberg
Andrew Tadie
Eleanor Tate

Warren Taylor
Beverly Taylor
Susan Thompson
James Tolman
Fred Troutman
Tom Trzyna
Kathleen Verduin
Suzanne Voltz
Donald von Dohlen
Steve Walsh
Lilian Walsh
Harry Watters
John G. West
David Whalen
Kevin Wildie
David Wohler
Gregory Wolfe
Ralph Wood
Suzanne Wood
Leslie Workman
John Wright